RACIAL
JUSTICE
AT WORK

RACIAL JUSTICE AT WORK

Practical Solutions
for Systemic Change

MARY-FRANCES WINTERS
& The Winters Group Team

BK

Berrett–Koehler Publishers, Inc.

Berrett-Koehler Publishers, Inc.
1333 Broadway, Suite 1000
Oakland, CA 94612-1921
Tel: (510) 817-2277/Fax: (510) 817-2278
www.bkconnection.com

ORDERING INFORMATION

QUANTITY SALES. Special discounts are available on quantity purchases by corporations, associations, and others. For details, contact the "Special Sales Department" at the Berrett-Koehler address above.

INDIVIDUAL SALES. Berrett-Koehler publications are available through most bookstores. They can also be ordered directly from Berrett-Koehler: Tel: (800) 929-2929; Fax: (802) 864-7626; www.bkconnection.com.

ORDERS FOR COLLEGE TEXTBOOK / COURSE ADOPTION USE. Please contact Berrett-Koehler: Tel: (800) 929-2929; Fax: (802) 864-7626.

Distributed to the U.S. trade and internationally by Penguin Random House Publisher Services.

Berrett-Koehler and the BK logo are registered trademarks of Berrett-Koehler Publishers, Inc.

Printed in the United States of America

Berrett-Koehler books are printed on long-lasting acid-free paper. When it is available, we choose paper that has been manufactured by environmentally responsible processes. These may include using trees grown in sustainable forests, incorporating recycled paper, minimizing chlorine in bleaching, or recycling the energy produced at the paper mill.

Library of Congress Cataloging-in-Publication Data
    Names: Winters, Mary-Frances, author.
    Title: Racial justice at work : practical solutions for systemic change / Mary-Frances Winters, The Winters Group Team.
    Description: First edition. | Oakland, CA : Berrett-Koehler Publishers, [2023] | Includes bibliographical references and index.
    Identifiers: LCCN 2022034445 (print) | LCCN 2022034446 (ebook) | ISBN 9781523003624 (paperback ; alk. paper) | ISBN 9781523003631 (pdf) | ISBN 9781523003648 (epub) | ISBN 9781523003655 (audio)
    Subjects: LCSH: Diversity in the workplace—United States. | Racial Justice—United States. | Social justice—United States. | United States—Race relations.
    Classification: LCC HF5549.5.M5 R344 2023 (print) | LCC HF5549.5.M5 (ebook) | DDC 331.13/3—dc23/eng/20220919
    LC record available at https://lccn.loc.gov/2022034445
    LC ebook record available at https://lccn.loc.gov/2022034446

FIRST EDITION

29 28 27 26 25 24 23 22 | 10 9 8 7 6 5 4 3 2 1

Book production: BookMatters; Cover design: Nita Ybarra; Cover illustration: Krystle Nicholas

CONTENTS

PREFACE

Note on terms: Language describing various identity groups is ever-changing. There is no universal agreement and, in our attempt to be respectful of different perspectives, we acknowledge that the terms we have chosen may not resonate with all readers. The term BIPOC *(Black, Indigenous, and people of color) is used in the book to recognize that while every identity has had its unique journey with racism, there are shared experiences that we attempt to capture. When not citing language directly from a study or quote, we use* Latine *to describe individuals who have historically been identified as Hispanic, Latino, or Latinx. Latine, created by LGBTQIA+ Spanish speakers, adopts the letter* e *from the Spanish language to represent gender neutrality.*[1] *SWANA is a decolonized term for the South West Asian/North African region that was created by its own community members to be used instead of names that are Eurocentric in origin, such as the Middle East or Near East.*[2]

We wrote *Racial Justice at Work: Practical Solutions for Systemic Change* in the midst of intense culture wars in the United States and other parts of the world. There are diametrically opposing views on the meaning of equality, equity, and justice—and who has the right to decide. At this critical juncture in our history of civil and human rights, *Racial Justice at Work* is an attempt to provide clarity and guidance for leaders in every sector, social justice advocates, and everybody who desires to create equitable workplace systems that truly work for all.

This book invites the reader to reimagine what is possible with chapters from different Winters Group team members who represent a variety of lived experiences, cultural backgrounds, and generations. The book focuses on Black, Indigenous, and people of color (BIPOC) in the workplace. It is a guidebook with actionable solutions for workers everywhere in every industry. It is especially crucial for leaders with decision-making power to create just and fair work environments.

Those who believe justice is not being served for BIPOC will have to be courageous and steadfast. Justice means that we face the ugly truth about systemic racism and the harm caused, and change those systems so that we can move closer to "liberty and justice for all." As culture wars intensify, we see attempts through proposed and enacted legislation to deny that systemic racism even exists.

Luckily, amid the attempts to uphold systems of racism are many counterefforts to enhance workplace equity, inclusion, and justice. Since the murder of George Floyd and other Black people in 2020, organizations have made bold commitments to combat systemic racism in the workplace, including aggressive hiring and philanthropic goals. We have seen a surge in organizations filling diversity-related roles. Research by LinkedIn found that the number of people with the title "head of diversity" more than doubled between 2015 and 2020, and in the sixteen months after the murder of George Floyd, it almost tripled.[3]

It is encouraging that many organizations recognize the need for such roles. Unfortunately, too much of the work continues to be performative (commonly referred to as "check the box"). According to Russell Reynolds Associates, chief diversity officers have an average tenure of only 1.8 years.[4] There is a great deal of effort put into hiring BIPOC and other programmatic activities such as employee resource groups and mentoring programs, but not enough emphasis on the organizational systems perpetuating inequities. The focus is on fixing the *people* rather than the *systems* that harm people. *Racial Justice at Work* focuses on correcting harmful systems. There are bold organizations, some of which are highlighted in the book, directing their efforts on systemic change. We need more.

The Winters Group has consulted with organizations for over three decades, and we realize that a justice-centered approach is very different from traditional corporate DEI work. Many leaders who signed up to focus on antiracism and social justice in their organizations did not understand the distinction between *equity* and *justice*. Many have even added the "J" to DEI (diversity, equity, and inclusion) and are struggling to operationalize it. There is resistance to the culture change required to center justice and the experiences of those most impacted by racism. This book acknowledges the adverse reaction to change and how to address it. By providing specific, actionable strategies, this book maps the intersection between traditional corporate solutions and those advocated in social justice spaces.

Racial Justice at Work reimagines policies, practices, procedures, and ways of working and being that foster fairness, equity, and opportunity for all. The recommendations in this book are bold and audacious. Some of the solutions may seem unrealistic, improbable, or even outlandish, especially in the backdrop of the culture wars. We invite you to be curious about those solutions you may disagree with and ask yourself why. For those recommendations that you might agree with but think will never happen, try to reimagine what would need to happen to make them a reality. If not what we recommend, then what?

Actualizing justice is not for the faint at heart, not for those who prioritize comfort over progress. It will not be easy as the culture wars intensify. It is for those who have the courage to act.

Is that you? If so, read *Racial Justice at Work.*

It's about Correcting Harm

MARY-FRANCES WINTERS

Founder and CEO

The Winters Group, Inc.

(she/her/hers)

After the murder of George Floyd in 2020 and the protests that ensued, there was a racial reckoning of sorts in the United States and around the world, with a focus specifically on inequities that persist for Black people. Even though there has been much legislation throughout history outlawing unequal treatment, Black people and other marginalized identities (Indigenous, Latine, Asian Americans, Native Hawaiians, Pacific Islanders, and the SWANA community)—referred to as BIPOC throughout the book—continue to suffer significant disparities in all aspects of society, including education, healthcare, the workplace, and the criminal justice system.

Racial Justice at Work explores workplace inequities and offers practical solutions to address them that go beyond equality, beyond equity to justice. Why *justice* and not racial *equity* at work? Even though the idea of equity is new for some organizations and not without its controversy, justice goes further. Most people really mean *equality*—treat everyone the same—when they use the term *equity*, which means differential treatment based on need. *Justice* means we will correct past inequities. *Racial Justice at Work* is written to examine the underlying systems that preserve the status quo and prevent us from achieving equity and justice.

While the term *social justice* is not new, and many of the civil rights laws are grounded in these ideals, the way we think about justice is transforming. *Social justice* can be defined as the way in which human rights are experienced in the everyday lives of people at every level of society. Social justice entails the fair distribution of wealth, opportunities, and privilege. And since we know that the distribution has not been fair, justice necessitates the redistribution of wealth opportunities and privilege. Justice-centered approaches require us to consider who has been or is harmed by workplace systems, who benefits from the status quo, and what we need to do to correct policies, practices, and belief systems.

Affirmative action in the United States is about social justice. Albeit controversial, the goal is to correct past discrimination and exclusion of certain groups in the workforce—called *protected classes*—by requiring employers with more than fifty employees who do more than $50,000 in business with the government to set hiring and promotion goals. These goals are designed to achieve parity—that is, equal representation based on labor force availability in government job classifications. Affirmative action is not without its critics. This legislation continues to be challenged as "reverse discrimination," and certain aspects have been upended over the years since it was first enforced by Executive Order 11246 in 1965.[1]

Affirmative action is primarily about hiring and promotion, a part of the HR function in organizations. Often diversity, equity, inclusion, and justice (DEIJ) are thought of primarily as HR issues. Chief diversity officers often report to the chief HR officer. This book examines what justice looks like beyond the HR office, revealing practices, policies, and systems that uphold the status quo and harm BIPOC in such areas as procurement, marketing and advertising, investment strategies, and software algorithms.

Racial Justice at Work is a series of essays written by members of The Winters Group team in two parts. Part I explores racial justice at work from a strategic perspective—opportunities such as justice-centered leadership approaches, addressing resistance to change, and becoming comfortable with racial justice concepts. Part II offers specific solutions to achieving racial justice in different organizational functions. You may find some redundancy in our thinking and recommendations. This is intentional for you to see justice from different interpretations and intersections.

After the murder of George Floyd in 2020, many corporate leaders claimed not to know that there was still such a significant racial divide. With this supposed newfound knowledge, they vowed to give more attention to racial inequities that persist in the workplace and society in general, specifically for Black employees. Corporate responses included more aggressive hiring and promotion goals, more attention to amplifying racial diversity in their marketing and advertising campaigns, increasing philanthropic dollars to Black-led organizations, and enhancing supplier diversity to include more BIPOC-led companies. These goals, while well-intended, are not likely to bring about sustained change. All of these ideas have been tried before to no avail.

We need new, radical remedies that disrupt these stubborn patterns of disproportionate outcomes. This book, while not exhaustive, offers justice-centered ideas to correct harm and remove barriers that continue to leave BIPOC employees disadvantaged in the workplace. We recognize that these ideas will seem very "radical" to some readers, and we expect they will be controversial and not without critics. We believe that if we are serious about racial justice, these are the types of remedies that organizations need to consider, and some already are doing so.

We focus primarily but not exclusively on racial justice related to Black employees because we believe that if we can figure out ways to create policies and practices geared at eliminating or at least alleviating the burdens faced by Black people in the workplace, they will also alleviate and perhaps one day eliminate injustices that continue to harm other marginalized groups—the Indigenous, Latine, Asian, SWANA, LGBTQIA+, people with disabilities, women, and those with intersectional identities.

Compounding the issues of racial injustice, of course, was the global COVID-19 pandemic, which has had its own set of repercussions for the workplace as a whole. And there is clear evidence that we are now in the throes of culture wars where so-called conservative values are clashing with so-called progressive values. I say "so-called" because as you look deeply into the polarization around certain social issues such as racial justice, reproductive rights, and LGBTQIA+ rights, for example, it is not clear what constitutes progressive or conservative. We are weaponizing terms that keep us from gaining clarity and from coming to any semblance of common ground. I write about the weaponization of terms in Chapter 2.

As a result of the pandemic, many people reevaluated their relationship with work. The Great Resignation, as it has been dubbed, resulted in millions of people leaving traditional jobs that were unfulfilling for a variety of reasons. Research shows that women and BIPOC led the mass exodus, primarily because of systems that perpetuated inequities, whether intentionally or unintentionally. "Quiet quitting" describes a trend where people who stay in the workplace are no longer willing to perform outside of their defined job description. Workers around the world are exhausted and demand a more humanistic approach to leading and managing.

The culture wars see us fighting over whose values will dominate on topics like critical race theory and whether it is or should be taught in schools; reproductive healthcare rights—decisions that can have more impact on women of color; gun control; and transgender rights (e.g., Florida's "Don't Say Gay" bill). Thamara Subramanian explores clashes of cultural values in Chapter 8, asserting that dominant group values that define only one right way leave little opportunity to include other ways of thinking and being. These cultural issues, which some might say are political in nature and therefore should not be discussed in the workplace, have a profound impact on workers and are being (and should be) discussed. The Winters Group has been asked to support employers in developing equitable policies around abortion rights and to lead discussions on gun violence. For example, a grocery store chain asked for listening sessions after the racially motivated killing of ten innocent Black people in Buffalo, New York, at the Tops supermarket in 2022. The Black employees of this other food store chain feared that they could be the target of something similar.

I believe that many organizations have good intentions as they grapple with the ongoing injustices in society. They are committed to seeking solutions that create inclusive, equitable, and just work environments. They recognize that they are not islands unto themselves and cannot ignore the external events that impact their employees. Yet progress continues to be slow. Organizational cultures are steeped in ways of being, which often unwittingly continues to harm Black and other marginalized identities.

This book aims to consider the complexities of all that I mentioned above and yet distill some very actionable approaches for reimagining a racially just workplace. It is about the three Ps—people, policies, and practices.

People. How do people from different racial identity groups experience the current systems? Who is impacted by the policies and practices? Who is harmed? Who benefits? Who holds the power and control to uphold unjust systems? People in power control systems. How do you support people in power to address the resistance (e.g., claims of reverse discrimination) that is inevitable when you are trying to change systems?

Which belief systems need to be challenged? Which belief systems are ignored or disregarded? As Thamara Subramanian asks in Chapter 8, how safe are BIPOC employees to speak up about their lived experiences? In Chapter 9, Scott Ferry says that employees will not feel safe until they are safe. Leaders will need to recognize the limitations of their own lens and center the experiences of those most impacted without judgment.

Policies. The purport of *Racial Justice at Work* is that we must go beyond the current notions of inclusion and belonging and strive for justice. If we do not, we will continue to make lackluster progress in achieving the espoused desire for true fairness. I love this definition of equity: *when we can no longer predict outcomes by one's identity.* Justice is the path to achieve that goal. We need to ask, what are some policies that disproportionately harm Black and other marginalized groups? How do we find and interrogate these policies? What is the process for evaluation and change? The book does not include an exhaustive identification of all policies that could potentially inhibit racial justice. Rather, it attempts to highlight some beyond traditional HR policies that may not immediately be considered.

Practices. Beyond written policies, what are accepted ways of being and doing that harm Black and other marginalized workers, yet go unchecked? For example, as Tami Jackson asks in Chapter 12, do we have notions of professionalism that uphold dominant culture norms and thwart individuals from contributing fully and authentically? In Chapter 17, Gabrielle Gayagoy Gonzalez offers how recruiting practices that favor referrals from current employees to fill job openings limit the pool of recruits. Often, representation of BIPOC employees is lower than the organization desires. Therefore, if the primary recruiting strategy is referrals, they will likely continue to get people from the dominant group in the employee population.

We have not succeeded in dismantling systems that perpetuate harm to marginalized communities. Many of the efforts have failed because they are programmatic, focusing on fixing the marginalized communities rather than fixing systems that uphold inequities. Even the well-researched and proven business case for diversity (that more diversity positively impacts organizational outcomes) isn't compelling enough to bring about sustained change.

Racial Justice at Work is framed around four key strategic requirements to uncover and correct systems: committing, understanding and acknowledging, reimagining, and actualizing.

Committing

Organizational leaders claimed to be committed to doing something different after George Floyd's murder, to achieve racial justice in the workplace. They asked for training and education on the history of racism. They wanted to teach their employees how to be "antiracists." They wanted comprehensive equity audits—or as some call them, civil rights audits—to not only examine the compliance aspects around nondiscrimination but also review the environment, including the attitudes and perceptions, especially of their Black employees. As time passes since the George Floyd murder that sparked the racial reckoning, we are beginning to see the commitment wane. There is much more resistance to digging deep into racial injustices. In Chapters 6 and 7, Kevin A. Carter goes into detail about how to recognize and address resistance using theories of culture change.

For example, we have experienced quite a bit of resistance to using terms that describe the systemic nature of racism, such as *white supremacy culture*. I discuss this in more detail in Chapter 2, on the weaponization of racial justice terms. The term *white supremacy culture* continues to be mischaracterized as labeling all white people as white supremacists—extreme hatemongers in white sheets—rather than being understood as a belief system, whether conscious or unconscious, that the ways of the dominant group are prioritized and seen as better than other cultural values.

The commitment to persevere and work through the backlash and resistance is necessary to achieve racial justice at work. In Chapter 4, I lay out the commitments that leaders need to make, including an acknowledgment that injustices prevail everywhere; accountability for outcomes; the need for individual learning and reflection; allocating ample and ongoing resources—and accepting resistance, conflict, and discomfort as a part of the path to success.

Understanding and Acknowledging

What is justice? What does it mean to be justice centered? These questions are answered in Chapter 1. Justice, as I stated earlier, requires us to repair harm and develop new ways of thinking and being that ask the questions, *Who will benefit from this decision? Who will be harmed by this decision?* This book does not cover the history of racism, but that is fundamental to understanding how to correct racially unjust systems. So many leaders and influencers claim not to have a historical comprehension of racism, and the attempts by some ultraconservatives to block such education make the work of racial justice that much harder. For example, Nikole Hannah-Jones's historical account of racism in her *The 1619 Project,* for which she won a Pulitzer Prize, has come under attack and has even been banned in certain school districts. We provide resources on where to find helpful historical references on our website at www.wintersgroup.com.

Understanding and acknowledging also means that we appreciate that actualizing racial justice in the workplace is fundamentally about culture change. It cannot be reduced to a litany of programmatic initiatives that become performative and do not focus on systems. Kevin A. Carter discusses the theory of culture change related to dismantling racism in Chapter 6. Understanding requires interrogating systems through comprehensive auditing. This has to be done transparently without fear of the consequences when disparities are uncovered. In Chapter 14, I discuss the problem with DEIJ data, including the historical penchant to mitigate legal risk by not allowing certain data to be interrogated. Often the legal perspective is that it is best that we don't know about it. In Chapter 15, Thamara Subramanian outlines a four-step process to interrogating data with a racial justice lens, including organizational alignment, uncovering overlooked insights, applying a racial equity and dominant culture analysis to the data, and transparently revealing the results, even when they are not positive, with actionable recommendations for change.

Understanding is also about listening to the lived experiences of employees by creating a culture where there are no negative repercussions for speaking up, as Katelyn Peterson points out in Chapter 10, "Closed Mouths Don't Get Justice," and as Scott Ferry points out in Chapter 9, "Employees Can't Be Safe until They Feel Safe." Other chapters in Part II are written to enhance understanding of hiring and recruiting systems that perpetuate bias with job descriptions that require excessive years of experience, as outlined by Gabrielle Gayagoy Gonzalez in Chapter 17; training approaches that can harm BIPOC learners by retraumatizing them with reminders of injustices, as pointed out by Leigh Morrison in Chapter 19; and procurement policies that harm BIPOC vendors with long payment terms, as shared by Mareisha N. Reese in Chapter 20.

Reimagining

We cannot reimagine something different until we understand the harm that current systems cause. Each chapter offers reimagined ways of thinking, being, and doing that dismantle the status quo. Chapters in Part I ask readers to reflect on what is possible and what could be if there was courage to challenge the current system. In Chapter 6, Kevin A. Carter writes: "You may strive for a bold new idea that proclaims your mission is alive and well or a grand gesture to say you are no longer part of the problem but part of the solution." That grand gesture for a leader might be taking a pay cut to fund reparations for BIPOC employees or paying employee resource group leaders for their extra work, as Leigh Morrison and Tami Jackson tell us about in Chapter 16.

Tami Jackson implores us in Chapter 12 to reimagine professionalism by challenging dominant group notions about what "professional" looks like in name, appearance, speech, attire, and more. Scott Ferry asks us in Chapter 13 to reimagine allyship as "more than putting a black box in a social media profile, sharing an Angela Davis quote, or starting meetings and seminars with a perfunctory land acknowledgment." Instead, he says, consider "the conversations that these gestures are theoretically meant to spark and find or make the spaces to *actually have them* with others who do not yet agree."

In Chapter 16, Leigh Morrison and Tami Jackson invite us to reimagine the possibility of reparations in the form of such things as funding

student loan debt or committing to designating a portion of philanthropic giving to reparations. Gabrielle Gayagoy Gonzalez offers what
reimagining hiring and recruiting with a justice-centered focus might
look like in Chapter 17, such as including requirements in job postings
such as "demonstrates an understanding of institutional racism and
bias." Mareisha N. Reese suggests in Chapter 20 that procurement
departments can reimagine policies that harm BIPOC-owned vendors by recognizing that one size does not fit all and adopting policies
that benefit BIPOC business owners, such as faster payment terms
and different data security requirements. Megan Ellinghausen asks
us to reimagine bias in technology in Chapter 21. She explores how to
dismantle algorithms that reinforce oppressive modes of racism and
discrimination. This can be realized by taking on a socially conscious
design that centers those most impacted, that puts justice ahead of
profit, and that prioritizes equity over efficiency.

Actualizing

It can be done. We can change systems to prioritize racial justice in
the workplace. There are organizations that are transforming their
ways of being and doing. The book offers examples of practices that
actualize racial justice.

Mareisha N. Reese offers an example of a justice- and equity-
centered approach in Facebook's "Receivables Financing Program."
Facebook launched the program in 2021 and stated that it "gives our
diverse suppliers exclusive access to affordable cash flow through their
unpaid invoices. Instead of waiting sixty or ninety days for your customers to pay, you can sell those invoices to Facebook for immediate
payment."[2] Who benefits? Both Facebook and the supplier benefit, as
Facebook does charge a nominal 0.5 percent interest. Who is harmed?
No one. While this is pretty innovative and very justice centered, it
would not be needed if large companies would set more reasonable
payment terms and be more flexible with small businesses that need
to be paid promptly (e.g., net ten days).

In Chapter 21, Megan Ellinghausen shares how some state and local governments are attempting to disrupt bias in artificial intelligence (AI) algorithms that disproportionately harm BIPOC in areas such as job selections and the ability to obtain insurance. In 2018, New York City produced the first legislation in the country to shine a light on how government agencies are using AI to make decisions about people and policies. Since then, over forty pieces of legislation have been introduced to study or regulate government agencies' use of AI. Illinois enacted a law in 2019 requiring private employers to notify job candidates when algorithmic hiring tools are being used, and Colorado passed a law in 2021 that creates a framework for evaluating insurance underwriting algorithms and bans the use of discriminatory algorithms in the industry.

Leigh Morrison and Tami Jackson, in Chapter 16, outline how reparations are being actualized. In 2020, Evanston, Illinois, approved the nation's first government reparations plan "to acknowledge the harm caused by discriminatory housing policies, practices, and inaction going back more than a century."[3] The $10 million plan will create grants for homeownership and improvement and mortgage assistance for Black residents descended from those who suffered housing discrimination in the city. This is just one of many examples emerging of organizations embarking on reparations initiatives. LinkedIn now pays its employee affinity group leaders additional above their salaries for their extra work in organizing and leading programs designed to support greater inclusion. Most often Black or other people of color are tapped for these positions.

Racial Justice at Work lays out the current systemic problems impacting people, policies, and practices and invites the reader to reimagine what is possible when we have the desire to persevere, learn for understanding, and actualize new systems that are just—and in the end, make us all better off.

PART I

REIMAGINING JUSTICE IN THE WORKPLACE

Racial Justice at Work is about exploring possibilities for something new, different, affirming, and sustaining. It is about uncovering the pervasive norms, assumptions, and worldviews that keep us from making the progress that will lead, once and for all, to a world that works for all. Part I focuses on theory and strategy—essentially the *why* for this work. What is racial justice, and how should we approach weaponized terms related to antiracism in a polarized political climate? How do we make the collective mental shift to a justice mindset? What does it look like for leaders to take a developmental approach to racial justice? How can an organization prepare for and address resistance to racial justice work? Why is it important to take a clear stand? Reading this part of the book will prepare you and your organization to embrace the mindset, skillset, and heartset to take the action steps outlined in Part II, "Actualizing Justice in the Workplace."

CHAPTER ONE

Defining
Justice

MARY-FRANCES WINTERS

Founder and CEO

The Winters Group, Inc.

(she/her/hers)

With liberty and justice for all...

—UNITED STATES PLEDGE OF ALLEGIANCE

Most of us in the United States are very familiar with this phrase. You, like me, probably recited the Pledge of Allegiance daily during your K–12 school years. The founding fathers did not mean justice for *all*. They intended justice for white men, and even though we have fought (literally) for justice in this country and others like South Africa for centuries, the promise has still not been realized.

Justice in Corporate Contexts Is New

Justice is a new term in the diversity lexicon, especially in the corporate world. The movement started with the term *diversity*. Some years later, *inclusion* was added, and more recently, *equity* and for some more progressive organizations, the term *justice* has been added, and we now have—DEIJ (diversity, equity, inclusion, and justice) or JEDI (justice, equity, diversity, and inclusion).

In recent years there have been more attempts to align popular corporate approaches to diversity, equity, inclusion, and justice (DEIJ) and the social justice framework used more often in the nonprofit sector. Even though the corporate and nonprofit organizations es-pouse the same desired outcomes, the path to achieving equity often looks very different. As a matter of fact, until recently (after the Black Lives Matter protests of 2020), "justice" was rarely included in orga-nizations' definitions or goals (especially in the corporate world). I daresay that even those organizations now using "justice" as a part of their nomenclature have different interpretations of what it means or how to execute it. This chapter focuses on defining *justice* and how the concept is manifesting in corporate settings.

Fairness Is Not Necessarily Justice

If asked to define *justice* in one word, many might say it is fairness. However, the idea of fairness is complex and nuanced. Psychologists have a phrase called *the fallacy of fairness* and define it as an individ-ual's attempt to apply similar rules to everyone in their lives. Fairness is subjective and is almost always interpreted from an interpersonal lens…you in relation to others. Our sense of fairness is based on our perceptions, which we form from our experiences. We can begin to overcome the fallacy of fairness by adjusting our thinking.

First, fairness is not absolute. It is not binary—meaning it is not either fair or unfair. It is relative and can be very complex.

Second, our sense of fairness is often based on what we have expe-rienced—others may have had different experiences to inform their sense of fairness.

Third, we must look beyond our own sense of fairness and think more broadly about fair and equitable systems. I am not suggesting that we should discount our sense of whether something is fair or not. I am pointing out that it may come from a limited perspective, and we need to learn to recognize the limitations of our lens.

What Is Justice If Not Fairness?

Justice can be categorized in one of several ways: *distributive* (deter-mining who gets what), *procedural* (determining how fairly people are treated), *retributive* (determining how people are punished for wrongdoing), *contributive* (everyone has the right to contribute to how society operates), and *restorative* (repairing what is broken and compensating victims for past harm).[1] The restorative aspect of justice is probably the most controversial and has gotten little traction in the workplace. This book incorporates elements of all of the different types of justice.

Corporate reasons for attending to social injustice have morphed over the years from compliance (legal mandates) in the '70s to assimilation (helping newcomers to the hallowed corporate halls "fit in") and morality rhetoric of the '80s to a capitalistic driven "business case for diversity" started in the '90s. This business case rationale, still popular today, advances the notion that as US demographics shift from majority white to majority Black and brown populations, a focus on hiring people from these groups will enhance the organization's profits. Diversity practitioners set out to "prove" that targeting consumer marketing efforts to the growing "minority" populations leads to positive financial returns. The mantra "diversity is not only the right thing to do but also the right thing to do for business" is a popular cliché touted by many corporate leaders attempting to merge the moral with the capitalistic.

It is certainly not a binary. Organizations can do good and be good at the same time. Intentionally applying a justice framework enhances overall organizational performance. For example, consider the emergence and growing popularity of B corporations—those that certify they will balance purpose with profits. B corporations are legally required to assess the impact of their decisions on workers, customers, suppliers, the community, and the environment. Nearly four thousand companies globally are certified B corporations, using business as a force for good.[2]

The compliance, assimilation, and "attracting new markets" arguments for advancing equity have generally prioritized profit over purpose or people. "The right thing to do" motivation for DEI in corporate spaces has been most often thought of in moral terms. While morality is important, it is different from justice. Morality is about a personal sense of right and wrong, whereas justice is about taking the necessary action to uphold one's moral code. Dr. Martin Luther King Jr. in his *Letter from Birmingham Jail*, argued that "a just law is a man-made code that squares with the moral law or the law of God.... I would be the first to advocate obeying just laws. One has not only a legal but a moral responsibility to obey just laws. Conversely, one has a moral responsibility to disobey unjust laws. I would agree with St. Augustine that 'an unjust law is no law at all.'"[3] In organizations, obeying unjust policies is akin to what Dr. Martin Luther King Jr. and St. Augustine called obeying unjust laws.

Mapping the intersection between past corporate diversity and in-clusion approaches and what is required to integrate sound social jus-tice actions requires understanding this nuanced difference between morality and justice. One can abhor racism from a moral perspective ("It is wrong!") but do little to bring justice. Organizations were quick to issue statements after the George Floyd murder that by and large acknowledged the immorality of the rampant examples of blatant racism but perhaps did little to recognize complicity and take actions toward justice.

We are witnessing more calls for justice from workers today.[4] No longer are they willing to let the leaders define effective DEIJ actions passively. BIPOC employees and aspiring allies educate themselves on inequitable internal and external policies. And many more are leaving corporate spaces that do not provide equitable experiences, as evidenced by the Great Resignation movement outlined in Chapter 3.

Organizations serious about justice must interrogate their policies with an equity and justice lens. At its core, it means asking: Who is harmed by our systems? Who benefits from them? How can we redis-tribute power so that everyone benefits? Chapter 15, by Thamara Sub-ramanian, provides a step-by-step approach for interrogating policies and practices with a justice-focused lens. Even before we conduct such interrogations and add the "J" to our work, we must have a clear definition of justice and the actions the organization will commit to actualizing it.

SUMMARY

- Justice is a newer concept in the corporate diversity, equity, and inclusion space, and there is a lack of understanding about what it means and how to actualize it.

- Justice is often defined as "fairness" from an interpersonal perspective. Psychologists describe *the fallacy of fairness* because of the nuances and subjectivity applied to the definition.

- We have to look beyond our personal sense of fairness and think more broadly about fair and equitable systems.

- Fairness is not necessarily justice.

- Justice can be defined as distributive, procedural, retributive, contributive, and restorative.

- Corporate reasons for attending to social injustice have morphed over the years from compliance to assimilation to morality to the capitalistic-driven "business case for diversity."

- The compliance, assimilation, and "attracting new markets" arguments for advancing equity have generally prioritized profit over people.

- Intentionally applying a justice framework to achieving DEI goals enhances overall organizational performance.

- Morality is about a personal sense of right and wrong, whereas justice is about taking the necessary action to uphold one's moral code.

DISCUSSION/REFLECTION QUESTIONS

1. If your organization has added "J" to its diversity, equity, and inclusion work, do you know what it means? Has it been clearly defined?

2. Is there resistance to the notion of correcting harm? Is this being interpreted as unfair because of the equality versus equity mindset?

3. What are some justice-centered actions that you can take personally to support centering the experiences of those most impacted?

CHAPTER TWO

The Minimization, Weaponization, and Demonization of Racial Justice Concepts

MARY-FRANCES WINTERS
Founder and CEO
The Winters Group, Inc.
(she/her/hers)

Fear does not care about facts.

—DR. MICHAEL BERNARD BECKWITH

I laughed (an incredulous laugh, mind you) when a roving news reporter asked random people if they were for or against critical race theory (CRT). One older white man said with disdain that he was definitely against it. The reporter then asked him what CRT was—he said he did not know but knew it was not good and should be banned in schools.

This account epitomizes my experience with many people when it comes to terms and concepts related to racial justice, CRT being just one of several where there are misunderstandings and "alternate" interpretations that cast the concept as bad and even evil. Others include "the Great Replacement Theory" and "white supremacy culture." Even though the book is not about white supremacy culture per se, CRT, or the Great Replacement Theory, they have become the target of widespread controversy. To understand racial justice at work, I think it is important to consider the attempts to minimize, weaponize, and demonize concepts such as these. There are many other terms that have been weaponized and demonized related to racial justice that I do not address in this chapter, such as "woke," political correctness, reparations, and Black Lives Matter.

In our hyper-polarized world of social media sound bites, binaries are exacerbated, and it seems that there is just as much rhetoric, or maybe even more, minimizing, weaponizing, and demonizing of these terms as there is engaging in thoughtful discourse to learn more. Therefore, I thought it would be helpful to include a chapter that gives a few examples in hopes of advancing curiosity and a more balanced understanding. Because racial justice is a complex, controversial topic, this chapter only covers examples of how even the idea of systemic racism is minimized and how CRT, white supremacy culture, and the Great Replacement Theory are weaponized and demonized. I define each of these concepts and provide specific illustrations.

Let me first define what I mean by *minimization, weaponization,* and *demonization* in this context. *Minimization* is to diminish the importance of something through words or actions. *Weaponization* is to intentionally spread lies or disinformation—taking an idea or concept out of context to advance a cause contrary to its original intent. *Demonization* is to portray something or someone as bad or evil.

Teach Us but Don't Make Us Uncomfortable

When I wrote *Black Fatigue: How Racism Erodes the Mind, Body, and Spirit* in 2020, I devoted a chapter to defining terms like *race, racism,* and *white supremacy* because there seemed to be so many saying that they were not aware that racism was still such an issue and that they were not knowledgeable about it. (The resources page on our website at www.wintersgroup.com offers a comprehensive list of definitions of antiracist terms from MP Associates, the Center for Assessment and Policy Development, and World Trust Educational Services.)

They said, teach us. As more people were exposed to antiracism education and concepts like white supremacy culture, the message changed to "If this is what antiracism is about, then we are not interested in learning more. It makes us uncomfortable." As a result, actions have been taken to weaponize and demonize racial justice work by even attempting to outlaw discourse. For example, Donald Trump, while in office, issued Executive Orders banning diversity training in government agencies and for government contractors that made participants "uncomfortable."[1] Once Joe Biden was elected president, he immediately rescinded the orders. In April 2022, the governor of Florida, Ron DeSantis, signed House Bill 7, a law dubbed the "anti-woke" act with similar limitations to Trump's Executive Orders on how employers can talk about race and gender.[2] Florida has also passed what is commonly known as the "Don't Say Gay" bill, Florida House Bill 1557, which prohibits teachers from mentioning sexual orientation or identity in grades K–3.[3]

As an example of minimization we face at The Winters Group, clients routinely ask us to modify language in our training that might make participants uncomfortable. I will talk more about these requests later in the chapter.

Fear of Punishment Increases Discomfort

The topic of racial justice can engender discomfort for a variety of reasons. For some who are open to learning, I think one of the main sources of discomfort is the fear of saying the "wrong thing" and the repercussions that might follow. I have heard something like this numerous times: "I have to admit I don't know much about the history of racism, and I don't want to offend anyone, so I am uncomfortable in settings where my ignorance might be exposed." Let's face it. There can be consequences for saying the wrong thing. Numerous high-profile individuals have been "punished" for saying something considered offensive to a particular identity group—from being suspended or even fired from their responsibilities.

Consider Kevin Hart's 2012 despicable homophobic jokes, which in 2019 cost him the Oscars hosting job. Many were outraged when Megyn Kelly was dismissive about displaying blackface in 2018. In the same year, Rosanne Barr lost her starring role in her TV sitcom for likening one of Obama's advisers, Valerie Jarrett, to a monkey. Both parties admonished Iowa Republican Congressman Steve King's remarks in a *New York Times* interview in 2019: "White nationalist, white supremacist, Western civilization—how did that language become offensive?"[4] As punishment, King was stripped of all of his committee assignments. He says his comments were mischaracterized, but he has a long history of insensitive remarks about Muslims, immigrants, and other nonwhite groups. Therefore, King's punishment seems warranted. In 2020 he lost his reelection bid. In 2022, John Demsey, a thirty-one-year Estée Lauder veteran and executive group president, who had been previously lauded for his diversity and inclusion efforts at the company, was asked to leave for reposting a racist meme using the "N" word. He said that he posted it without reading it. He was contrite and issued a very long apology. Also, in 2022, Whoopi Goldberg was suspended from *The View* for two weeks after saying on the show that race was not a factor in the Holocaust. She, too, offered an apology.

There certainly should be some type of accountability for racist rhetoric, especially for high-profile people with great influence. However, does the punishment in and of itself lead to systemic change? Such reactions may be somewhat performative if they are not followed up with some deep discussion and education. If the standard solution is punishment, let's move on—we are not advancing racial justice. It is a form of minimizing. In Chapter 11, Rochelle Younan-Montgomery offers restorative dialogue techniques to repair the harm that such incidents cause BIPOC. (For the purpose of this book, BIPOC refers to Black, Indigenous, and people of color.)

I want to be clear. The goal is not to alleviate discomfort. It is to create a space for learning. Discomfort is a necessary part of most learning journeys. Consider a skill that you have learned. Think about the early stages of mastering that skill, such as riding a bike. I know I fell off plenty of times—skinned my knees, making me uncomfortable. The point is we will make mistakes along the racial justice path. Learning happens when we are willing to own our mistakes, learn from them, and use the experience to change our behaviors. Only when a critical mass of people engage in their own learning will we begin to change systems.

Minimizing and Even Denying the Existence of Systemic Racism

Minimizing and denying systemic racism can be another way "discomfort" manifests. If we claim that we are making too much of racism or that it does not exist, we do not have to experience discomfort. Systemic racism is a set of systems and structures that advantage the dominant group (e.g., white people) and disadvantage other groups. Systemic racism involves one group having the power to enact institutional policies and practices that harm BIPOC.

Here are some sentiments that minimize or even deny the existence of systemic racism. "That happened a long time ago. Why are we still talking about slavery?" Or it might look like absolving oneself from collective accountability with sentiments like, "This has nothing to do with me. I am not responsible for what my ancestors did." Another way I have heard it expressed as a comparison to their ethnicity is, "My ancestors were Irish immigrants (or some other white immigrant group), and they also suffered from racism, but we don't keep dwelling on it." Or, "Everyone has the same opportunities to succeed. We cannot be held accountable for outcomes."

This last argument is made in opposition to *equity* as contrasted with *equality*. *Equality* means we treat everyone the same (i.e., same opportunity). *Equity* means we consider the different needs of people based on past discrimination that continues to cause disparate outcomes. Senator Lindsey Graham, Republican from South Carolina, is one of many conservative politicians who has publicly denied the existence of systemic racism. He said on Fox News in 2021: "Our systems are not racist. America is not a racist country. Within every society, you have bad actors."[5] In a report issued in 2021, the British Commission on Race and Ethnic Disparities denied the existence of systemic racism in Great Britain, claiming geography, family influence, socioeconomic background, culture, and religion have a more significant impact on life outcomes than the existence of racism.[6] The UN Working Group of Experts on People of African Descent categorically rejected and condemned the analysis and findings of the report.[7]

This book presumes the existence of systemic racism.

The Weaponization and Demonization of CRT

Glenn Youngkin, Virginia's governor, elected in 2021, based his campaign on weaponizing and demonizing CRT. In his first few days in office, he issued an Executive Order banning the teaching of divisive topics in school, specifically naming CRT.[8] The fact is, CRT was never taught in Virginia schools or any school district. In fact, CRT is not a topic that is generally taught in K–12 schools across the US. A study by the Southern Poverty Law Center in 2011 found that thirty-five states received a rating of F for their coverage of civil rights content in the curriculum. Four other states earned a D rating, while only three states were rated with an A.

Most people do not even know what CRT is, as mentioned in the example at the beginning of this chapter. In a 2021 study by Northwestern University of more than nineteen thousand random Americans, 73 percent could not define it.[9] Yet, because of how it has been demonized and weaponized, many people are against it. According to the same survey, only 27 percent of Americans had a favorable perception of CRT, yet 52 percent supported "teaching about how racism continues to impact American society today."

So what is CRT anyway? Kimberlé Crenshaw, Black woman scholar, attorney, and executive director of the African American Policy Forum, is credited with coining the term *critical race theory* in the late 1980s to understand why laws were not working as intended to create equity for BIPOC.[10] It is a course taught in some law schools and other graduate courses of study. She has demystified CRT as "not a thing but rather a way to look at a thing." She said: "It is a way to study the enduring racial inequities in this country and ask the question 'why.'" CRT does not teach that all white people are racists. CRT seeks to understand why racial disparities continue to persist. CRT does not teach that the rule of law does not exist as the detractors espouse. It teaches that the rule of law has not been fair or just for BIPOC.

CRT gets a lot of attention from politicians, talk show hosts, and the news media. It is seen as such a threat that more than forty states have introduced legislation to ban CRT or limit how racism and sexism can be discussed in education, including K–12 and at the college level.[11] Some of these bills also seek to ban diversity training in government, like Florida's legislation. Conservative politicians have used CRT as one of their key talking points, like Glenn Youngkin denouncing it as Marxist, racist bigotry. Senator Ted Cruz (Republican of Texas) said that CRT is just as racist as the Klansmen.[12]

Those who oppose CRT oppose teaching the truth about racism in this country. We don't have to face the "uncomfortable" truth if we deny and ban it. As more contemporary scholars like Nikole Hannah-Jones (*The 1619 Project*) and Ibram X. Kendi (author of *How to Be an Antiracist* and *Stamped from the Beginning*) gain popularity by telling the untold stories of racism in this country, there is a groundswell of opposition. Scholars who advance racial justice are often demonized. For those weaponizing and demonizing the concept, any mention of racism could be interpreted as CRT and therefore evil. Educating ourselves on what is true and false is critical to achieving racial justice.

White Supremacy Culture Concept Is Minimized, Weaponized, and Demonized

I remember the first time I introduced the idea of white supremacy culture to a group of mostly white senior leaders. I expected some pushback, but I was optimistic that the topic would engender curiosity. I was very wrong. The response was anger and denial. I thought I was cautious to set up the discussion by distinguishing between a white supremacist and white supremacy culture—the former, a person who openly advances racist beliefs and actions, and the latter a system that upholds the values of the dominant group (i.e., those who hold power) as the only "right way" of being and doing. This was a training session for a longtime client. We lost the contract soon after.

For many white people, the very idea of suggesting that there is even a "white culture," let alone one that is "supreme," is totally antithetical to their belief system. Over the almost forty years of doing DEI work, I have often heard from white participants in sessions that they do not feel they have a culture. "Culture" is ascribed to those "other" groups. In hindsight, I should have realized that introducing a concept as complex as white supremacy culture to people who likely had not thought of themselves as a part of a culture defined by their race would not go well. Pew Research conducts a survey that asks, to what extent is your race core to your identity? Nearly 75 percent of Black people, 59 percent of Hispanic, and 56 percent of Asian Americans answer that it is extremely or very important, while only 15 percent of white people do so (Figure 2.1).[13]

Because of the lack of connection to their race as a part of their identity and lack of a sense of being a part of a racial culture, white people may not only minimize but deny the existence of a white supremacy culture. They are not able to conceive of such a thing. That stands to reason because when you are a part of the dominant group, all that relates to it is normal for you. It can be impossible to see how BIPOC might experience the culture differently unless you are open to such a possibility. The fish-in-water analogy works to support our understanding. The fish does not know that it is swimming in water until you take it out of the water. We all swim in the dominant culture water. The problem is that BIPOC often find that the water is deeper and more toxic and too often end up drowning.

The term *white supremacy culture* is a way of understanding how systemic racism is ingrained in many of the systems we take for granted as the *best* or *only* way. The term has become so demonized many of our clients ask us to change the language to *dominant culture*. Those willing to lean into the concept a bit more accept *white normative culture*. Clients tell us that leaders feel personally attacked and are uncomfortable with the discussion when we use the term

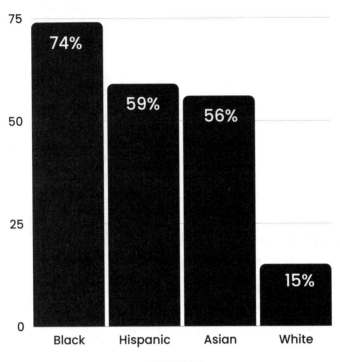

Is race/ethnicity important to how you see yourself?

FIGURE 2.1.

Percentage of People Who Believe Race or Ethnicity Is Core to Their Identity, 2019

SOURCE: The Winters Group based on data from Pew Research Center

white supremacy culture. Even though *dominant culture* translates to "white," as white people hold power, it is somehow more palatable not to connect the characteristics to a racial group explicitly. I understand that the term *white supremacist* carries great negativity as people associate it with the KKK and other hate groups.

The goal for greater racial understanding is to learn to distinguish between white supremacists and white supremacy culture. White supremacists subscribe to a belief system that white people are the superior race and therefore should dominate to the exclusion or elimination of other races. On the other hand, white supremacy culture is the operating assumption that white people and their ideas, thoughts, beliefs, and actions are superior to BIPOC and their ideas, thoughts, beliefs, and actions.[14] This typically plays out unconsciously as the unquestioned, completely accepted norms, behaviors, beliefs, values, and symbols passed down by communication and imitation from one generation to the next.

Trainers and facilitators Tema Okun and Kenneth Jones are credited with advancing the theory of white supremacy culture in a 1999 paper based on their experiences in teaching and consulting in antiracism.[15] As a result of the resurgence of interest in antiracism training after the murder of George Floyd in 2020, Okun developed a website to add more clarity and context. Okun's website says: "My intention is to say that white supremacy culture trains *all* of us to internalize attitudes and behaviors that do not serve *any* of us well." She says that the characteristics are not binaries—good or bad—but in excess and to the exclusion of other ways of doing or being. They are harmful to all of us and even more to BIPOC.[16]

My attempt in this chapter is not to explain how each of the interrelated characteristics Okun advances might exemplify a white dominant culture. I refer you to the resources referenced in this chapter. To support your understanding, though, I encourage you to think about: Who gets to decide what is right? Acceptable? Normal? And how do these "standards" harm BIPOC? I offer a few examples here.

Epistemicide

I am reminded of a story a former client tells. He is a gay Latine DEIJ professional. When defending his PhD dissertation, his professor rejected two of his sources as not credible and said he would not be granted his PhD referencing the Latine scholars he had chosen. They were not considered the experts on that topic, and he should replace them with European scholars. My client said that the scholars he selected advanced similar theories to the European ones but were not as well known. He wanted to amplify their voices. Not only were the Latine scholars disadvantaged by a system that assumes white scholarship is supreme, but all of society is also. It is a form of epistemicide.

Portuguese sociologist Boaventura de Sousa Santos is credited with coining the term *epistemicide*, the erasure of Indigenous knowledge and ways of being. In his book *Epistemologies of the South: Justice Against Epistemicide*, he outlines how colonization, in addition to the violence against humans, also eradicated Indigenous knowledge. As just one example, in South America before colonization, agriculture was balanced with nature through complex agroecology systems that included religious and cultural values. European colonizers abandoned these ways during the Spanish conquest to maximize profit at the expense of biodiversity. Who got to decide? There are many other examples of epistemicide, including adhering to Western medical models rejecting Eastern and Indigenous healing approaches, loss of Native languages, religions, and teaching methods. The dominant culture gets to decide the "right" way.

Only One Right Way

In Chapter 12, Tami Jackson questions "only one right way" in how we define *professionalism* and who gets to decide what is professional. From hairstyles to dress codes, the norm is decided by the dominant group. In 2018, for instance, a young Black high school wrestler in New Jersey sporting dreadlocks was about to start his match when he was informed by a white referee that he would need to cut his dreadlocks or forfeit the match. A video of the young man having his dreadlocks cut by a white trainer soon went viral.[17] Can you imagine the psychological impact of this incident on this young man? In addition to dreadlocks, schools have banned braids, corn rows, and other styles that are considered "Black" to the point of needing a law, the CROWN Act, passed in the US House of Representatives in 2021, prohibiting discrimination on the basis of hairstyle because the dominant group was deciding what was acceptable and normal. CROWN stands for "Creating a Respectful and Open World for Natural Hair"; it has yet to pass the US Senate.

Bigger Is Better

Another white supremacy culture characteristic is: Bigger is always better. We see this manifest in unquestioned capitalism. If public corporations don't exceed last quarter's earnings, they are dinged by Wall Street. This often leads to decisions that prioritize profit over people. We saw this starting in the '70s with massive worker layoffs. This approach to maintaining "acceptable" profit margins when the economy is down is now accepted and even expected. In his 2007 book *The Disposable American*, reporter Louis Uchitelle describes the devastating psychological impact on individuals at all income levels, and BIPOC are more impacted by these events as more often the "last hired and first fired."

Consider that in 2021, CEOs made 254 times more than the average worker. The Economic Policy Institute estimates that CEO pay has increased by 1,322 percent since 1978, compared to 18 percent for the typical worker over this period.[18] Who benefits from a bigger is always better ideology? Those who are in power and make the decisions that benefit them. We see this manifest in tax laws enacted to advantage the wealthiest in society, who are by and large white. People on the bottom of the income hierarchy suffer the most, and BIPOC as a group are more likely to be on that bottom rung.

Either/or thinking is another characteristic that Okun advances. For example, capitalism in and of itself is not necessarily all bad, but it is not all good either. With either/or thinking, if one does not embrace capitalism without question as the best system, they may be labeled socialist or Marxist, or something deemed even worse—another example of "only one right way" to think or believe. Capitalism leads to power hoarding (another characteristic of white supremacy culture), upholding wealth inequality, and short-term thinking (e.g., the need to increase profit every quarter). Of course, there are also many positive aspects of a capitalist society, such as free markets and innovation. Again, who gets to decide who can fully participate and benefit from capitalism? Who gets exploited in such systems? History tells us that it is BIPOC and other nondominant groups. These are complex issues, and I am not a scholar on capitalism. My objective is to encourage more thoughtful discourse that is not based on binaries to be able to consider possibilities that benefit all rather than disproportionately benefitting dominant groups.

Right to Comfort

One of Okun's characteristics of white supremacy culture is the right to comfort. The notion that white people should not be made to feel "uncomfortable" is one of the key premises of the laws being passed to ban diversity training mentioned earlier. Even without the potential legislation, I regularly hear clients' sentiments like, "We need to be careful not to make our leaders too uncomfortable, or we will lose them, and it is important to keep them engaged." Who gets to decide the "discomfort" tolerance?

Should it be acceptable for BIPOC to be uncomfortable in work environments that are unwelcoming and exclusive but not for dominant groups? And again, who gets to decide? It is necessary to have a foundational understanding of the history of racism to understand white supremacy culture, to be able to critically self-reflect and accept that the water we all swim in is based on a racial hierarchy. White is at the top of the hierarchy.

You may not like the feeling when you hear the term *white supremacy culture*. The term has been socialized into our lexicon, and rather than reducing it to a binary of "I believe it or I don't" (it's good, or it's bad), if you hold the dominant identity of white, I encourage you to go deeper and self-reflect on the things that you consider normal, universal, unquestionably right. Where do those ideals come from, and is it possible that they represent an underlying, perhaps unconscious belief that your ways are better than those of other racial identities?

The Great Replacement Theory

Fueling these ardent and growing attempts to censure thoughtful discourse on racism is the propagation of the Great Replacement Theory—that nonwhite immigrants will replace the white majority, gaining the political power to "win" the culture war and thus dismantling white supremacy.[19] Also called "the White Replacement Theory," it is the belief that there are forces intentionally working to change the racial mix of the country and they must be stopped even if it means violence.

Here is how this concept is weaponized. There are many examples of how the dominant group throughout history has engaged in "replacement theory" attempts to replace BIPOC. Consider the Indian Removal Act, which led to the infamous Trail of Tears. Starting in 1830, more than one hundred thousand Native Americans were forced to abandon their homes and move to Indian territory, with more than four thousand dying on the journey because white settlers wanted the valuable land.[20]

The emergence of urban Chinatowns resulted from the displacement of Chinese people in the 1870s. The anti-Chinese movement was marked by massacres, riots, evictions, and legal restrictions on where Chinese immigrants could live and work—rural Chinatowns were destroyed, forcing many Chinese immigrants into urban areas. Today, Chinese people are being "replaced" in urban Chinatowns, where the number of white residents in Chinatown is growing at a faster rate than the overall population in those cities.[21] Chinese people are getting priced out of these housing markets and replaced with white people, a form of gentrification.

Gentrification is when an economically disadvantaged area of a city experiences an influx of middle-class or wealthy people who renovate and rebuild homes and businesses, often resulting in an increase in property values and the displacement of original, usually poorer residents of a neighborhood.[22] Gentrification has displaced BIPOC in many major cities in the United States over the past four decades. BIPOC are being forced to move from communities, where in many cases they have generations of history, where they can no longer afford to live, into neighborhoods that are even more depressed.

Racial justice requires us to seek the truth. The truth about the Great Replacement Theory is that there is no organized attempt to replace white people—population shifts based on birthrates are doing that—but there is a long and continuing history of organized attempts to displace and replace BIPOC.

SUMMARY

- Many racial justice concepts are minimized, weaponized, and demonized.

- *Minimization* is to diminish the importance of something through words or actions. *Weaponization* is to spread lies or disinformation intentionally, and *demonization* is to portray something or someone as evil.

- Many white people are uncomfortable discussing race. The fear of being wrong and, as a consequence, "punished" exacerbates the discomfort in exploring racial justice concepts. Racial justice requires us to give grace and space for learning while holding people accountable for racist words and actions.

- Systemic racism is minimized or denied by suggesting it is something of the past or only happens at the interpersonal level by a "few bad actors."

- Critical race theory (CRT) is weaponized and demonized. It is an academic term to describe a way of examining the persistence of systemic racism and asking why. It is not taught in K–12 settings. It is typically a graduate-level college course.

- White supremacy culture is a way of understanding how systemic racism is ingrained in many of the systems we take for granted, and may not be conscious of, as the best or only way. White supremacy culture is confused with white supremacists—people who subscribe to a belief system that white people are the superior race and therefore should dominate to the exclusion or elimination of other races.

- The Great Replacement Theory is demonized as an intentional attempt of BIPOC to replace white people. The truth is that dominant groups have engaged in replacing BIPOC for centuries.

DISCUSSION/REFLECTION QUESTIONS

1. Why is it important to understand how racial justice terms are minimized, weaponized, and demonized?

2. What can we do to gain more knowledge about what is true, not true, confusing, and ambiguous?

3. What can you do to ensure that you are a part of the discourse to correct inaccurate and harmful interpretations of racial justice terms?

4. What can you do if you identify as white to enhance your ability to lean into your discomfort? If you are BIPOC, what is your capacity to offer grace and space for mistakes without feeling that you are obligated to teach white people about racial injustices?

CHAPTER THREE

Operationalizing Justice:
A Radical Shift in Consciousness

LEIGH MORRISON
Learning and Innovation Manager
The Winters Group, Inc.
(she/her/hers)

I believe a future where harm is the anomaly is already rooting
in our communities...we generate small pockets of movement
so irresistibly accountable that people come running toward
us, expecting they will be welcomed, flawed and whole, by a
community committed to growth; knowing that there is a place
in this violent, punitive world that is already committed to, and
practicing, a healing and transformative iteration of justice.

—ADRIENNE MAREE BROWN

Perhaps your organization was one of many that jumped to action during the racial reckoning of 2020. You likely made donations, hosted antiracism trainings or listening sessions, and distributed statements to various stakeholders to communicate solidarity with people experiencing the impact of racism. Your momentum may have waned since then—whether due to uncertainty about how to navigate backlash from internal or external stakeholders, lack of funding or staffing to support racial justice efforts, or other priorities taking precedent in an increasingly complex world. You are far from alone... and welcome back. Your commitment is critical.

In January 2021, we witnessed an insurrection against the US government by a mob composed of white supremacists intent on preventing the peaceful transfer of power. In stark contrast to the violent suppression of peaceful protests by Black activists and allies spurred by the murder of George Floyd,[1] this event was met with a striking lack of resistance from law enforcement.[2] These events together illustrated in no uncertain terms how racism continues to permeate US culture, politics, and institutions.

Resistance to racial justice work is robust and escalating in our era of fear and misinformation as Kevin A. Carter point out in Chapter 6. Racist conspiracy theories are reaching wider audiences. Inflammatory rhetoric from conservative pundits has fueled censorship of historical truths in school curriculum.[3] Conservative lawmakers are passing laws that restrict voting rights and make it illegal to conduct diversity training that makes (white) people uncomfortable.[4] Recent events make it increasingly clear how much work is needed to even begin approaching a society in which race is no longer a predictor of outcome.

In this book, The Winters Group team invites you to explore a radical shift in consciousness critical to this moment. This shift calls us to interrogate how white supremacy culture is rooted in our worldviews, through priorities placed in many Western cultures on characteristics like individualism, "quantity over quality," right to comfort, and power hoarding, among others.[5] In the workplace, this shift can encompass everything from how we market and advertise, to changes in HR policies and practices, to payment terms for diverse suppliers, and much more. Because white supremacy culture is the water we swim in, many of us have accepted it as normal. We may be oblivious to how it harms all of us—with an additional burden often placed on marginalized communities.

This radical shift in consciousness requires us to embrace possibilities that may initially feel "out of the question"—because many of us have never really used a justice-centered lens to correct persistent inequities. We must push past the assumption that these possibilities are "unrealistic" or too far-reaching; in fact, they may be our only hope of reaching far enough. Encouragingly, possibility models for meaningful change and correcting harm are increasing in prevalence and proving their potential throughout institutions historically steeped in systemic racism, from banking to media to government. Some examples:

- In October 2020, JPMorgan Chase allocated $30 billion toward addressing structural barriers to racial equity perpetuated by the banking industry.[6] Funds are directed toward expanding affordable housing for Black and Latine households, growing Black- and Latine-owned businesses, and improving access to financial health and banking in Black and Latine communities.[7] This was followed in August 2022 by Bank of America's announcement of its new Community Affordable Loan Solution program, which offers first-time homebuyers in Black and Latine communities mortgages with no down payments or closing costs.[8]

- In February 2022, the *Baltimore Sun* published an editorial titled "We are deeply and profoundly sorry: For decades, the *Baltimore Sun* promoted policies that oppressed Black Marylanders; we are working to make amends."[9] Rather than offering the familiar vague promises of support and solidarity, this article acknowledged specific examples of racist harm caused by the newspaper's policies and publications, defined tangible actions to disrupt and correct this harm, and solicited readers' direct input.

- In August 2022, the Biden administration announced a Student Debt Relief Plan, including expansion of income-based repayment support and the cancellation of up to $20,000 of student debt for recipients of Pell Grants and up to $10,000 for nonrecipients with income below $125,000. Historically marginalized communities remain underrepresented in both completion of higher-education degrees and in higher-paying jobs, while simultaneously shouldering disproportionate amounts of student debt. Policy interventions like debt relief and restructuring compensation have the potential to meaningfully reduce race-based and other identity-centered wealth disparities.[10]

Each of these examples spells hope and offers the possibility for justice-centered progress that can sustainably disrupt entrenched systemic inequities. Each of them was made possible through significant—one might say, radical—shifts in thinking and approaches that have been accepted for too long. Radical changes in practices that will support us in operationalizing justice begin with understanding how and why the very terms of justice are being intentionally cast in a negative light.

Demonization of Progress

Affirmative action. Representative leadership. Redistributing resources. Compensation transparency. Collective bargaining. Education about historical and current manifestations of racism. Dismantling white supremacy culture. Conversation about power and privilege. Open acknowledgment of mistakes and harm. Reparations.

These terms may send shivers down the spines of organizational leaders—and it is no wonder, given that some have become demonized in subsets of US and Western cultures to the point that many people have deeply negative associations with them. (In Chapter 2, Mary-Frances Winters highlights other terms that have also been demonized.) Yet if we assume these concepts are antithetical to running a successful organization, make no mistake: this is due to our conditioning in a capitalism-centered, white supremacist culture to which these concepts pose a threat. Realizing just and antiracist organizations will require divesting from these assumptions. Importantly, this will require defining success more broadly than organizations may be accustomed to and recognizing that *the thriving of organizations is inseparable from the thriving of individuals who comprise them.*

Contrary to what dominant rhetoric that distances us from solutions might have us believe (*We just aren't ready for this … we've made progress, but change takes time.*), real solutions to ongoing injustices are in reach, and stakeholders expect action. Forward-thinking organizational leaders must affirm accurate information, embrace bold policy change, and commit to working through resistance they will inevitably encounter in the critical pursuit of racial justice. Kevin A. Carter advises on this in Chapters 6 and 7. We must move toward justice-centered approaches in our thinking, being, and doing. The intense countermovements to the racial reckoning unfolding today seek to undo progress with lies and deception. This moment calls those who say we are committed to racial justice to do something.

Stakeholders Expect Change

Advocates for racial justice are increasingly demanding that organizations make changes.[11] In light of the Great Resignation, organizations are finding themselves unable to brush off racist incidents and harm caused in today's climate, as employees[12] and consumers[13] alike hold them accountable. Simultaneously, those that fail to retain historically marginalized employee groups develop or maintain reputations as hostile work environments. Consider:

- **Demand for diversity and inclusion.** A survey conducted by Glassdoor in 2020 found that three out of four job seekers indicate a diverse workforce is an important consideration for them when evaluating job offers. Furthermore, almost half of Black and Latine employees and job seekers have quit a job after experiencing or witnessing workplace discrimination.[14]

- **Rising legal action.** Organizations as varied as the National Football League,[15] art museums,[16] and craft breweries have been met with accusations of, and lawsuits surrounding, racism and gender-based discrimination. The tech industry—one of many struggling with representation in overwhelmingly white and male workforces[17]—routinely makes the news. In the fall of 2021 a federal court ruled that Tesla must pay $137 million to a former worker due to racist abuse he experienced there.[18] A similar suit has been filed at Google,[19] which also recently settled a gender-based pay discrimination lawsuit for $118 million.[20] Activision recently settled in an $18 million payout to victims of sexual harassment.[21]

- **Employee walkouts and consumer boycotts.** Netflix,[22] Wayfair,[23] and Disney[24] have contended with employee walkouts and customer boycotts based on their complacency and involvement in amplifying transphobic content, supplying furnishings to migrant detention camps, and the passage of Florida's "Don't Say Gay" laws, respectively.

- **Support for unionization.** In a landmark vote in April 2022, Amazon workers at a Staten Island warehouse became the first Amazon employees to successfully overcome years of corporate lobbying when they voted to unionize to support their rights and safety.[25] This effort, organized by a diverse coalition of employees, directly responded to low wages, high turnover, questionable safety practices, and intense "productivity monitoring."[26] Employees at an Apple Store in Maryland voted to form the company's first US union in June 2022.[27] To date, 160 Starbucks stores have voted to unionize after a first location's successful union vote in December 2021. After seven Starbucks union organizers were fired, a federal judge ordered them reinstated.[28]

- **Call for transparency.** Today, 87 percent of job seekers desire workplace transparency.[29] Millennials value trust more than any previous generation and are twenty-two times more likely to stay long-term in high-trust organizations. However, this trend extends further: Gen Xers and Baby Boomers are sixteen and thirteen times more likely to stay, respectively.[30]

These facts provide a small snapshot of the many ways that complicity and "business as usual" is proving increasingly unsustainable—a trend that will no doubt continue as the demographics of our workforce evolve and conversations about justice continue to make strides in the public consciousness.

More organizations than not are struggling with dysfunction that has been normalized through dominant culture and history (*We've always done it this way!*). What will set some organizations apart from others during this era is how open and responsive they are to employee concerns. Leaders who prioritize listening, fostering trust, and accountability will likely succeed. Those unwilling to lean into discomfort that is requisite to progress are likely to revert to "familiar dysfunction"[31]—a particularly unsustainable path in a culture increasingly focused on accountability for harm.

Organizations Are Being Called to Lead the Way

So-called culture wars are in full force. Backlash to "woke supremacy" and antiracism work is—as white supremacy is intended to function—creating noise and distraction. Those committed to upholding white supremacy are appropriating the language of harm and "divisiveness" to confuse people into complacency and inaction. In the midst of it all, we are each faced with a choice about which side of history we will be on. We cannot allow this noise to distract us from the work at hand or drown out the moral and historical truths we must affirm at this moment[32]—or risk slipping further into the grips of xenophobia and authoritarianism.[33]

The 2021 Edelman Trust Barometer, a report published annually on global trends surrounding trust, found that more Americans trust CEOs than the institutions of government and the media.[34] This extraordinary trend has key implications for the role of organizations and their leaders in disrupting persistent systemic injustice. Many organizations are new to navigating harmful events with a justice-centered lens, and may struggle to respond. Our team urges leaders to address events promptly and avoid burdening those traumatically impacted by racist events with teaching their colleagues about their experiences. To promote longer-term sustainability, prioritize wellness by increasing access to benefits like mental health support and paid time off. Certain events also call for targeted policy responses; in light of the overturning of *Roe v. Wade*, we encourage increasing access to reproductive healthcare through insurance coverage and funding relocation expenses for those whose rights are in peril.

This book outlines the value of possible models like these and longer-term strategies to prevent and disrupt injustice. Because our team believes in the value of ongoing reflection and change accompanying our practices, as we compiled these chapters, we devoted time toward reflecting on how these topics show up in ourselves and our organization and continually asking ourselves: where can we do better? As we continue to build critical capacity around long-overdue cultural change, we encourage you to make this commitment with us. We invite you to reach out to us on social media to share about changes your organization has made, connections this book sparks for you, and commitments you will make going forward.

SUMMARY

- While many organizations have embraced externally focused and shorter-term steps to address racial injustices, much broader shifts to organizational approaches are needed to sustain change.

- "Business as usual" is failing in a time when employees and consumers alike are demanding accountability from organizations and businesses for the harm they have been complicit in or caused.

- In the context of unprecedented employee turnover spurred by the Great Resignation, most job seekers are prioritizing diverse and inclusive workplaces supported by transparency and cultures of trust.

- The backlash to racial justice work is a predictable response with countless historical precedents; it is designed to divide people and distract from the reality that everyone can benefit from changes that support equity and justice.

- As distrust in government and the media continues to manifest, organizations and their leaders occupy a critical role in guiding public opinion and setting precedents around social issues.

- As employees rethink their relationships to work, it is becoming increasingly difficult to separate the thriving of employees from the thriving of organizations to which they belong. Commitment to and progress toward racial equity will benefit employees, employers, and social progress alike.

DISCUSSION/REFLECTION QUESTIONS

1. What associations do you have with concepts like affirmative action, compensation transparency, and reparations? Are they positive or negative? Where did they originate?

2. How would you characterize the level of trust in your organization? What has supported or impeded it? How might this relate to retention, turnover, and other dynamics?

3. To what extent has your organizational leadership been involved in antiracism work? Have you adopted external-facing and short-term responses to racial injustice, comprehensive internal efforts for policy and culture change, or both?

4. What resistance have you encountered, or do you anticipate, to justice-centered efforts in your organization? How can you use themes addressed in this chapter to make a case for longer-term, sustainable investments in justice initiatives?

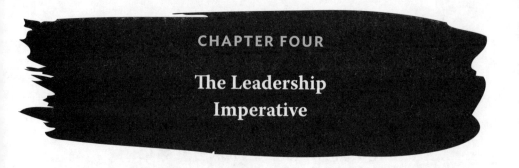

CHAPTER FOUR

The Leadership Imperative

MARY-FRANCES WINTERS
Founder and CEO
The Winters Group, Inc.
(she/her/hers)

> Not everything that is faced can be changed; but
> nothing can be changed until it is faced.
>
> —JAMES BALDWIN

If we are going to operationalize justice in organizations, we will have to start hiring and promoting people into power positions who understand what a justice-centered approach entails and are not afraid to work through the resistance, which Kevin A. Carter writes about in Chapters 6 and 7. Conflict and discomfort will surely be a part of the process. A number of other contributors to this book have questioned the sincerity of the commitment that organizations made to racial justice in the wake of recent Black Lives Matter protests. It did not take long before we started to experience backpedaling from the forceful declarations many organizations made to prioritize antiracism. I used to ask if the racial reckoning would be a moment or a movement. I am afraid it may now be turning into a memory.

In their quest to placate the dominant group (those with systemic power, privilege, and social status), I find that organizational leaders are taking the path of least resistance. They hear from those who have their ear that "this antiracism stuff is going too far." "What about me and my group?" They are also being influenced by accounts of white people feeling uncomfortable, targeted, and de-prioritized. In some organizations, leaders express anger and resentment about engaging in antiracism work. I reviewed the results of an equity audit The Winters Group conducted for a client. One of the essential findings was that key stakeholders (leaders) were against and even hostile to diversity, equity, and inclusion efforts in the organization.

As a result of the resistance, we are being asked to expand learning content to include other historically marginalized groups beyond Black/African Americans and to use language that is more palatable to white people. In essence, as usual, we are being asked to center the feelings of the dominant group (white people). I have no problem including content on other marginalized groups beyond Black/African Americans. However, every racial and ethnic group has had a unique history of oppression. We actually do a disservice, and it is disrespectful to people of color, when we lump everybody together as if the experiences are all the same—and to boot, do it in a ninety-minute session.

As a result of the racial protests of 2020, organizations vowed to address anti-Black racism specifically. This does not mean that other forms of racism are less important and do not demand attention; the recent rise in anti-Asian racism and antisemitism are prime examples. We believe that focusing on anti-Black racism—a response to the unique ways the US was built on anti-Blackness and continues to perpetuate compounded inequities—will also benefit our understanding of other forms of racism and actions that can mitigate them too. We encourage organizations to give appropriate attention to each "-ism" separately.

It is one thing to espouse antiracist values and another to live them. Espousal is an important first step. Before the recent racial reawakening, most organizations did not even use the term *antiracism*. And still, this language is rarely included in corporate communications. Antiracism is new territory for many leaders. Some may not have fully understood what they were signing up for when they vowed to address anti-Black racism. Leaders need to make good on their commitments made since George Floyd's murder, and the Black Lives Matter protests that erupted around the globe as a result. While pushback was expected, I don't think leaders gave enough attention to how they would address it.

I was recently piloting a learning experience on racism with the CEO and direct reports of a major organization. We introduced the concept of white supremacy culture, and there was indeed major pushback. One of the leaders said they needed to reevaluate how to brand this as inclusion training and not use the term *racism* or *white supremacy culture* so as not to make participants too uncomfortable. I reminded them that it might be too late to sanitize the language and "soften" the content, as they had committed publicly to engage in antiracism training. The leader seemed surprised that such a commitment had been made. I explained that antiracism education is very different from diversity, inclusion, and belonging training. Antiracism work is based on a specific body of research and ideologies that have not been introduced in many corporate spaces. Core to antiracism education is understanding concepts such as white supremacy culture.

As a result of this type of resistance, The Winters Group introduced five leadership commitments that we think are critical to embrace before embarking on antiracism work.

1. **Acknowledge that systemic inequity, injustice, and exclusion are real and exist everywhere.** Some leaders are still skeptical that racism is as insidious as it is, especially in their organizations. If you don't believe that it exists, obviously, you will not give it priority. When you believe it, it is easier to embrace the ideologies and language that help us understand racism and dismantle it.

Lately several leaders have asked if they should organize listening- or healing-type sessions every time some injustice occurs, as such events seem to be happening daily around the world. As a practical way to operationalize justice and acknowledge the reality of the unjust world that we exist in, I recommend institutionalizing space for listening and discussion on a regular cadence where people can opt in as they choose. For example, schedule monthly virtual conversations in different parts of the world for sharing and healing.

2. **Know you (as the leader) are responsible and accountable for creating and sustaining equity and justice.** Leaders must stand up to the resisters and be willing to take action—including parting ways with those not on board. I talked with a potential client recently who is asking us to coach a leader who made some racist comments. The HR lead said, "We are not going to fire him. This is just the way he is, and I don't think he really means it." I learned that the incident happened in 2019, and people in the organization experience this leader as bombastic and arrogant. Why is he still there if the organization is committed to being antiracist?

If you are serious about antiracism, some really tough decisions will have to be made about who gets to be a leader. It starts with who you hire and promote. Do you assess potential leaders on their perspectives on diversity, equity, and inclusion? Do you emphasize your commitment to antiracism and expected behaviors? What measures are in place to hold leaders accountable?

As an example of leadership commitment, The Winters Group was recently invited to present our solution to a major tech firm as a part of their selection process for a consulting partner. The CEO participated in the interview along with the DEI team. He was very engaged, asked probing questions, and demonstrated his interest in ensuring they picked the right partner. Leaders need to be visible and involved in the work.

3. **Be willing to engage in your own reflection and learning, recognizing personal work is necessary to drive broader change.** Leaders too often think antiracism learning should focus on their teams and not them. They come late and leave early from the training sessions or don't show up at all. While I acknowledge

that leaders are busy and unexpected events may come up, they must prioritize their own learning. As an example of engaging in education, one of our clients retained The Winters Group to meet for one hour every other week for a year with him and his direct reports in a developmental learning journey where we unpacked concepts like white supremacy culture. I coached the CEO monthly. At the end of the year, leaders could all point to new behaviors, changes in policies and practices that fostered a justice-centered approach.

4. **Prioritize and allocate ample resources to sustain this work.** Too often, we hear from the DEI lead that there is a "limited budget" for this work. We know that many times the DEI office is understaffed. Additionally, people with no background in DEI are tapped to do this work as "volunteers" just because they are BIPOC. We are working with an organization that pulled someone from the manufacturing floor to coordinate inclusion. He asked me recently how he could better manage the immense stress and toll attempting to perform in a role for which he has limited experience, other than his identity as a Black man. This should not be his responsibility. Do not equate someone's identity with qualifications to effectively lead DEIJ work, and do not expect BIPOC to take on extra work without appropriate compensation. DEIJ should be a formal part of every leader's job description—from first-level manager up to the CEO.

5. **Accept resistance, conflict, and discomfort as requisite to progress.** Be proactive in anticipating resistance and develop effective strategies to address it. Here is a process to follow:

   ▸ Senior leaders should establish expectations for all other leaders and employees. Tie them to existing values in your organization.
   ▸ Communicate non-negotiables such as "We will use the anti-racism language. Training and education will be mandatory, and we expect you to be supportive and willing to learn."

▸ Establish real consequences for not demonstrating behaviors previously communicated and supported by the organization's values.

In Chapter 7, Kevin A. Carter outlines the various steps for addressing resistance.

SUMMARY

- Racial justice requires committed leadership willing to stand up against inevitable resistance.

- Leaders need to acknowledge the persistence of racism in society and their organizations.

- Leaders must recognize the need to "do their own work." toward understanding their biases and hold their direct reports accountable to do the same.

- Ample resources must be allocated to antiracism work, understanding that it is a long-term, continuous effort.

DISCUSSION/REFLECTION QUESTIONS

1. If you are a leader, what is your actual level of commitment? Are you willing to work through the resistance?

2. How are you going to hold others accountable?

3. How will you share the vision with others in the organization? What are the non-negotiables?

4. Even if you are not a leader based on your position, what is your sphere of influence to impact change? Where can you lead?

CHAPTER FIVE

A Developmental Approach to Racial Justice

TERRENCE HAREWOOD, PhD
Vice President, Learning and Innovation
The Winters Group, Inc.
(he/him/his)

> One has the capability to make more equitable decisions
> from an intercultural mindset than a monocultural mindset.
>
> —MITCHELL R. HAMMER, PhD

Amid the conversation on racial reckoning worldwide and in the United States, many organizations have been sprinting, jumping, and hopping to get on the racial justice bandwagon. Whether the motivation toward embracing racial justice has been primarily performative or premised on a genuine commitment to centering the experiences of those most marginalized and repairing past harms, many approaches to racial justice have been ill-conceived. Through their learning and development efforts at work, many organizations, consultants, trainers, and social justice advocates have been conducting training that often requires participants to engage and to do things for which they are not developmentally prepared.[1] Racial justice educational experiences and development initiatives that require people to sprint before they have effectively warmed up or conducted the necessary conditioning are doomed for "failure" before they begin.

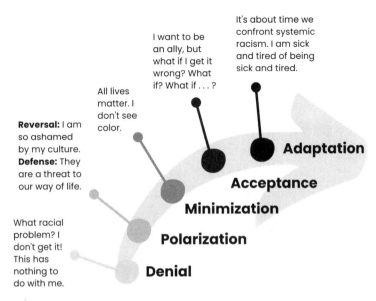

FIGURE 5.1.

The Intercultural Development Continuum

SOURCE: The Winters Group based on data from Intercultural Development Continuum, developed by Mitchell R. Hammer, and adapted from Milton Bennett's Developmental Model of Intercultural Sensitivity (DMIS)

The purpose of this chapter is to describe how leaders might employ a constructivist developmental approach to operationalize racial justice at work. By considering where leaders, employees, and the organization are developmentally and building out learning experiences accordingly, we will see an increase in organizational culture change over time. To explore this approach, we invite you to imagine individual, structural, and systemwide change through a narrative of two leaders in a midsized organization in the Midwest. Although neither the organization nor the characters described here are real, this story is inspired by actual events and people. I will use this story to illustrate what an organization's development journey could look like.

I will explore researcher Mitchell R. Hammer's Intercultural Developmental Continuum (IDC),[2] an adaptation of theorist Milton Bennett's earlier Developmental Model of Intercultural Sensitivity (DMIS),[3] and his accompanying assessment of intercultural competence, the Intercultural Development Inventory (IDI). These can be used to actualize workplace racial justice when combined with other approaches like unconscious bias and antiracism learning experiences.

The IDI provides essential quantitative data that help us decide how to design, sequence, and customize professional development learning experiences for entities representing various sectors, sizes, and make-up (Figure 5.1). The continuum moves from denial at the very early stages of development to adaptation, where one is adept at bridging cultural differences. Let's explore our story where one of the main characters, Jake, advances along the developmental continuum, moving from the earliest monocultural stage, as he is challenged and supported by Claudia. She is operating from the intercultural stage of adaptation, which is furthest along the IDC continuum, with her own set of developmental challenges.

The Context

Jake Smith is a fourth-generation CEO at Cherokee, Inc., a midsized, family-owned business in the Midwest. The home office remains in the original building where the company was founded in 1898. Although Cherokee, Inc. has maintained a relatively strong reputation in the community over the years, it has periodically been the subject of widespread controversy. For instance, tribal leaders and racial justice advocates have vehemently objected to the company's appropriation of the Cherokee Nation and People's name over the years. The company's leaders have continually ignored or dismissed the complaints. The local newspaper quoted Jake as saying, "I don't see what's the big deal. A name is a name. My grandfather chose that name because he liked it, not for any other reason." Jake continued: "I don't get it. I went to high school with a Black girl—wait, can I even say Black these days?—whose name was Cherokee Walker. How come no one ever asked her to change her name?"

Jake and other leaders at Cherokee, Inc. boast about their strong organizational culture; they laud the many traditions that date back to when the company was founded. More than half of the current leaders started at entry-level positions and rose through the ranks. Jake and other leaders agree that "we have a true meritocracy here."

But BIPOC leaders who work, or have worked, at the company over the years maintain a different perspective about the company. Claudia Jones, an African American female and self-proclaimed diversity, equity, inclusion, and justice (DEIJ) advocate, has worked as a human resource professional at Cherokee, Inc. for the past thirteen years. She is the longest-standing BIPOC employee at the company. Claudia has a strong background in antiracism and has consistently challenged Jake and other leaders to examine institutionalized racist practices that create oppressive working conditions for BIPOC employees. She complained about the dismal recruitment, retention, and termination rates of BIPOC employees and the high number of discrimination claims against leaders and other white employees over the years. In a recent meeting with senior leaders, Claudia expressed the following:

- Leadership has not been intentional in its diversity and inclusion efforts for far too long.

- As an organization, they have ignored how policies and practices have disproportionately impacted BIPOC employees.

- Out-of-touch leaders often say they are "glad there is no racism here" and "don't understand what all of this conversation about Black Lives Matter is about."

- Exit interviews show that the BIPOC employees who have left the company did not feel as though they belonged at that organization; they experienced being disrespected by leaders and other staff. When they expressed concerns, they were often dismissed by human resource professionals as just "overreacting."

- There is no formal employee orientation in this organization. Leaders believe and express that each employee should be able to "figure out how things are done around here quite easily."

- Jake, the current leaders, and leaders before them have dismissed the claims as unnecessary whining.

Turn of Events

The situation at Cherokee, Inc. came to a head-on collision during the summer of 2020. Even as businesses in the community were being attacked and set afire after the senseless murder of George Floyd, Jake and other leaders insisted: "This has nothing to do with us. We treat our Black employees well." Imagine the shock when Claudia approached Jake with a list of demands signed by all BIPOC employees at the company. The list included:

- Form a task force to develop strategies to recruit and retain more BIPOC staff and leaders in the organization.
- Revise policies and practices to ensure BIPOC employees experience a greater sense of belonging.
- Establish equitable pay for all BIPOC staff on par with their white colleagues.
- Mandate diversity, equity, and justice workshops for all staff.
- Require antiracist training and executive coaching for all leaders.

Jake and the leadership team ignore these demands. Like previous events, they believe "this too will blow off." In this case, however, it does not blow off. After ten days without a response from Jake, *all* BIPOC employees, along with several of their white colleagues, walked off the job and refused to return until Jake provided a reasonable response.

Jake will not be able to "see" the need to implement these "demands." As far as he is concerned, everyone gets along well, and there are many reasons BIPOC employees left that had nothing to do with their race. He believes that the company should not react to external events.

Jake's response frustrates Claudia.

Understanding the Situation through the Lens of the IDC

The Intercultural Development Continuum (IDC), adapted from Milton Bennett's Developmental Model of Intercultural Sensitivity (DMIS), is a model that posits five developmental orientations: denial, polarization, minimization, acceptance, and adaptation. The **denial orientation** is the earliest of these stages, where leaders typically demonstrate a nascent capacity to engage cultural differences. Leaders who operate from the denial orientation have had relatively little exposure to people who are culturally different from themselves and tend to engage in ways that are experienced as more task oriented. As tasks are done, leaders here are less likely to consider the significance of culture or identity as important variables that impact how work is accomplished and success is measured. A common assumption among leaders operating from the denial frame of mind is that it is the individual employee's responsibility to figure out the inner workings of the organization. Conversations about racial justice are likely to fall flat if they are brought up to the leaders using conventional antiracist approaches or traditional activist strategies, where the focus might be considered confrontational.

Note: Data show that fewer than 4 percent of leaders operate from this denial developmental orientation.

Claudia recently completed an IDI Qualifying seminar to be certified to use the Intercultural Development Continuum (IDC). At first, Claudia, who prides herself on being a staunch antiracism advocate, was somewhat resistant to the IDI-guided development approach. She has long been convinced that antiracism is the only thing that can solve racism. Nonetheless, she agrees to try it, first on herself to engage in her intercultural development, then to see how it supports her efforts to operationalize racial justice at Cherokee, Inc. She keeps remembering a statement from her IDI training, which suggested "the further leaders are along the IDC, the greater their capacity to create organizational policies, practices, and structures that promote and bring about equity."[4] Jake is at the earliest developmental stage of denial. Claudia is operating from adaptation and realizes now that her lists of demands were perhaps more than Jake could handle.

Frustration and Setbacks

Jake despises this feeling of being ambushed by his employees but is willing to meet some of the demands. He notices how other organizations, including many of his competitors, are responding. Jake begins to get worried about how his company will look in the eyes of the public. He is concerned about how this could impact the company's image and, ultimately, the bottom line.

Claudia helps Jake to see how diversity is good for business. Jake and key HR leaders distribute a memo stating that the company will sponsor an annual multicultural food day. Jake also orders a task force to explore hiring more BIPOC employees, which results in the hiring of six new BIPOC employees for entry-level positions at Cherokee, Inc. Though this may stop short of a significant increase in the hiring of BIPOC-identified employees, there is change and new challenges for Jake as well as the organization.

Pushback from Leadership

As more BIPOC employees join the Cherokee, Inc. workplace, Jake feels conflicted as he engages in dialogue with other leaders and continues to hear from Claudia that he needs to do more. Claudia shares that there have been several complaints from new BIPOC employees about the unreasonable organizational policies. For instance, the company has recently instituted a policy stating that "all employees are prohibited from wearing unprofessional hairstyles such as dreadlocks, Nubian knots, braids, afros, etc." The company also mandated that all employees speak only English while at work. While some leaders have defended these policies by saying, "they have to learn how to do things the way we do things around here," Jake feels ashamed about all the statements he hears from his leadership. He is beginning to see himself as white, and for the first time he notices

Aspects of Polarization

Many organizations operate from a place of polarization of cultural differences, the second stage of the IDC. According to research conducted by IDI, LLC, as many as 15 percent of leaders and a similar number of organizations operate from this development orientation. Some leaders and employees may struggle to make sense of increased cultural diversity in the workplace. These organizations become particularly vulnerable to intergroup, and cross-cultural conflict as individuals and the organization are asked to look at cultural differences differently.

Let us suppose the core leadership is operating and looking at the organization from this developmental orientation. In that case, they will likely respond to this complexity by polarizing differences—seeing the world through an "us versus them" lens. According to Hammer, this "us versus them" approach to differences can take one of two forms: *polarization-defense* or *polarization-reversal*. Both have profound implications for how racial justice might be addressed at work and the challenges faced as the organization seeks to do so.

In *polarization-defense*, leaders may believe that having employees from diverse backgrounds could threaten "the way we do things around here." This is usually coupled with a negative evaluation, including stereotyping of individuals perceived as culturally different and general feelings of mistrust toward them.

To defend the organizational culture and preserve the status quo or privileges associated with "our culture," HR policies and practices are often deployed to align employees' behaviors and beliefs with dominant organizational cultural practices. Unlike the standardized "sink or swim" human resource method that characterized organizations operating from denial orientation, onboarding from polarization orientation is hiring those who are "like us" in the dominant organizational culture or indoctrinating new BIPOC into the ways things get done within the organization. Conversations about race or culture are perceived as threatening, handled in divisive ways, and tend to be heavily discouraged.

Some leaders and employees may exhibit a strong sense of judgment at *polarization-reversal*. However, in this case, the negative evaluation and judgment are toward members of their own culture while expressing a more positive judgment toward BIPOC and people from other cultures. One impetus for this perspective is often motivated by a desire to disassociate oneself from something that is found to be shameful about one's culture. The result is often a form of performative allyship, where members from the dominant culture may profess solidarity with the cause of racial justice.

that all of the members of the executive team are white. He listens to the discussions in the media about the disparities in wealth, health, and education outcomes and the fundamental flaws in the penal and juvenile justice systems. He wants to do more but is concerned about the possible backlash.

At first, Jake's strong rhetoric and statements about "white people need to get on board" convey to some white employees that the organization has changed dramatically. Jake admits for the first time that he had benefitted from white privilege. He admonishes his fellow leaders to consider how their old-fashioned ways would eventually run the company into the ground. "I don't know how us white people can be so racist and refuse to do anything about it," he said. "We can't keep stuck in the past. Those Black employees work so hard and make such a contribution. They have endured so much. We can learn so much from them." Developmentally Jake has moved from denial to polarization on the IDC. He operates from *polarization-reversal*, whereas some other leaders operate at *polarization-defense*. Both aspects of polarization are described in the description of polarization above.

What can Claudia do to advance racial justice at her job, given a polarization orientation? The developmental support for those at polarization is to shift their focuses away from differences and to explore cultural similarities. Claudia could remind the leaders of the organization's values which state that they create a welcoming environment for everyone. At this stage, it is vital to highlight the commonalities—the shared values. Claudia must also attend to her developmental challenges, which we will address below.

Another Developmental Shift on the Horizon

As Jake continues to push senior leadership to hire more BIPOC within the organization, Claudia observes their responses and takes stock of some of the conversations happening across the organization. One leader expresses: "I don't see why we must lower our standards in order to have more quotas around here. We are doing fine and have been for years without them." Another employee shares that "all this ruckus about Black Lives Matter should be restricted from our workplace." The more Jake pushes, the more the leaders double down on their cries for stricter policies and more rules—more polarization. As such, the organization faces challenges that will only be effectively navigated by asking questions and exploring shared goals.

But Jake remains relentless. In fact, to prove his sincerity, Jake asks Claudia if he can attend church service with her and perhaps join her at her home for dinner with her family following the church service. Surprised, Claudia agrees. So, on Sunday, Jake arrives at church to meet Claudia. He is wearing a multicolored dashiki he purchased from a flea market the day before. He knew the church was primarily African American, so he believed wearing this shirt would help him fit in. He brought his camera, and he plans to take selfies with the church pastor and Claudia and her family. Jake is convinced that the leaders back at Cherokee, Inc. will come around if they can see him posing with these Black people. During the service, the pastor preached about the horrific events of September 11, 2001, and called upon the congregation to remember to "love thy neighbor."

At home after the service, Claudia cannot resist. She has to give Jake some critical feedback about his choice to wear the dashiki. She explains the concept of cultural appropriation to him and assures him that she knows he meant well. Jake takes the criticism very well. The following day at work, Jake announces Claudia's promotion to a new role as "chief" diversity officer, reporting directly to the vice president of human resources. He then asks her to coordinate mandatory diversity training for everyone starting next quarter.

Claudia is surprised to hear all of this coming from Jake. It was like he had an epiphany. She is even more surprised when she hears Jake rationalize it by saying diversity adds immense value to the organization and that it will be important to have some standard policies that reflect this value. He seems genuinely interested in increasing the level of diversity in the organization. He says, "I realize now that this diversity can help increase our bottom line and can make us more competitive. We have to be colorblind. I attended church with

Minimization Orientation of the IDC:
Sameness and Equality at the Forefront

The changes implemented by Jake and what they mean for the dominant organizational approach reflect a shift toward the *minimization orientation* along the IDC. At this developmental stage, where about 65 percent of people operate, organizational policies and practices fall under the umbrella of a universalism approach. The primary focus here is establishing and instituting common procedures and policies to ensure everyone is treated fairly and equally. The emphasis here is likely on complying with Equal Employment Opportunity Commission (EEOC) policies and a push to have everyone value diversity and demonstrate that in a particular way. The organization may rewrite values, mission, and vision statements to reflect this new value on diversity and create a common language used to reflect this value.

Organizations and leaders like Jake, who have entered the minimization stage of their development, are likely to be genuine in their efforts to increase diversity and may invest resources in hiring for diversity. However, when leaders haven't fully developed a comfort with the differences of people from diverse backgrounds and their own cultural identities, onboarding and day-to-day interactions convey to those who are "other" that conformity is necessary to be seen as a fit or to achieve success within the organization. This shows up in standardized policies, procedures, and daily cultural exchanges.

Leaders are more likely to attend to differences in personality at the individual level. They operate in a way that conveys it is our commonalities, not differences that truly matter.

Furthermore, at minimization, leaders, and organizations are particularly vulnerable to microaggressions, as individual efforts to be nice or do the right thing are often not experienced in the manner intended. People from other cultures may experience and make sense of some of the same behaviors differently from those who represent the dominant culture. BIPOC and other employees who experience an offense may often feel pressure to fit in or go along to get along, or just cope so as not to risk their jobs, career advancement opportunities, or being stereotyped. The fatigue associated with such choices often leads BIPOC employees to leave or simply cope with surviving within the organization.

Claudia yesterday and was reminded that at the end of the day, 'we are all God's children.' We all want to feel safe and to be heard and to take care of our families." Claudia recognizes that these are great strides toward actualizing justice within their organization, and there is evidence that there is still more work to be done. Jake has moved along the continuum from polarization-reversal to minimization.

Claudia knows that engaging the organization in deep self-reflection is what is needed. Individuals at the minimization developmental orientation are likely to start recognizing their privileges. Reflections on how some of their intersectional identities might garner certain privileges while others may cause them to be targeted for discrimination are likely to challenge and support them at this developmental stage. Examining organizational policies and practices to uncover underlying assumptions and reimagine them through the lenses of diversity, equity, inclusion, and justice may be what the organization is prime for at this developmental stage.

The Journey Continues—Dealing with Discomfort

Jake and other leaders have accepted the common humanity of people, which is reflected in changes made within the organization. Despite the growth, Jake and other leaders are still uncomfortable and unclear about how to address differences. Tom, the vice president of marketing, complains: "Our people are not ready for this. We have to be careful that we don't alienate our hard-working employees in an effort to pacify BIPOC." Tom might still be operating from a polarization-defense mindset.

Jake has asked Claudia to develop some employee resource groups (ERGs) to create a "safe space" for BIPOC to voice their concerns. Tom again intimates: "See, that is exactly what I mean. Is there going to be a white ERG?" Claudia can see that progress is being made, though she still feels frustrated by the slow pace of organizational change. She poses this question regularly to shift her focus: "Do I want to be right, or do I want to be effective?" She periodically asks herself, "What is my role here? What are my goals here? And how can I keep doing this without losing my soul here?" While there are times when she grows increasingly frustrated, she uses these recentering questions to help her meet Jake and the organization where they are developmentally. These frustrations and challenges Claudia experiences are typical of her developmental orientation of adaptation. We will explore that more later. Because of her capacity to hold more complex perspectives about differences, she is no longer triggered when she hears Jake say, "All lives matter," in response to news or events surrounding the Black Lives Matter movement.

Claudia is deliberate in her practices and how she frames the work of justice for herself and others. For instance, she intentionally uses the phrase *white dominant culture* instead of *white supremacy culture* in her monthly workshops with the staff and her conversations with Jake. Although she struggles with this choice internally, she knows that leaders are not developmentally ready to fully grasp the concept of white supremacy culture and chooses to use white dominant culture as a strategy. Even though she faces regular backlash from BIPOC employees, who accuse her of being too soft on racism at work, and from many white employees who feel that her "reverse-racism" agenda puts them at risk of being replaced, she accepts that the work toward justice is a developmental journey characterized by slow incremental change. She also becomes frustrated by the number of BIPOC who, just in the interest of fitting in, seem to be quiet and don't participate and are going along to get along. Again, this frustration is typical for a leader like Claudia, who operates from the developmental orientation of adaptation.

Jake is becoming significantly more self-reflective. He orders a DNA kit from an ancestry site to learn more about his family background. He has started asking himself what it means to have white skin and to be male, Christian, and heterosexual-identified. In addition, Jake and the leaders at Cherokee, Inc., have started exploring the history of the organization. Jake falls back into feeling guilty at times, but he can snap back and get curious about how the organization has been engaging in differences. They have decided to review the holiday and leave policy first to understand how white dominant culture might be showing up. The more they learn, the more they want to know.

As part of the new onboarding process, new hires are paired with mentors with shared racial identities. Claudia finds herself smiling some days as she reflects on how many leaders and employees are beginning to recognize and acknowledge the existence of privilege, what it is, and developing knowledge around the differences in how organizational policies privilege and disadvantage employees from diverse cultural backgrounds. BIPOC are now also questioning whether the self-silencing, code-switching, and going along to get along or to move up strategies are healthy. Through self-reflection and commitment to learning more, they are becoming curious about the experiences of other cultures. They are beginning to seek out knowledge about the experiences of people from cultural backgrounds different from their own.

But when Claudia tries to push the needle, she is met with some resistance. At a meeting with the senior leaders, Claudia decides to mention the phrase *white supremacy culture*. After sharing the excerpts from Tema Okun's Web posting, "(divorcing) White Supremacy Culture: Coming Home to Who We Really Are," Claudia experiences some immediate pushback. (Please refer to Chapters 2 and 3 for a more detailed discussion of white supremacy culture.) One leader shares: "I am concerned that if we continue to explore the language of white supremacy culture at work, employees might use this as a weapon. And, because we taught it to them here at work, they may be using it against us to reject such things as standard written English at work, with a claim that we are 'worshiping the written word,' for example."

How can Claudia make sense of this resistance? Did Claudia introduce this framing too soon? Would this have been better coming from Jake as the person with the most power in the organization?

Seeing as the Other: Acceptance Orientation

Acceptance is the first of two intercultural stages captured in the IDC. About 15 percent of those who take the IDI operate from this orientation. It is characterized by a sense of curiosity about cultural differences. When the shift toward acceptance orientation occurs, there is a general recognition of patterns of cultural differences. HR practices and policies are more likely to consider the lived experiences of people from racially and culturally diverse backgrounds.

As the conversations turn from *white dominant culture* to *white supremacy culture* at work, individuals and organizations operating from this developmental stage might experience anxiety. Intellectually, they may accept the need for justice and might also be able to acknowledge the need to repair past harms. However, they may struggle to identify strategies to operationalize this at work. They may be anxious that employees, now armed with the knowledge of the unwritten codes of white supremacy culture, may use the "master's tools to dismantle the master's house."

Addressing these types of conflicts or ethical dilemmas at work is not yet part of the mindset, heartset, or skillset of leaders and employees operating from the developmental orientation of acceptance. They may become overwhelmed with a need to make the perfect decision and may find themselves struggling with analysis-paralysis as they work to actualize racial justice at work. This is not to suggest that some important decisions will not be made.

Adaptation Orientation:
Authenticity Is More Important Than Perfection

Claudia is aware that the organization and leadership will need more support as some of the changes at Cherokee, Inc., although well-intentioned, were poorly implemented, and many of the professed policies were not implemented. Leaders here struggle to hold each other accountable, but there is evidence that leaders are becoming increasingly more vulnerable and curious about cultural differences. Claudia observes that leaders may need to develop more cultural humility and a deeper capacity to take risks if the organization is to live out its new mission of "actualizing racial justice at work."

This is something that Jake and the leaders struggle with. These high-functioning leaders are used to making important decisions that drive the organization. Many leaders express anxiety when they are asked to develop a policy or even take a stand on an issue related to racial justice. They often pivot the decision to subcommittees, form task forces, write white papers, and still struggle to make decisions. Claudia has engaged a consultant from The Winters Group to help support them. During one workshop, one leader exclaims: "As a white leader, we only have one chance to get it right. In this cancel culture, it is better to not do anything than to do it wrong." Jake finds that this analysis-paralysis is the new challenge for his company.

Although her organization's journey toward racial justice continues, Claudia is a lot more optimistic today than when she began. It has taken about five years, but she can see her efforts paying off. She is glad that she resisted the temptation to quit the organization on so many separate occasions due to the lack of understanding, responsibility, and reflexivity of the organization and its leadership and the fatigue she experienced.

Claudia exemplifies many of these symptoms throughout the story and can still be effective as she maintains a developmental focus. Although organizations seldom make it to the adaptation stage, many leaders, like Jake, can exert considerable influence on the organizational culture when they reach this stage of their development. Jake has also finally made it to this adaptation stage, and it shows up in his bold actions. For instance, recognizing the harm caused to many BIPOC communities, Jake has made several decisions to repair the harm. Although many senior leaders have advised Jake to "let bygones be bygones" or simply "just let go of the past," Jake is acutely aware of the fact that his family's wealth, and the success of his company, would not have come had it not been for the displacement of many BIPOC communities.

He sees that through the company's misguided belief in meritocracy, they had caused significant harm to BIPOC employees emotionally,

The Journey to Adaptation

If the leaders and employees are willing to engage in cultural humility by trying out new approaches, taking the risk, reflecting on their actions, and modifying their thinking and behavior regularly, they are likely to arrive at the developmental orientation of *adaptation* to cultural differences. At this level, not only are leaders able to more effectively deconstruct problems associated with the taken-for-granted thinking and behaviors that are ingrained in white supremacy culture at work, but they are also much more capable of making tough decisions that advance the work of racial justice than at earlier developmental stages. About 2 percent of people who take the IDI operate from this mindset.

Adaptation is reached through a high level of exposure, experiences, and deliberate education and reflection about complex cultural differences. These contribute to an increased capacity to be reflexive and to be able to modify one's thinking and one's behavior appropriately, effectively, and authentically when one is navigating cultural differences. Leaders can better deconstruct oppressive systems and identify subtle and important ways in which white supremacy culture operates. But holding an adaptation worldview does not come without its challenges. Frustration and impatience with people operating from earlier developmental orientations are common. They may also experience an emotional tug-of-war as they wrestle with achieving broader intercultural organizational goals and being true to who they are in authentic ways. Furthermore, individuals commonly experience burnout.

psychologically, relationally, and professionally. In response, Jake has made a clear and compelling case for a salary-equity adjustment. As a responsive leader who embraces a clearer understanding of justice and equity, his passion and authenticity as he communicates an apology, commitment, and the new policies land surprisingly well with employees. Jake has also made the decision to rename the company from Cherokee, Inc. as a step toward redressing the harm. HR policies are more likely to be mutually adaptive and actualize racial justice when sufficient leaders and stakeholders operate from this developmental orientation.

SUMMARY

- Through the experiences of Claudia, Jake, senior leaders, and the employees at Cherokee, Inc., in this chapter we have described the stages in a developmental journey toward actualizing racial justice at work and what they could look like.

- Using the lens of the Intercultural Development Continuum, we have outlined typical developmental issues and potential strategies that could be used at the various stages.

- We invite you to consider how you might employ this developmental framework at your institution or with your clients to actualize racial justice at work.

DISCUSSION/REFLECTION QUESTIONS

1. Which developmental stage did you see your organization operating from throughout this chapter?

2. What challenges are you encountering currently, and how does this developmental framework help you pinpoint what might be happening at your organization?

3. Given the common challenges outlined at each developmental stage, what developmental stage–appropriate strategies might you employ to operationalize racial justice at your work?

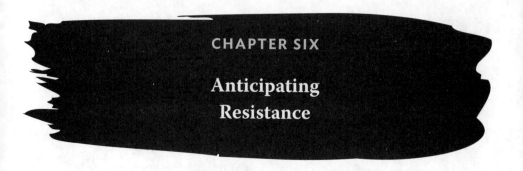

CHAPTER SIX

Anticipating Resistance

KEVIN A. CARTER

Vice President, Strategy and Assessments

The Winters Group, Inc.

(he/him/his)

I hope I have been a catalytic agent for change. I firmly
believe that none of us should be satisfied by the status
quo. The business community must recognize its
responsibility to eradicate racism and inequality.

—KENNETH CHENAULT

"Culture eats strategy for breakfast," Peter Drucker stated. Even if you
have a well-crafted strategy, people must be enthusiastic about implementing that strategy. If they are not on board or are active resisters,
you stand no chance of implementing the plan. Operationalizing racial justice is about culture change, and organizational cultures resist
change by their very nature. This chapter is the first of two focusing
on anticipating and addressing resistance. An organization's culture
comprises individual mindsets, behaviors, and commitment. That is
why it is essential to recognize how personal attitudes, beliefs, and
actions at various levels of the organization will positively or negatively influence the implementation of diversity, equity, inclusion, and
justice (DEIJ).

For example, we had an onslaught of requests for what we call justice-centered equity audits soon after the murder of George Floyd. Organizations espousing an aspiration to embed equity policies, procedures, and practices recognized that a current-state assessment was the first step in becoming antiracist. However, we soon learned that while top leadership endorsed such an examination, those same leaders resisted implementing the findings of those assessments. Some companies met our results with denial and defensiveness or even questioned the validity of our methodologies.

This resistance prompted us to alter our approach. We recognized the need to anticipate and address the resistance before embarking on the equity audit. The first step is identifying the threat of loss people are experiencing.

The Challenge

DEIJ work is a transformational change management process. People and their emotions are more important than rational and technical analysis or solutions. So how, specifically, can we use that fact to achieve better buy-in? We have found that stakeholders must know the human responses to change before starting racial justice work.

First, change can be:

- Developmental, such as learning a new skill.

- Transitional, such as learning or altering a process.

- Transformational, such as reshaping a business strategy or shifting a work culture.

Second, change also has a:

- Technical side related to effective and efficient project management toward a solution or outcome.

- Process side pertaining to the methods and theories used.

- People side, because employees need to embrace and adopt the solution.

Third, change has an emotional impact.

DEIJ is transformational, people-focused, and emotional work; as such, it is complex and often polarizing. Therefore, we start an engagement via executive alignment sessions with all relevant stakeholders exploring how their behaviors are fostering a supportive organizational culture. We invite participants to assess their readiness to take a justice-centered approach. Our approach contains two components: *incorporating change management theory* and *aligning solutions to the appropriate level within the organization.*

Component 1: Incorporate Change Management Theory

We start with sharing change management theories,[1] such as the one shown in Figure 6.1. The figure illustrates the intersection of change management and organizational-level theory—adapting concepts from the Prosci ADKAR Model,[2] the Kübler-Ross Change Curve[3] models of change, and the Intercultural Developmental Continuum[4]—that predicts how individuals and organizations respond to cultural (including racial) differences. Next, we assess the employees and management: how much disinterest, ambivalence, and anxiety about being an antiracist organization is at play? Is there a denial by employees that any change is even needed? Do many people minimize the need to change their behavior toward anyone different? Again, it takes significant effort to "see around the corner—see what others do not yet see, speak into the future."

We ask participants where they think their organization is on the change continuum in Figure 6.1. Often different blocs within the company have diverging opinions, providing a valuable lens into the organizational culture. For example, the CEO is usually more optimistic about the organization's DEIJ commitment and readiness than middle managers. Revealing these different perspectives offers an opportunity to level-set expectations and acknowledge the potential derailers in implementing the audit findings.

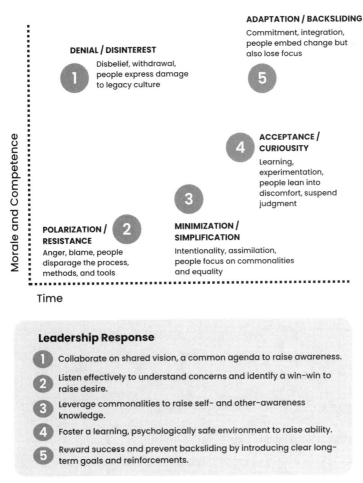

FIGURE 6.1.

Adaptation of Change Management Models

SOURCE: The Winters Group based on the Kübler-Ross Change Curve, Intercultural Development Continuum, and The Prosci ADKAR Model

We discuss how change can engender a sense of loss and ask them to consider their organization's most relevant fears and anxieties. People experience fears in any or all the areas below:

- **Security:** employees no longer feel in control.

- **Competence:** workers become embarrassed when faced with new tasks because it is hard to admit you do not know how to do something.

- **Relationships:** people often lose their sense of belonging to a team, a group, or an organization.

- **Sense of direction:** meaning and mission often become unclear.

- **Territory:** there is a feeling of uncertainty about workspace or job responsibilities people once felt "belonged" to them.

This sense of loss may manifest in these ways:

- **Disinterest:** withdrawal, attention turned to the past, concern about damage to the legacy culture.

- **Resistance:** anger, blame, anxiety, depression, and noncompliance.

- **Simplification:** activity is pursued by advocates but not enough to upset the status quo.

- **Frustration:** overpreparation, confusion, chaos; energy and innovative ideas might lack coherence.

- **Backsliding:** committed participants look for the next challenge, but others question the "return on investment."

What can we do to mitigate these responses?

- **During disinterest:** Confront individuals with information. Explain that the change will happen. Delineate what to expect and suggest actions to adjust to the change. Allow them time to let things sink in, and then arrange a planning/discussion session.

- **During resistance:** Listen, acknowledge feelings, respond empathetically, and encourage support. Do not try to talk people out of their feelings or tell them to change or pull together. If you accept their response, they will continue telling you how they feel.

- **During simplification:** Respond to concerns about mission and values. Discover the ways people may feel harmed or excluded. Begin to develop learning that moves from simplicity ("Don't all people just want to be respected?") to complexity ("How are women, people of color, or any nondominant group being specifically marginalized?").

Resistance to Change: Macro, Meso, Micro

To foster change, align action to level.

	Macro: organizational or societal	Meso: department, unit, or team	Micro: individual (bio-psycho-socio readiness)
Awareness	The organization makes clear the need for the change.	Unit, department, or team (UDT) leaders embed the need for the change in communications, meetings, and interactions.	Individuals are aware of how they will develop or grow to support the change.
Desire	The organization communicates a compelling future state or vision.	UDT leaders communicate how the group and its members will benefit from the change.	Individuals believe the needed change will benefit them.
Knowledge	The organization obtains and disseminates the necessary knowledge for the change.	UDT leaders align and connect new knowledge to existing policies, procedures, and practices.	Individuals connect the new knowledge and behavioral change to individual benefits.
Ability	The organization establishes a learning culture.	UDT leaders provide opportunities for individuals to grow abilities and skills.	Individuals gain new competencies that better themselves, the team, and organization.
Reinforcements	The organization holds itself accountable through transparent rewards and penalties.	UDT leaders embed new competencies into team goals and performance expectations.	Individuals are rewarded based on alignment with the change.

Source: The Winters Group

- **During frustration:** Concentrate on priorities and connect learning to behavioral change. Follow up on projects underway. Set short-term goals. Conduct brainstorming and planning sessions.

- **During backsliding:** Set long-term goals. Concentrate on teambuilding and communication. Acknowledge and reward those responding to the change. Make gains visible, explicit, and tied to plans.

Component 2: Align Action
to the Appropriate Level within the Organization

We next assess DEIJ implementation on macro-, meso-, and micro-levels.[5] The table on the previous page uses the Prosci ADKAR Model and the Intercultural Developmental Continuum in the rows to identify the stages of successful change management. In the figure's columns, the Kübler-Ross Change Curve and level theory models show what steps should be implemented at the organizational, work team, and individual levels. For example, a leader who has only communicated the macro importance of DEIJ change (the benefit for the organization) has not raised widespread awareness of why the change matters. They will also need to clarify how it benefits the meso- and micro-levels, the team, and individuals. Macro recommendations tend to be organizational goals, strategies, and tactics. Meso recommendations should be related to team performance, culture, and relationships. Micro recommendations should be related to personal knowledge, behaviors, and wellness.

Macro

The macro-level establishes or reconfirms an organization's vision, mission, goals, and strategies through an equity and justice-centered lens (as shown in the strategy planning process in Figure 6.2).

At the macro-level, the goal is for leaders who can envision aligned and supportive behavior:

1. GOALS

High level, aspirational, big picture

Ex. Improve representation of BIPOC at all levels of the organization

4. ACCOUNTABILITY MEASURES

Quantitative and qualitative evidence that goals have been achieved

Ex. Number of HBCU graduates interviewed and hired

Continuously Be, Learn, Do, and Improve

2. STRATEGIES

Aligned, integrated approach to achieve goals

Ex. Engage divisional leaders in setting realistic goals by division

3. ACTIONS

Clear, assigned, and supported steps to execute strategies

Ex. HR Team will develop goals based off hiring projections and present them to leadership in quarter 2

FIGURE 6.2.

An Example of Goals, Strategies, Actions, and Accountability Measures That Center Justice

SOURCE: The Winters Group

+ Senior leaders must understand the theories of change, transformational stages, and what to expect at each stage—they need to identify the organization's current stage and whether there is backsliding.

+ Executives are accountable for understanding what they need to learn about themselves and what they need to change to become antiracist individuals. They must become or "be" the change they want to foster within the organization.

- Senior leaders implementing DEIJ strategies should break the implementation down into projects. Component project examples: setting up a governance structure and process, a communications cadence and focus, data availability and transparency, a learning experience and curriculum to foster competencies, and an accountability process.

- Organizations must establish RASCI (responsible, accountable, supporting, consulting, informing) process teams to clarify everyone's role and ensure collaboration. For example, different strategy teams may need the same data (shared measurement).

Meso

At the meso-level, middle managers tasked with implementing change can derail it.

Racial equity is such a big and complex issue that middle managers can feel overwhelmed, resulting in inaction and helplessness. Macro-level planning not supported by meso team wins will lead to failure and exhaustion. The most effective remedy is a meso approach that *celebrates wins*,[6] by focusing on:

- Concrete outcomes that go beyond creative ideas and promises.

- A long-term goal of in-depth changes and shifts in attitude, mindset, routines, beliefs, or values.

- Change at the local or departmental level because only that level allows people to meet complexity and turbulence effectively and change systems.

- Specific steps that make an essential contribution to a shared ambition.

The following three tables walk you through those three critical steps. In addition, the tables provide you with the characteristics, indicators, questions, and contraindicators of team wins. *In this chapter, we detail the analysis process, and in the next chapter, we will walk you through an example to use the process to center justice.*

STEP 1 Identify and Value Team Wins

Characteristic	Indicator	Contra-indicator
Outcome	• Visible results	• Promises and ideas only
Change	• Second and third-order change	• More of the same low-hanging fruit
Level	• Local or intermediate	• Large scale, best practice
Impact	• Creates or adds to the shared ambition	• Slight loss for a few people or a significant loss for one or more people

Source: Catrien J.A.M. Termeer and Art Dewulf

In this first step, we seek concrete outcomes that are in-depth changes to routines, beliefs, or values. A characteristic of the change is that it is second- and third-order, which means it is something new and comes from a quest for continuous improvement. Because people either leave organizations or gain buy-in from middle managers, the local or intermediate impact must be clear and aligned with the macro-level strategies. Most important, does the action create shared ambition rather than a "win or lose" situation for the manager and their direct reports?

As a part of step 2, ask whether a team action can scale up, broaden, or deepen progress in addressing racism. First, people should feel their efforts can have a larger influence; it is energizing and contagious. Second, the visible results of a single team should increase the chances of success for other teams. Third, there should be a bandwagon effect whereby people do it simply because others are doing it. These mechanisms contribute to the dispersion and accumulation of organizational wins. As team wins multiply, they are more likely to result in sustained changes. People may gradually gain confidence in the positive effects, thereby contributing to widespread acceptance.

For step 3 in the meso-level wins framework, organize or embed your victories into organizational or societal policies, processes, practices, and cultures. Use the following table to think systematically about the reverberated effect of each change in your initiatives.

STEP 2 Analyze Whether Propelling Mechanisms Are Present in Team Wins

Propelling mechanism	Indicators
Energizing	• Enthusiasm and empowerment are present
Learning by doing	• Learning outcomes guide new experiments
Logic of attraction	• Other communities notice, know, and value the win
Bandwagon	• Win can be highlighted and celebrated

Source: Catrien J.A.M. Termeer and Art Dewulf

STEP 3 Embed Team Wins in Policies, Processes, Practices, and Culture

Aspect	Examples	Questions
Policies: principles, rules, and guidelines an organization uses to reach its long-term goals	• Code of conduct • Health and safety • Compensation and benefits • Social justice	• Does the team win encourage us to rethink or reexamine a policy?
Processes: the way individuals or products and procedures across departments reach the desired outcome	• Product development • Sales • Procurement • Talent onboarding • Customer support	• Does the team win become embedded within or outside the process? • Does the team win benefit process owners?
Practices: the way tasks, goals, or actions are completed in a place of business	• Behaviors • Skills • Competencies	• How will this team win change behaviors? • How will this team win add skills? • How will this team win establish competencies?
Culture: the emotions, implicit assumptions, norms, and beliefs of being within an organization	• Symbols • Interactions • Relationships • Stories • Rituals • Beliefs	• What will stakeholders think about this team win? • How will this team win make stakeholders feel? • How does this team win align with or alter beliefs?

Source: Catrien J.A.M. Termeer and Art Dewulf

Conclusion

As Americans grapple with unprecedented stress and anxiety due to complex social issues with long historical roots, you might look for your organization's "big win." You may strive for a bold new idea that proclaims your mission is alive and well or a grand gesture to say you are no longer part of the problem but part of the solution. This chapter provides a methodology to identify and implement solutions despite the probability of entrenched old attitudes. Should you find those old habits of exclusion and injustice hobbling your organization's run into the fair and equitable future, read on.

Chapter 7, "Addressing Resistance," focuses on meso- and micro-level change management. At the meso-level, your objective is fostering concrete team wins that have an energizing, bandwagon, and contagious effect. Your aim is to have a a non-anxious, affirming, and committed presence at the micro-level. You will need to help an organization, its teams, and individuals acknowledge and respond to the discomfort of operationalizing racial justice. We often feel we must "know" or "do" something different to center justice. However, because centering justice is transformational, emotional, and often polarizing work, we must "be" something different. A leader must become a non-anxious, affirming, and committed presence to cultivate sustaining advocacy, among others.[7]

SUMMARY

- Creating antiracist cultures requires the ability to apply a racial justice lens to theories of change.

- Change across an organization is more methodical and can be more effective when you divide the organization into levels (such as macro-, meso-, and micro-) and apply appropriate standards and strategies to each.

- Culture change is difficult. Culture change with a racial justice priority is even more difficult.

- Resistance must be expected, anticipated, and addressed by change agents before embarking on a racial justice initiative.

DISCUSSION/REFLECTION QUESTIONS

1. Has your organization committed to culture change with a racial justice lens? To what extent are you ready to embrace the complexity of the work?

2. Who are the champions for culture change in the organization? What ideas do you have to help everyone get on board in your context?

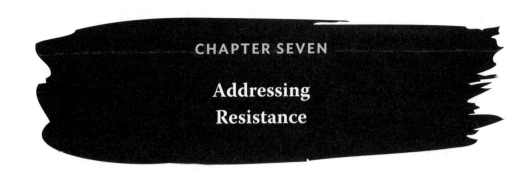

CHAPTER SEVEN

Addressing Resistance

KEVIN A. CARTER

Vice President, Strategy and Assessments

The Winters Group, Inc.

(he/him/his)

> In a racist society it is not enough to be non-racist,
> we must be anti-racist.
>
> —ANGELA DAVIS, PHD

Diversity, equity, inclusion, and justice (DEIJ) is transformational, people-focused, and emotional work; it is complex and often polarizing. Progress happens when you implement a two-pronged approach:

1. Embedding change management, such as the adaptation of the Kübler-Ross Change Curve, discussed in Chapter 6, and

2. Using organizational-level theory.

This chapter uses the method detailed in Chapter 6, "Anticipating Resistance," to provide practical advice for diagnosing and turning around an organization whose efforts to change are being stonewalled. We begin where the prior chapter ended: at the meso-level, where people are most likely to foster or hinder change. We then describe how leadership (the micro-level) can help an organization overcome resistance, especially in leading by example. Executive leadership is

Action Items for Centering Justice				
Action items	Step 1 (Y/N)	Step 2 (Y/N)	Step 3 (Y/N)	Team win (Y/N)
Align employee equity to the Core Values Index (CVI), which is part of each employee's performance review	Y	Y	Y	Y
Find opportunities to sponsor or advocate stretch roles for Black, Indigenous, and people of color (BIPOC)	N	NA	NA	N
Institute and train all people managers on racial hiring goals	N	NA	NA	N

Source: The Winters Group

micro-level because they are the smallest unit of analysis with the great potential to impact the whole organization. In addition, leaders' direct interaction and involvement within their social settings will foster the organizational culture. Finally, we provide resources that anyone can use at any level to take a social-justice temperature check and facilitate an appropriate attitude adjustment.

To help clarify how this systematic approach derails resistance, above are hypothetical actions for a company fighting headwinds in adopting a social-justice viewpoint and practice.

Throughout this chapter, we will use a sample checklist of centering justice actions on discussing the meso- and micro-level approaches. The first action involves aligning employee equity to the Core Value Index (CVI).[1] The CVI is an assessment that reveals a person's core values and offers recommendations for better aligning your behaviors to your core values. It is an assessment that every employee completes at this company and is central to employee onboarding. The second action involves sponsoring Black, Indigenous, and people of color (BIPOC) for stretch roles. *Stretch roles* are jobs for which a person has most, but not all, of the required experience. And the third action is instituting racial hiring goals. It is legal to establish numerical goals or targets. Goals and targets can be described as "aim to double the percentage of Black, Latine, or Asian Americans in senior manager by 2024." It is illegal to have rigid quotas or set-asides. Quotas or set-asides can be described as "the next five people we hire in X job must be women" or "we need ten Black people in Y job."

Our business challenge or question is: which of these actions has the most potential to anticipate and address resistance to centering justice? And by *centering justice*, we mean embedding sustainable policies, practices, or procedures that repair harm, provide opportunities, and empower employees, particularly traditionally marginalized employees.

Step 1. Identify and Value Team Wins

As discussed in Chapter 6, identifying and valuing team wins is Step 1. Let's look at the first possible action. *Align employee equity to the Core Values Index, which is part of each employee's performance review.* This action, of the three listed, has the highest potential to become a contagious team win to center justice. Every employee is already using the assessment. It is visible and potentially even measurable, as all leaders create developmental plans aligned with their respective Core Values Indexes (CVIs). Moreover, adding the concept of equity (i.e., fostering fairness by treating people differently) to the CVI is equivalent to making a second- or a third-order change—and potentially creating even a radically new practice. This action can also be leveraged at a team level to foster shared ambition.

Finally, no one loses if this action is implemented, and when it is, the other two action items become natural extensions. In other words, *Action Item 1* creates positive momentum for *Action Items 2* and *3*. For example, suppose leadership believes that learning and fostering racial equity aligns with individual CVIs and team objectives. In that case, they will more eagerly embrace racial hiring goals and advocate for stretch roles for BIPOC employees.

For example, my CVI is Merchant/Innovator. The merchant dominant value means building and sustaining relationships is central to my life's strategy. Therefore, I am constantly working to know and understand the truth about myself and others. The secondary innovator value means understanding and compassion are central to my life strategy. The principles of equity, fairness, and advocacy central to justice can be easily aligned for all employee CVI profiles, and *Action Items* 2 and 3 can be examples of modeling the value.

Step 2. Analyze Whether Propelling
Mechanisms Are Present in Team Wins

Action Item 1 also meets the requirements of Step 2; it has tremendous potential as a propelling mechanism. It is energizing. People learn by doing, and it connects people across various departments. Most important, it fosters behavioral change. For example, wouldn't it be energizing to know that you and your team are engaging in a behavior that aligns with your core values?

Action Item 1 also requires self-reflection. For example, managers ask themselves, how might I unconsciously or unintentionally be devaluing the experiences of women, LGBTQIA+, or disabled individuals? Does such behavior align with my core value as measured by the CVI? The CVI is not imposing a core value on an individual but uncovering principles individuals believe are essential to their being. Because the first action incorporates equity and centering justice into the CVI, it has the attributes of attraction as a propelling mechanism that we discussed in Chapter 6. Because the CVI is already incorporated into performance reviews and behavioral competencies, organizations can highlight and celebrate wins and internalize behavioral change.

Step 3. Embed Team Wins into Policies,
Processes, Practices, and Culture

The first action item also progresses through this third step, incorporating wins into policies, processes, and culture. For example, let's say the feedback I have received is that my challenges lie in my conscious and unconscious biases. I have been told that these challenges are barriers to exhibiting my core values and finding shared purpose with others, particularly those different than myself. The following questions could be embedded within my development plan and 360 feedback to center justice:

- Do I examine my thoughts, language, and behavior for assumptions?

- Do I address personal biases by considering the viewpoints of others?

- Do I build relationships to acknowledge, appreciate, and learn from similar and different individuals?

- Do I seek to understand individuals rather than see them as group representatives?

We've focused on the first action item because it creates a win-win for the manager and catalyzes the two actions that follow it. In our example, the last two action items would also be significant wins that require substantial corporate and personal commitment. However, people can quickly sabotage these actions. For example, it's unclear why instituting the hiring or advocacy benefits the leader or manager. These are not poor or unnecessary action items; they're essential in any well-crafted diversity, equity, inclusion, and justice strategy. However, we focused on the first action item because it's the most self-reinforcing *place to start*.

Micro

At the micro-level, each executive leader, or people manager, is the fulcrum or levering point to model competencies and behaviors to center justice. Addressing resistance to change is most challenging on the micro-level, but it's a fantastic opportunity to alter an organization's culture. Leaders centering justice help others discover and cherish their uniqueness, so people gravitate toward them; they attract allies and deter enemies. *In addressing inequity issues, whether political, racial, ethnic, or other factors, these leaders call out the harm* and *provide the balm that improves the whole organization.* With this balanced approach, they enable people to conduct a self-examination of their biases and stereotypes.[2]

These leaders can take a well-defined stand and remain meaningfully connected to others across intersectionality *and conflict*. We all have aspects that define our identity: our race, thinking style, personality, or status as a husband, wife, grandmother, disabled or nondisabled person. These leaders help us understand these unique aspects of ourselves and how they shape our worldview. They find strength in self-examination and reflection and can hear and appreciate others' concerns without taking a dimmer view of themselves. They see connections or similarities among people and then forge deeper analysis.

For example, during a session discussing perfectionism, a white male participant said: "We can all feel the sting of perfectionism, or never measuring up; it is not unique to women or BIPOC employees." An executive within the organization said: "Yes, reflect on how 'not measuring up' feels; sit with it. Now imagine if you are made to feel that way purely because of your sexual orientation or skin color, and policies and practices are intentionally put in place so you consistently feel that way. Do you see both the shared commonality and the painful difference?"

Leaders centering justice are an organization's emotional immune system, non-anxious, affirming, and committed presence resisting triangulation and holding themselves and others responsible for self-reflection, personal growth, and action.

Triangulation is a form of manipulation that aims to divide and conquer. Someone uses indirect communication, often talking behind someone's back, to stop an initiative. It is a failure of nerve pattern. Leaders who center justice prevent a leadership team from engaging in triangulation and other failures of nerve patterns. Leaders centering justice ensure no one in the ranks of middle management of an organization has the power to skirt responsibility to center justice or to pretend change has happened when it has not.[3]

Leaders centering justice recognize and address the pain of stereotypes, bias, and racism and close windows to escape addressing these issues. These leaders model and insist upon the emotional maturity needed to execute a bold plan to foster racial equity. Since organizational culture comprises individual mindsets, behavior, and commitment, leaders need to model attitudes, beliefs, and responsibilities of DEIJ to influence individuals and change corporate culture.

The Intercultural Development Continuum (IDC) (modified from the Developmental Model of Intercultural Sensitivity initially proposed by Milton Bennett, PhD) is worth studying (see https://idi inventory.com/generalinformation/the-intercultural-development -continuum-idc/). It gives details and examples to illustrate an essential truth: we can more successfully address racial inequity by (a) understanding culturally learned differences, (b) recognizing commonalities between oneself and others, and (c) using this insight to facilitate shared wisdom.

The Importance of Supporting Leaders

At the micro-level, a leader centering justice receives and, eventually, can provide the necessary coaching and support to hold others accountable to DEIJ goals. Justice cannot be operationalized in organizational cultures unwilling to work through the various resistance levels. It is complex and can be emotionally draining and painful. Leaders must engage in this work with open hearts and minds. *Leaders must ensure that their behavior fosters tailwinds and not headwinds to operationalize justice.*

Exercises to Address Resistance

The table that follows is an exercise to help anyone or any group (at any level) in your organization assess weak points to centering justice and address them. Which elements could you be more intentional about using to foster diversity, equity, inclusion, and justice within your organization?

Our final exercise in addressing resistance is a spot-check to help people at all levels of your organization recognize their resistance. Our fundamental principle is that a justice lens must be internalized

Resistance to Change—Micro Exercise
Bio, Psycho, Socio Readiness

Which of these elements could you be more intentional about on a consistent basis?

Bio readiness	Psycho readiness	Socio readiness
• I am aware of how family, culture, and experiences affect how I think and behave.	• I foster a psychologically safe environment to acknowledge, discuss, and address emotional and polarizing issues.	• I consistently find ways to show appreciation during stressful and uncertain situations.
• I am aware of neurodiversity and how to leverage it for success.	• I instill confidence in others that views and perspectives will be acknowledged and considered.	• I cultivate a broad and culturally diverse network of individuals to exchange ideas and make decisions.
• I nurture body and spirit in a manner that fosters hope, empathy, and grace.	• I am aware of unique talent(s) or strength(s) and how to nurture them.	• I use my power in visible and subtle ways to include people and discourage exclusion.

Source: The Winters Group

to be operational. The table that follows shows how breakout groups during a session responded to these questions: What do you envision yourself doing differently based on this DEIJ purpose statement? What help, support, or information do you need to manifest your vision of modeling the DEIJ purpose genuinely? There is tremendous synergy and clarity in encouraging individuals to write down and share what their commitment to DEIJ will look like to others.

Commitment Assumption Testing

What do you envision yourself doing differently based on this DEIJ purpose statement? What help, support, or information do you need to manifest your vision of modeling the DEIJ purpose genuinely?

Breakout Group 1

• I will seek to understand all communities better.

• I will reinforce why we as a company are doing this work.

• I will help to educate on DEIJ with our team members.

• I will work to help change the previous internal history of the company and why representation matters internally.

- I will lead with empathy and curiosity.
- I will offer grace when others are just beginning this journey.
- I will be ok with being comfortable with being uncomfortable.
- I will do my part to emphasize that our DEIJ purpose statement should be just as important as our mission and vision when presenting.
- I will do my part to reinforce our purpose statement with our values.
- I will continue to educate myself without waiting for resources to be given to me.
- I will emphasize the importance of our company allowing time during work hours to learn about DEIJ.
- I will continue to set goals and hold others and myself accountable.

Breakout Group 2

Envision:

- I will take responsibility to bring people up to the same page as this group to understand how we got here.
- I will integrate the purpose statement in how I carry out my job responsibilities.
- As I educate myself, I will talk about it more in many settings.

Needs:

- I will actively learn of the disparities to help champion changes for health equity.
- I will create a venue to share and get support for the things we are doing. A format for talking through the how in which each of us will go about this.

Breakout Group 3

- I will seek to understand those that have a different perspective and/or opinion and then have a dialogue to try to better understand the others' viewpoint.
- I will allow myself and team to have space to grow and reflect on DEIJ.
- I need buy in from all levels of the company.

Breakout Group 4

- Last sentence is the most powerful, helps us stay aspirational.
- I will care about more than just our clients, but our communities and members just as much (if not more).
- I will stay focused on and aware of why we are doing this.
- I need to know what I can be doing differently to bring the whole organization along on this journey; I will create opportunities for open conversations about our goals.
- I will be a north star for the company and EEs, and help us course correct when we go astray (along with our values).
- I will keep us in our lane.

Breakout Group 5

- I will put diverse candidates on a path to success and being at the table to make decisions.

- I will develop education and training to put us in place to fulfill our DEIJ purpose.

- I will create and coach diverse employees on reasonable pathways to promotion. I will hold myself accountable to coach employees toward these pathways.

- I will create a succession pool of existing diverse candidates for leadership roles.

- I will create and support a targeted and intentional intern program.

- I will recognize I don't have all the answers and will be open to mentorship and education on how to achieve these things.

- I will be committed to meeting people where they're at, listening to understand their unique perspectives and how our purpose statement is meaningful and important to their role, their teams, and to our org.

Source: The Winters Group

Encourage Self-Care for Sustainability

Because people must make a change and have individual histories, families, levels of wellness, and communities, be sure your organization fosters self-care so members can stick with the often-tiring work of centering justice. Offer wellness support and encourage people to know how to care for and strengthen themselves and their networks.

Conclusion

This chapter offers ideas and examples to show how to embed justice throughout your organization. Notably, while commitment is often needed from the "top of the house," we know progress stalls when your ground floor and walls are not solid and steady. You will set the tone for others to follow with self-awareness and proactive behavior. At the micro-level, you will need to be the change you want others to adopt. You will need this unwaning commitment to inspire, coach, and empower teams at the meso-level. Middle managers grapple with many challenges: talent development, strategy alignment, and team performance. We have shared a three-step process to help you identify initiatives that create momentum and support with these individuals, who usually have their finger on the organization's pulse.

SUMMARY

* Operationalizing racial justice is transformational, people-focused, and emotional cultural change; as such, it is complex and often polarizing.

* Reflect on how people react to change and the appropriate response to gain their buy-in and support.

* The change needs to happen at a macro-, meso-, and micro-level. Your challenge is creating a vision, mission, and strategies for the future state, creating collaborative work teams, and coaching individuals.

* Your objective is to have a DEIJ strategic plan where leaders can envision aligned, committed, and supportive behavior at the macro-level goals.

* At the meso-level, your objective is fostering concrete team wins that have an energizing, bandwagon, and contagious effect.

* Your objective is to have a non-anxious, affirming, and committed presence at the micro-level. You will need to help an organization, its teams, and individuals acknowledge and respond to the discomfort of operationalizing racial justice.

* Because operationalizing justice can be very emotionally taxing, find ways to support your body, mind, and spirit.

DISCUSSION/REFLECTION QUESTIONS

1. Are you familiar with and applying the Prosci ADKAR (i.e., Awareness, Desire, Knowledge, Ability, and Reinforcements) change management model to personal and professional change efforts? What stage in the change management process are your organization, teams, and individual workers? Are you ready to respond appropriately?

2. What sorts of struggles do you have in operationalizing justice? For example, is it hard to:

   ▸ Develop a clear and compelling vision and plan?
   ▸ Get team buy-in to the plan?
   ▸ Help people acknowledge the pain and discomfort of racial inequality?

3. How much time are you taking to aid your physical, psychological, and relational health? How are your eating, exercising, and sleeping habits affected as you operationalize racial equity? What about your networks and friendships?

CHAPTER EIGHT

Neutrality Isn't Neutral: Whose Values Do We Value in the Workplace?

THAMARA SUBRAMANIAN

Equity Audit and Strategy Manager

The Winters Group, Inc.

(she/her/hers)

> Your beliefs become your thoughts,
> Your thoughts become your words,
> Your words become your actions,
> Your actions become your habits,
> Your habits become your values,
> Your values become your destiny.
>
> —MAHATMA GANDHI

Justice is not neutral.

After decades of keeping politics, conflict, and anything beyond the job description out of the workplace, we are recognizing the collective harm and inequities that often arise as a result of organizations' commitment to being "impartial," "neutral," or "apolitical."

Consumer researchers surveyed 168 managers across various industries about brands taking sociopolitical stances.[1] Researchers found that regardless of the manager's political affiliation, surveyed managers saw a fictitious organization that did not support inclusive policies such as LGBTQIA+ and reproductive rights as less committed to community and social responsibility and less profitable. So do we need to shift from a neutral workplace, and how does this relate to creating a just workplace?

Neutrality Upholds the Status Quo

Neutrality stems from the *intent* to reduce harm, but its impact can be seen as detached, bereft of emotion, and exacerbating harm. Neutrality preserves the status quo without acknowledging the complexity associated with different cultural values and the harm we continue to perpetuate against marginalized groups. Neutrality is more about equality than equity. *Equality* asks us to treat everyone the same. *Equity* requires us to treat people differently based on different needs. Equal rights laws in the US require employers to refrain from neutral policies that may have a "disproportionate effect" on certain groups of employees[2] as it is a form of discrimination.

However, even with such legislation, we continue to practice equality and neutrality. The result? Initiatives or changes that support equity and justice at the workplace are often framed by skeptical leaders and other employees as pushing a progressive "agenda" that goes against the status quo instead of the true intent: amplifying our diverse values. This negative connotation creates more resistance and polarization by misconstruing what justice is, halting DEI initiatives, and stifling change. In actuality, justice aligns the intent of being inclusive with the impact of reducing harm and increasing benefit for *all* in the workplace.

Operationalizing justice requires us to be intentional in programs, policies, and behaviors in validating ways of thinking and being other than those that prioritize dominant (white) cultural norms. We must intentionally create equity by bringing validity and power to values, truths, and ways of being, living, and thriving that have been dismissed as "unpractical," "not our culture," "inefficient," or "wrong" compared to the dominant culture.

Examples of white-centered values can be seen in our colloquial language. Think of the English idioms: "to each their own" and "it's a shark-eat-shark world." These common phrases are indicative of an individualistic, competitive cultural norm. We see this in the competitive nature of promotions and professional growth. Yet, in Japanese culture, harmony or group cohesiveness is valued more than being the best within a group of colleagues. Instead of looking at the value of a promotion and raise as only affecting the individual, the implications of how these actions would change the work and team dynamics are considered first. Collaboration is valued as part of the decision-making process instead of competition. It is a more justice-centered approach to assess the impact of decisions on the entire team.

As another example, the white dominant culture values the written word over verbal interaction. African cultures, however, value verbal communication. As the saying goes, "much can be lost in the translation" if we only rely on the written word. This can lead to opportunities for misinterpretation and misunderstanding with less attention to nuance and context that is integral to employees' realities and workplace experience.

Examples of Multicultural Value Systems

Edwin Nichols, PhD, created a framework, "Philosophical Aspects of Cultural Difference,"[3] that highlights some of the various cultural differences that inform culturally differing (but equally valid) systems of value, summarized in the table below:

Culturally Differing Systems of Value

Racial/ethnic culture group	Axiology: How do we define value?	Epistemology: How do we know what we know?
European	Human-Object: **Acquiring the object** is most valued	Cognitive—We know through measurement
African Latine	Human-Human: **Interpersonal relationship** is most valued	Affective—We know through symbols and feeling
Asian	Human-Group: Group **social cohesion** is most valued	Conative—We know through transcendent experience
Indigenous to the Americas	Human-Multiverse: **Balance of relations** between humans and other beings and spirits across past and present is most valued	Affective / Active—We know through activity and symbols

Source: The Winters Group based on "Philosophical Aspects of Cultural Difference"

Disrupting Either/Or Value Systems

The problem isn't that these systems of value differ, but rather that we value one set of values more than the others, further solidifying the roots of injustice and inequity across underrepresented groups. For example, Asian Americans, albeit known to make higher salaries than most other racial/ethnic groups in America, are least likely to get promoted to management of any other racial/ethnic group.[4] What may be lacking in many people's understandings of the "why" is the Eastern value of harmony and collectivism being interpreted with bias. In the cultural context of white American individualism, behaviors associated with collectiveness may be construed as a weakness or lack of proactiveness. What would a world be like where we valued collaboration as much as competition? How can we start operationalizing alternative ways of thinking, being, and living?

Actions to Center Multicultural Values

Here are some actions to consider embedding in your organization or personal life based on Nichols's framework outlined in the table above.

Interpersonal Interaction: Validating and empowering achievement beyond metrics and written rules

* Reassess your policies to remove either/or thinking. For example, zero tolerance policies may create harm by not leaving room for exceptions of misinterpretations of behavior. Gender binary language—such as "he" or "she," may exclude those who define as nonbinary, without a gender pronoun, or an alternate pronoun such as "they" or "Ze."

* Collect and embed qualitative data and metrics as part of company performance measurements.

* Create open-ended descriptive performance reviews instead of quantitative measures.

- Engage in dialogue with community leaders to identify ways to offer time and resources (beyond just financial resources) to underserved communities as part of an external DEI strategy.

Social Cohesion:
Embracing collective accountability and collaborative achievement

- Offer full-team performance rewards instead of individual employee awards.

- Provide mentorship opportunities for BIPOC leaders and emerging leaders to engage in meaningful relationships across job levels.

- Delineate leadership responsibilities by incorporating staff representation.

- Offer extra resources and support for employees with joint families (i.e., living with elderly people).

Transcendent Experience:
Engaging with our historical past to repair harm for the future

- Consult local Indigenous leaders regarding best practices for environmental conservation and creating climate-conscious organizational practices.

- Repair harm through your internal and external DEIJ strategy, such as offering financial compensation for BIPOC affinity group leaders or providing unrestricted grant funding to BIPOC businesses.

- Offer alternative healing services and BIPOC mental health professionals as part of your health and wellness benefits, such as Tai Chi, Ayurveda, chiropractic care, or group spiritual practices.

- Incorporate music and other performing arts in your DEIJ learning and development programs.

Operationalizing justice means not just centering the experiences of those most impacted by oppression but also centering their values. Ensuring diverse values are seen, respected, and rewarded begins the journey toward equitable and just lives inside and outside the workplace. That's the work of liberation.

SUMMARY

- Justice requires shifting from neutral organization practices and policies to honoring and recognizing multicultural values.

- Neutrality can perpetuate inequities and be a barrier to shifting toward acknowledging and repairing harm.

- Our definition of neutrality is rooted in traditional workplace values from white dominant European values of acquiring and measuring impact while dismissing values from other non-Western cultures.

- Multicultural values and ways of being include an emphasis on interpersonal interaction and instinct (African and Latine), social cohesion and harmony in nature (Asian), and connection to history, symbols, and rhythm (Indigenous to Americas).

- Embedding multicultural values in the workplace is a way to shift from neutral to just. Employees can do this by validating achievement beyond metrics and written rules, embracing collective accountability, and engaging with our historical past to repair policies that cause harm.

- We all benefit from incorporating more than one way of being and doing.

DISCUSSION/REFLECTION QUESTIONS

1. What are the expected behaviors that we associate with our organization's values?

2. How can we expand our organization's mission, vision, and values to incorporate multicultural value systems?

3. What value systems do you find hardest to embed in your workplace culture and why?

PART II

ACTUALIZING JUSTICE IN THE WORKPLACE

Part II explores ways to implement racial justice using practical, albeit difficult, approaches. Some of these solutions may seem out of reach for organizations steeped in dominant culture norms, without the wherewithal to embrace radical change. How do we cultivate the psychological safety needed to foster trust and open communication? What are ways to invite others to be accountable for change using restorative dialogue? Can we redefine concepts such as professionalism and allyship so that they genuinely center those disproportionately disadvantaged in the workplace? How can we more effectively use quantitative and qualitative data to create a complete picture of where we are as an organization and where we want to go on our journey to realize racial justice?

What are some practical approaches to correct harm with reparations? What recruiting, hiring, and other human resources practices and policies should we rethink so that application is equitable and considers an employee's intersectionalities? What type of learning and development needs to be reimagined to ensure everyone from leaders to frontline staff have the knowledge and skills they need to apply a justice lens to their work? What steps can we take to remake our workplaces into those that prioritize wellbeing and address the additional burden for BIPOC workers? How do current procurement practices cause harm to BIPOC vendors, and what new policies can we enact to achieve fairness?

In what ways can we disrupt bias and race-based discrimination in technology? How can we better use marketing and advertising to amplify antiracist narratives? What does corporate social responsibility and philanthropy look like when we center racial justice? The answers to these questions and more are illuminated in this section.

CHAPTER NINE

Employees Can't Be Safe until They Feel Safe

SCOTT FERRY

Lead Instructional Designer

The Winters Group, Inc.

(he/him/his)

Justice is truth in action.

—BENJAMIN DISRAELI

Over the past fifty years, reams of research[1] have been published around the idea of psychological safety, an aspect of organizational culture that cultivates openness, engagement, and positive change. It is the feeling among employees that employers and managers will not punish them for speaking up. As David Altman from the Center for Creative Leadership puts it: "People need to feel comfortable speaking up, asking naive questions, and disagreeing with the status quo to create ideas that make a real difference.... It doesn't mean that everybody is nice all the time. It means you embrace the conflict and speak up, knowing that your team has your back and you have their backs." While most of the literature in this area has focused on team dynamics and organizational hierarchy—including the business case for psychological safety[2]—the current zeitgeist requires we refine it even further with an eye toward justice: *A just organization ensures that Black and POC employees are psychologically safe.*

The majority of organizations in the US are still hierarchical in their structures. Generally speaking, org charts are a nominal variation of "executives are positioned above upper management, which in turn stands above middle management, which then oversees the general staff population." There may be more levels, different terminology, or perhaps even a nice-looking horizontal layout, but at its core, this structure has become the operating paradigm in staffing. There are plenty of benefits of utilizing such a structure, and it can be highly effective in producing an organization's desired outcomes, whatever they may be. The adage too often remains true, though: "Bad news doesn't travel up."

More to the point: bad news doesn't travel up *if no one feels safe sharing bad news.* Likewise, good ideas die a quick death along with the bad news if employees expect their ideas to be overlooked, criticized, or dismissed out of hand. Put another way—the traditional workplace hierarchy often suppresses growth and change by suppressing bad news *and* good ideas due to employees not feeling psychologically safe.[3] "Often" is the operative word there, for it doesn't have to be so.

It takes a concerted effort from the team and company leaders to create a psychologically safe working environment, especially for Black and POC employees. Leaders have to be willing to receive open, honest feedback and not feel threatened by ideas from those lower in the hierarchy—especially employees of color—and cultivate a culture where everyone *feels* safe sharing.

Saying "You're Safe" Doesn't Make Employees Safe, Trust Does

In the design process with clients, it's incredibly common for leaders of organizations to overestimate the extent to which their Black and POC employees feel safe. This, in turn, leads to frustration when employees express concern over their lack of autonomy, power, or job security; their fear of speaking truth to power; and the oppressive, or outright racist, policies that oppress them.

To put an even finer point on it: it's not enough to *say* employees can speak freely to make it so. Employees must truly *feel* it. Regardless of mission and vision statements, press releases, or public commitments, employees' lived experiences are an organization's actual reality. The rest is just wallpaper. Understanding that feelings of safety stem largely from feelings of trust built up and maintained over time, we can at least begin to create psychologically safe workplaces by adopting a few norms.

Model Authenticity and Vulnerability

If leaders are unable or unwilling to be vulnerable with their teams, their teams will respond in kind. However, a leader who admits mistakes, speaks openly about their fears, and understands and shares their limitations can, through modeling, instill the same openness in their employees. From a racial justice perspective, this may look like a white leader acknowledging their white privilege or openly questioning whether company practices uphold white supremacy. This stands in direct contrast to, say, holding a listening session with Black employees with no prior discussion or acknowledgment of systemic and organizational racism. Practically speaking, this also sends a clear message to all employees that the organization is committed to hearing feedback and implementing change as necessary, rather than adhering to the typical culture wherein those who critically question the organization are denied opportunities for career advancement and leadership.

Choose Curiosity and Vulnerability over Judgment and Defensiveness

When an employee shares their criticism, it can be easy to respond in defensiveness or to project blame back onto the employee. Leaders can opt to walk another path, though. When faced with criticism, choose curiosity and vulnerability: validate their feelings (again, employees' lived experience *is* reality); probe for more details; ask for suggestions and recommendations; use equity-centered processes to rebuild policies, procedures, and structures.

Using equity-centered processes and principles effectively incorporates curiosity, vulnerability, and validation of others' perspectives and experiences. When leaders attempt to center equity while still using traditional top-down processes, it often becomes approval-seeking or concept-vetting. Equity-centered processes, on the other hand, involve those perspectives from the beginning, and the group then co-designs solutions that meet the needs of those most impacted. For example, if an organization is looking to create a less hierarchical, more equitable organizational structure, traditional methods would be akin to the executive team discussing the current problem, the future goals, and potential solutions. Through further conversations, the executive team decides on a particular solution. Then the executive team develops the solution; the executive team seeks feedback from middle managers first; the executive team makes adjustments to the solution or rejects feedback and moves forward; the executive team rolls out the new org chart.

Equity-centered processes, however, would look something like this:

- The project leader holds a meeting with a wide variety of stakeholders and voices—people of varying identities and job levels—and leads the group in identifying the problem(s) with the current structure, setting goals for the initiative, and brainstorming potential approaches and solutions.

- The group decides on a solution, or perhaps two or three, to flesh out further, utilizing the collective knowledge, perspectives, and experiences of those involved.

- Once a single solution has been identified and workshopped, it is presented to the executive team for discussion and feedback. (It's critical to note here that leadership should enter this conversation actively looking for ways to approve the plan, even if it is unexpected or far different from the one they envisioned.)

- The new structure is rolled out to the whole organization.

Leaders can use equity-centered processes on large-scale projects, like the one outlined, or small-scale ones, such as the flow and structure of team meetings. It's a good idea to practice this approach with lower-stakes projects so that when a high-stakes project begins, leadership is familiar with and ready to use these equity-centered design principles.

A large part of equity-centered design is modeling that leadership is committed to inclusion and belonging, ready to innovate in ways that center equity, and open to and receptive to feedback and new ideas. This is crucial because how leaders react to feedback and new ideas does far more to establish—or undermine—psychological safety than any amount of "my door is always open" statements and 360-degree feedback processes can ever hope to accomplish.

Welcoming employees through an open office door only to immediately shut it on new, heretofore unconsidered possibilities reinforces that true psychological safety is reserved for those whose voices are already heard, whose ideas are already centered above others. But a leader who prioritizes psychological safety also relishes innovation, creativity, iteration, and constructive interrogation of internal practices. Such a leader will not only *invite* input from all stakeholders, but she will also engage with it with an eye toward possibility, toward finding ways to say "yes" rather than looking for justification to say "no."

Recognize the Limitations of Your Own Lens

A leader's experience is inherently different than that of lower-level employees. Even in an organization that exemplifies equity and openness, the CEO will necessarily have a vastly different experience than the newest intro-level hire. This dichotomy is part and parcel of traditional org chart structures. Leaders who recognize and evaluate this disparity of experience will find it much easier to receive critical feedback and adopt new ideas. Put another way—leaders often see in 2-D, limited by their perceptions and experiences. When you recognize this limitation and, to torture the metaphor a bit more, put on a pair of 3-D glasses, your employees' reality will pop into stark relief. It is much easier to lay a solid foundation for psychological safety when leaders understand and internalize that they have a limited view of reality—that their experience is not their employees' experience—and that what is "safe" for dominant groups is not necessarily safe for all.

It's important to acknowledge that a leader may feel *too* vulnerable in openly recognizing the limitation of their own lens or may feel that they're opening themselves up to making a mistake—even potentially causing harm. It's equally important that you not let this stop you. When recognizing the limitations of your perspective and experience, consider using language such as this:

- "I know I'm only viewing this from my perspective and through the lens of my own experiences, so I want to open the floor to others. What did I miss? What am I not seeing?"

- "Thank you for sharing your experience! I hadn't considered it from that angle, and I appreciate you widening my perspective."

- "That's really interesting. Would you mind expounding on that? I'd love to hear more about how you see it from your perspective."

Center the Experiences of Those Most Impacted

Systemic racism exists. White supremacy exists. People can and do argue with this, but those arguments are rarely, if ever, in good faith—and they are always wrong. To wit: Black women die three times more often while giving birth than white women;[4] the year 2021 saw the highest number of reported hate crimes in over a decade, 62 percent of which were race-based;[5] in 2022, only six CEOs of Fortune 500 companies were Black—and only twenty-four Black CEOs have ever headed a Fortune 500 company.[6] And lest one think that correlation and causation are detached from the latter statistic, a 2016 study by *Administrative Science Quarterly* found that BIPOC job candidates who "whitened" their résumés by scrubbing them of any potential race-identifying information (names, scholarships, professional organization memberships, etc.) were more than *twice as likely* to receive a call back than those same applicants when they submitted non-whitened résumés.[7]

Unfortunately, statistics like these are far too long a list for these pages. Suffice it to say, the research and the data are clear. Recognizing this truth is the first crucial step in centering the experiences of Black and POC employees. Interrogating organizational systems through the lens of employees most impacted by racism and white supremacy can surface unseen aspects of organizational culture that uphold those systems. Doing so openly—through such strategies as equity-centered design, utilization of outside consultants, and long-term, in-depth learning experiences—will show employees that questioning the status quo is not only okay but actively encouraged, which begets psychological safety.

Leaders who use these suggestions as operating norms actively show a true commitment to justice. And a clear commitment to justice is the most effective way to lay a foundation for employees' psychological safety—far more so than virtue signaling and performative wokeness.

SUMMARY

* An inclusive leader continuously strives to create and maintain a psychologically safe workplace for all employees.

* True psychological safety is when employees *feel* safe, not when they're *told* they're safe; it is created by impact, not intent.

* Building a psychologically safe culture begins with authentic, vulnerable, and nonjudgmental leadership.

* Leaders naturally view their workplace through their own lenses. Be realistic and honest about what employee experiences you can and cannot directly relate to, honor the validity of personal experiences, and listen to learn from them. Understand that those most impacted by systems of oppression and injustice also need psychological safety in the workplace and should therefore be centered in the decision-making and culture-change processes.

DISCUSSION/REFLECTION QUESTIONS

1. If you were to survey your colleagues and employees, would they say the workplace is currently psychologically safe? Why or why not?

2. What feels like psychological safety to one person may feel unsafe or oppressive to another. Whose sense of safety should you prioritize in such a situation? How can you balance or mitigate this tension?

3. How can you invite feedback and new ideas in your organization so that people feel comfortable contributing and speaking openly?

4. Think of a time that you made a flawed decision or came to a flawed conclusion due to the limitations of your lens. What could you have done at this moment to broaden your perspective?

5. Identify an upcoming opportunity that you'll have to model vulnerability. What will you say or share that will help bring others along?

CHAPTER TEN

Closed Mouths
Don't Get Justice

KATELYN PETERSON
Lead Client Success Account Manager
The Winters Group, Inc.
(she/her/hers)

My silences had not protected me.
Your silences will not protect you.

—AUDRE LORDE

Have you ever heard the saying "closed mouths don't get fed," possibly in a song or film or quoted by your favorite entertainer? There may be different interpretations of what this means, but this idiom was instilled in my family based on the common understanding being "if you don't speak up, you will not get what you want."

Another common phrase is "silence is golden," or how about the opposite, "say what you mean and mean what you say." While these expressions may seem like universal advice that applies equally to everyone, they do not. Silence is not golden for BIPOC and other marginalized groups who continue to face injustices, but silence often feels safer. These groups have too often not been afforded the safety in the workplace to "say what you mean and mean what you say." Too often, BIPOC voices, true personalities, and vernacular are not welcome in workplace environments. They are minimized, stigmatized, and or misunderstood.

Silence will not lead to justice. Only when we are able to authentically, respectfully, and without repercussions say what we mean and mean what we say will we move closer to equity and justice. We must enhance our understanding of why silence often feels like the only option in the workplace. Whether it be not speaking up for ourselves or not speaking up for others, we must build our awareness and understanding of the injustices around us and overcome the fear often associated with speaking up. A speak-up culture actually leads to a more engaged and productive workplace.

According to research,[1] a speak-up culture is a workplace culture that values and encourages employees to express their fears, provide feedback, ask questions, raise concerns, and make suggestions without fear of retaliation or any other kind of harm. Unfortunately, we still have a long way to go to actualize such a culture, especially for BIPOC.

Understand the History of Silence

Dominant groups that held power over others have forced marginalized people into silence as a mechanism for survival. Enslaved Blacks were beaten or worse for saying anything that might be interpreted by their master as disrespectful. These fears continued through the Jim Crow era, where even a look could lead to lynching. The infamous Emmett Till lynching occurred because Carolyn Bryant Donham accused the fourteen-year-old boy of whistling at her, which is what led to his murder. Thus, "silence is golden" really meant silence is "survival."

There was and still is a huge risk in speaking up, but because closed mouths don't get fed, many courageous advocates for justice did speak up, and many paid the price with their lives. During the Civil Rights Movement of the '60s and '70s, a number of civil rights leaders were killed because of their demands for equality and justice, with the most famous being Dr. Martin Luther King Jr. Even in the midst of these risks and sacrifices, speaking up has and does lead to change. All of the legislation aimed at creating a just society was passed because people spoke up.

So why would silence still be needed for survival in many work-places? This history has embedded intergenerational fear and fatigue into the psyches of many marginalized groups. And the repercussion of speaking up is not just in the past but continues in many workplace cultures. Research shows that BIPOC have a greater fear of speaking up. In a 2015 *Forbes* article,[2] a woman of Indian heritage lamented that she was only perceived as "good" if she did not speak up. When Black women speak up, they are often labeled as "angry." A study[3] showed that when people of color advocated for diversity and equity in the workplace, managers saw them as less competent. BIPOC often "minimize" their identities in noninclusive workplaces and use a strategy of "going along to get along" and simply concur with dominant group perspectives. In Mary-Frances Winters's book *We Can't Talk about That at Work! How to Talk about Race, Religion, Politics and Other Polarizing Topics*,[4] she points out that we have been taught not to talk about topics that might be considered polarizing. The racial justice challenge is to increase awareness of workplace inequities and provide employees with the skills to speak up so all can be "fed."

Increase Awareness and Knowledge of Workplace Injustices

We cannot speak up for injustices if we are not aware of what they sound like or look like. Educating ourselves on the history of oppression in our society is important. However, it will take a lifetime and dedication to ongoing learning to amass the skills to recognize and speak up when we witness injustice. In addition, it will require changing workplace cultures so that speaking up is considered the norm and valued—an opportunity to grow and learn and not something to be punished. We can start by being more adept at recognizing microaggressions. Research shows that even microaggressions that are not blatantly obvious are just as harmful as more overt expressions of discrimination.[5] Microaggressions are defined as the everyday, subtle, intentional—and oftentimes unintentional—interactions or behaviors that communicate bias toward historically marginalized groups.[6]

Microaggressions may be targeted toward someone because of their race, gender, sexual orientation, nationality, age, weight, or any other aspect of their intersectional, social, or personal identity.

Many may not be aware of microaggressions because they lack education and because many workplace cultures encourage employees to keep their heads down at work and stick to what is in the job description. Lindsey Sank Davis et al. identifies "invisibility of unintentional bias" as a psychological dilemma associated with prejudice becoming so socialized that we are often unaware of biased behavior.[7] Education on an individual and organizational level is a key component in increasing awareness to break the silence. Microaggressions themselves can show in multiple forms. Davis and coauthors break down the complexities of microaggressions and the three possible forms: microassaults, microinsults, and microinvalidations.

Microassaults. When a person purposefully behaves or speaks in a racist way or uses racist symbols. This may be exemplified through racist jokes or joking about racism with knowledge of the harm but insisting it is harmless and just a joke.

Microinsults. Verbal and nonverbal behaviors that demean a person's race and express rudeness and insensitivity. People that use microinsults can either be aware or unaware of their racism. This is evident when asking demeaning questions of "how did you get this job or role?" as if it implies a surprise or shock that someone of color is in that position.

Microinvalidations. Forms of communication that attempt to negate, exclude, or ignore a person based on their race. People that give out microinvalidations usually deny that they were being racist. This often shows up as unfair treatment or questioning directed toward people of color but never asked to a dominant culture or white employee.

In Mary-Frances Winters's book *Black Fatigue: How Racism Erodes the Mind, Body, and Spirit*, she intentionally crosses out "micro" and calls them "assaults," "insults," and "invalidations" with these examples for Black women in the workplace:

Microassaults

- Why are you so angry?
- Why do you people always call the race card?
- You have so much passion. Maybe you need to tone it down for the meeting.
- I don't think that hairstyle is appropriate for work.
- You are pretty for a dark-skinned girl (this is colorism).
- You are different (meaning "different from other Black women").
- We had a Black woman a few years ago in our department. She was really nice, but it did not work out.

Microinsults

- You are so articulate.
- Mispronouncing one's name over and over again.
- Can I touch your hair?
- What is the Black woman's perspective on this?
- Showing surprise that you are in your role ("Oh, *you're* the manager").
- I have a good friend who is a Black woman.

Microinvalidations

- Mansplaining/whitesplaining: a white man or woman who explains to a Black woman about her own experience.
- Ignoring a Black woman's input and accepting the same idea from a white person.
- Being mistaken for the other Black woman (We All Look Alike Syndrome).

- You should be proud of how far your people have come.

- Being constantly excluded from meeting invites when you should be included.

- Being ignored in meetings (invisibility).

- Defensiveness ("I had that happen to me too").

Understanding the impact of microaggressions is just one type of injustice in the workplace. Additional injustices that may be present include:

- Lack of representation and diversity in an organization, or specifically leadership roles, with little to no recognition or interrogation.

- Avoiding conversations about external events that may be disproportionally impacting BIPOC employees.

- Policies and procedures that may perpetuate inequities and discourage speaking up.

Responding to Workplace Injustices

Mary-Frances Winters says in *We Can't Talk about That at Work!* that we do not talk about polarizing topics because we do not know how. She believes it is a skill to be developed. I will focus here on the skills necessary to address the microaggressions described in the last section. Generally, microaggressions should be called out at the moment if there is enough psychological and physical safety to do so. Addressing the behavior when it happens is usually the best time to share how it made the receiver feel. There could be three perspectives of what occurred—the viewpoint of the receiver, the perpetrator, and possibly bystanders or allies.

The Receiver

The receiver is the recipient of the microaggression. What should the receiver do when confronted with such behavior?

The receiver should pause, take a deep breath, and do some quick self-reflection. Why did this feel like an inequity? Next, ask the perpetrator to clarify their comment to ensure there is no misunderstanding. If it still feels like one of the microaggressions described above, the receiver might say something like, "I would like to share how that comment made me feel if you are willing to listen." It is important for the receiver to gauge how the perpetrator will take the feedback. In some instances, "silence might be golden" because of the emotional labor required to address the injustice. If the receiver decides to proceed, it might sound something like, "I am assuming positive intent but let me share the impact that comment had on me." This is an opportunity to educate. While it should not be the receiver's responsibility to educate, it is a choice. The receiver must attend to their own well-being and that might mean not pursuing a discussion about the microaggression.

If the receiver decides not to address the comment at the moment, it will be important to document what was said so that if the organization decides to address it later, the behavior has been captured as accurately as possible.

The Perpetrator

Being identified as a perpetrator of an unjust comment or action, especially a microaggression, does not mean you are a bad person. If accused of a microaggression:

Try not to be defensive. Out of fear, perpetrators may immediately go into defense mode if feeling attacked or being called biased or racist when that wasn't their intent. Even so, harm was caused, and it was probably difficult for the receiver or bystander to speak up. Assess the situation by being open to answering curious questions and seeing the scenario from the receiver's perspective. Demonstrate empathy. Defensiveness can inhibit the possibility of learning what has taken place. Instead, acknowledge the harm, listen, and reflect.

Acknowledge the hurt caused, apologize, and reflect. Refusing to take responsibility for harm caused does not make the situation any less hurtful or make it disappear. If anything, it makes it seem as if you acted intentionally with hopes of getting away with it. Understanding the weight of the situation means listening to learn how you have caused harm, apologizing for your role in doing so, and reflecting on how to ensure that it doesn't continue happening. Ignorance can only be used as an excuse for so long. Being identified as someone that has caused traumatic feelings to another is all it should take to want to increase cultural competence in an effort to ensure the behavior is not repeated.

The Bystander/Ally

A bystander can be someone who hears or sees unjust behavior but does nothing. A positive bystander will intervene, as would an ally. Allies may have a deeper commitment than a bystander. Allyship is a lifelong process of building relationships with marginalized communities based on trust, consistency, and accountability. They must be viewed as allies by the communities they are in allyship with. NiCole Buchanan, a professor of psychology at Michigan State University who leads workshops on reducing harassment and bias, states that "allyship is about what you do at the moment, but it's also what you do proactively to make sure that these things don't happen." Scott Ferry helps us better understand allyship in Chapter 13.

Even the most well-meaning bystanders or allies may not speak up because they don't know what to say, are worried that they will say the wrong thing, or will not come off as well-meaning as they intended. Psychologists offer a few ways bystanders can intervene[8] in some capacity by:

- **Planning ahead.** Increasing cultural competence and the skills to intervene requires practice and ongoing acknowledgment, just like any other skill. Practicing what to say or do in a moment of injustice will help gain the confidence needed to speak up when one actually happens.

- **Tailoring the approach to the situation.** A generic response to witnessing an uncomfortable encounter as a bystander may show up as simply asking the perpetrator and/or receiver to walk away or attempting to distract from what is happening. A tailored response to a situation identifies what is happening and fosters curiosity and conversation. A tailored response can be more impactful and empathetic than a generic one. If you are stepping in as a bystander/ally, you might clarify the perpetrator's intent so that the receiver does not have to do it (lessening the burden on the receiver).

In some cases, we may disarm a microaggression by saying, "I do not agree with that perspective." In other cases, it may be helpful to call direct attention to a subtle microaggression by asking if there is evidence in support of a statement. Planning ahead will help tremendously in tailoring what to say depending on the scenario. Try researching and learning more about microaggressions beyond the definitions and examples provided here. Practice alone or with a friend or colleague how you would react and what you may say if it occurred in front of you.

- **Speaking for yourself.** Even if the receiver speaking up does help confirm that an injustice has taken place, bystanders or allies should still speak for themselves and in the first person based on the feeling evoked from the situation and what they witnessed, rather than adding on any additional assumptions. Use "I" statements. "I felt uncomfortable by that comment," rather than "you are making them feel uncomfortable."

- **Targeting the behavior, not the person.** The goal is not to belittle the perpetrator. Demonstrating curiosity as a bystander can be more effective in helping the perpetrator realize wrongdoing rather than having them become defensive. This suggests using questions such as "What do you mean by that?" or "Are you aware of how that might be interpreted?" There is always a chance that perpetrators may still become defensive, but the bystander, who has been practicing, now has the opportunity to create a long-lasting effect by modeling curiosity and creating space for further dialogue. John Dovidio, a professor emeritus of psychology at Yale University, considers not taking that opportunity as "throwing away one of the most powerful weapons you have to create change, which is a person's desire to modify their own behavior."

Justice Is Justice Inside and Outside of the Workplace

Actualizing justice in the workplace should look the same as seeking justice in society. Marginalized communities are fighting every day, seeking justice for their communities and families. Justice in the workplace should have the same resolve as fighting for justice for a family member, friend, neighbor, or even stranger. We need to examine how power and dominant norms outside the workplace show up inside the workplace. Our workplace communities can come together to speak up against microaggressions as well as overt acts of discrimination toward marginalized coworkers and colleagues.

It takes a village in the workplace just the same as it does in our communities. It requires disrupting systems of injustice that allow microaggressions to continue, systems that continue to silence marginalized groups, and intractable systems of power. Our words hold more power and meaning than we believe, but breaking the silence is just the beginning. Now we must rid the silence forever.

SUMMARY

- Silence is not always golden and takes on many meanings for different communities and situations.

- Actualizing justice requires that we break the silence and stand up for ourselves and others by overcoming our fears and being well-prepared.

- Even the most subtle acts of discrimination, intentional or unintentional, hold just as much power as excessive and obvious acts in and outside the workplace.

- Microaggressions can show up in multiple forms, such as microassaults, microinsults, and microinvalidations.

- When speaking up, receivers should consider the context and their own self-care.

- Bystanders/allies may feel more prepared to intervene by planning ahead, tailoring their approach to the situation, and responding by speaking for themselves and targeting the behavior, not the person.

- Perpetrators need to try not to be defensive and to acknowledge the hurt caused, apologize, and reflect.

DISCUSSION/REFLECTION QUESTIONS

1. Is there a time in your life when you were negatively impacted by your own silence or someone else's?

2. Have you ever witnessed or been the target of a microaggression or overt act of discrimination and stayed silent? What was the outcome, and do you wish you could have done anything differently?

3. How will you plan ahead if you become the receiver, bystander, or perpetrator in an unjust situation?

CHAPTER ELEVEN

Accountability through Restorative Dialogue

ROCHELLE YOUNAN-MONTGOMERY

Instructional Designer

The Winters Group, Inc.

(she/her/hers)

> When held in a sense of mutual care and commitment to
> learning, conflict is generative. Conflict deepens alignment
> by clarifying our assumptions, motivations, and strategies.
> Working through conflict heals and brings us closer to the
> relationships we need to actually get to our vision.
>
> —JOVIDA ROSS AND WEYAM GHADBIAN

Justice and accountability are inextricably linked. To operationalize justice in our day-to-day work, we must always center those who are most impacted by racism and white supremacy and be accountable for our missteps. In a white dominant culture of avoidance, blame, and denial, this can feel like a tall order. There is no shortage of opportunities to dig into uncomfortable conversations, and even well-intentioned attempts can end in re-traumatization. How can we heal wounds and bring accountability? How can we move toward justice on an interpersonal level without succumbing to pitfalls? How can we avoid:

- Letting our rage take over?
- Acting from a place of saviorism?
- Shutting down?
- Weaponizing our wokeness?
- Lingering in shame?
- White folks overstating intent and refusing to acknowledge impact (BIPOC folks are really tired of this, by the way).

Restorative conversation models offer a way forward for folks committed to staying in the game for the long haul.

Restorative Dialogue in Practice

Restorative dialogue holds the key to actualizing interpersonal accountability. I experienced this early in my career when I was subject to persistent microaggressions from a colleague. Fuming and isolated, I considered quitting. My supervisor noticed that I was quieter and more subdued than usual and asked if I was doing okay (we had a trusting relationship). I had internalized a sense of shame and felt reluctant to share. She gently pressed a bit more, and I let her in on what had been going on. She asked if I would be willing to engage in a mediated conversation to make things right. Reluctantly, I agreed.

She arranged a meeting with the three of us and served as our guide for the discussion, taking great care to ensure we both had an opportunity to share our experiences. She asked a series of open-ended questions:

- From your perspective, tell the story of what happened.
- How have you been affected?
- What can be done to make things right or as right as possible?
- What feelings and needs are still with you?

We fumbled through, sharing our respective experiences. The conversation didn't exactly "resolve" the tension, but it did change my colleague's behavior. Crucially, the process created a space in which I felt seen, heard, and validated. I was floored at how my supervisor held us each with care and compassion while simultaneously setting clear expectations about behavior that would not be tolerated.

First Slow Down and Get Curious

Most people struggle to have direct, difficult conversations. We usually have little to no capacity to engage in constructive discussions and instead spend endless amounts of energy deflecting responsibility and tending to our wounds.

When we have been made aware of how we've caused harm to another, it is often painful. Maybe we said or did something that was racist. Perhaps we made a transphobic joke without realizing it was problematic. Maybe we did something ableist during a team meeting. Maybe we misgendered someone. When things like this happen, we most often experience shame, guilt, and excessive self-critique. Our nervous system kicks into the fight, flight, or freeze response, and we rarely respond from a place of humility and resourcefulness.

On the flip side, perhaps we have been on the receiving end of harmful toxic behavior from someone with more power (institutionally or identity-based). I know how this feels. In response to a suggestion for more equitable hiring practices, I was told by my cisgender, white male supervisor: "I don't mean to be an asshole, but I just need you to do your job." He also said things like, "We don't need training on microaggressions. We all know what a microaggression is." Meanwhile, I was witnessing him perpetuate racial microaggressions toward the women of color on my team, myself included.

At the lowest point, he instructed these same women to limit the use of their voices in meetings (this was formally written in their performance reviews). I later learned his underlying fear was that these women might make our white male president uncomfortable by voicing concerns about the program. Although it felt awkward, I engaged him in dialogue about these things often. Not much changed as a result. After about a year, I made the decision to leave with the support of my therapist and loving community. I had no other work lined up, but it had become clear that the cost was too great for my mental and emotional health.

Here's the thing, folks. If we are committed to the work of anti-racism and justice, we need to get comfortable slowing down enough to own our mistakes. Conflict is a *normal* part of any organizational dynamic. Consider for a moment your typical reaction to being invited into accountability. Do you tend to shut down? Do you minimize the situation? Maybe it feels tempting to justify your actions—to hyper-focus on your intent instead of acknowledging the impact ("I'm not like those other white people…"). What might it feel like to slow down and sense what is coming up for you at that moment? Or to liberate yourself from the need to be perfect, right, or even "woke"? Though it's rarely easy, I have come to treasure the gift of loving accountability and remain grateful to those who took the time to educate me.

We're All in Process

In 2018, I led a diversity training session at a community college. We discussed microaggressions and the myriad of ways they manifest in the college community. I repeatedly used the term *differently abled* to refer to folks living with disabilities. Afterward, someone who worked in our Disability Service Center approached me. She offered that while she understands the term *differently abled* seems inclusive, its use can have a derogatory impact because it sanitizes disability. My cheeks grew hot from embarrassment, and my heart started racing. I sensed a shame spiral coming on like a tornado in the distance, ready to obliterate everything in its path—starting with my ego. After a quick breath and a reminder to myself that we're all in process, I thanked her. I remembered I am free to be imperfect, even as a facilitator, and chose to have compassion for myself and gratitude for her courage. As a result of the exchange, we developed a close friendship based on a mutual desire to deepen our learning.

Learning to get curious about our emotional responses can help us move toward taking productive action instead of lingering in shame and denial. This can look like taking time to just "be" with what is coming up for you. Nonjudgment can be the first step toward curiosity. Going on a walk, listening to music, sitting still, and deep breathing are just a few ways that we can learn to accept the reality of what is—and gain clarity to make a better choice moving forward. Consider what helps you reground into the fullness of your humanity. Return to this when you are feeling charged and overwhelmed with emotion. Imagine what would happen if, instead of rushing the process, you gave yourself permission to truly feel what you're feeling. You might be surprised by the clarity that comes with taking time to *feel*, to *slow down*, to *just be*.

Helpful Tools

Once you have gained clarity about your experience of a given situation, you may decide to enter a conversation. For those seeking to lean into accountability, a restorative dialogical framework is an invaluable aid in structuring difficult, emotionally charged conversations.

The purpose of a restorative dialogue is simply to help us try new ways of engaging with one another. Here are a few tools to get you started. This may sound obvious, but there is no guarantee that you will be met with a willingness to engage. Always give someone the ability to opt out and get comfortable with nonresolution as a possible outcome.

Turning Towards Each Other:
A Conflict Workbook

Following are some recommended questions to consider from a powerful workbook created by Jovida Ross and Weyam Ghadbian. I encourage you to take focused time to answer these reflection questions and process them out loud with someone you trust.

- What do I hope this conversation will make possible? What are my core needs underneath the tension I feel?

- What am I telling myself about this situation? How might my emotional history be shaping or influencing these stories? Is there anything I want to ask the other person to clarify?

- What can I do to support myself in this conversation?

- What's my fear about this conversation? What would help me meet that fear in a grounded way?

- What do I want to listen for in this conversation? What will support me to be open to hearing potentially difficult truths?

- How could love show up in this conversation?

Open the Front Door (OTFD)

The OTFD tool can be helpful when you want to communicate something clearly amid a heightened emotional response. It draws on key aspects of Nonviolent Communication (NVC) as developed by Marshall B. Rosenberg, PhD. NVC teaches us how to say what's true for us without criticizing others, as well as receiving criticism without loss of self-esteem.[1]

- **Observe**: Concrete, factual observations, not evaluative, "I noticed…"

- **Think**: Thoughts based on observation, "I think…"

- **Feel**: Emotions, "I feel…"

- **Desire**: Specific request or inquiry about the desired outcome, "I would like…"

Here's an example using OTFD:

I noticed my colleague was trying to express her idea, but she kept getting interrupted. I think we should be intentional in providing space for everyone to share thoughts. I'm feeling frustrated that this is happening. I would like to request we hold space equally for us all to chime in. Is everyone open to going around one by one and sharing that way?

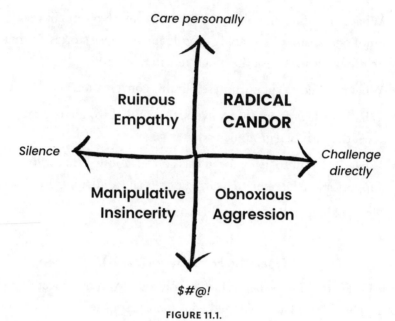

FIGURE 11.1.
Radical Candor **Framework**
SOURCE: The Winters Group based on *Radical Candor*

Radical Candor

Radical Candor provides a compass for candid conversations (Figure 11.1). Creator Kim Scott describes it as *"caring personally* while *challenging directly.* At its core, *Radical Candor* is guidance and feedback that's both kind and clear, specific and sincere." This is similar to what my boss exemplified when she so beautifully mediated that difficult conversation. According to Scott, the other most common forms of feedback are *obnoxious aggression, ruinous empathy,* and *manipulative insincerity.*[2]

She describes each one in more detail:

- **Obnoxious aggression,** also called brutal honesty or front stabbing, is what happens when you challenge someone directly but don't show you care about them personally. It's praise that doesn't feel sincere or criticism and feedback that isn't delivered kindly.

- **Ruinous empathy** is what happens when you want to spare someone's short-term feelings, so you don't tell them something they need to know. You *care personally* but fail to *challenge directly*. It's praise that isn't specific enough to help the person understand positive feedback or criticism that is sugarcoated and unclear. Or simply silence. *Ruinous empathy* may feel nice or safe but is ultimately unhelpful and even damaging.

- **Manipulative insincerity**—backstabbing, political or passive-aggressive behavior—is what happens when you neither *care personally* nor *challenge directly*. It's praise that is insincere, flattery to a person's face, and harsh criticism behind their back. Often it's a self-protective reaction to *obnoxious aggression*.

Anatomy of Trust: "BRAVING"

Researcher and storyteller Brené Brown has developed seven elements that are proven to help teams build and restore trust. She uses the acronym BRAVING to explain the seven main elements of trust. Brown says, "The BRAVING Inventory can be used as a rumble tool—a conversation guide to use with colleagues that walks us through the conversation from a place of curiosity, learning, and ultimately trust-building."[3]

- **Boundaries.** Setting boundaries is making clear what's okay and what's not okay and why.

- **Reliability.** You do what you say you'll do. At work, this means staying aware of your competencies and limitations so you don't overpromise and are able to deliver on commitments and balance competing priorities.

- **Accountability.** You own your mistakes, apologize, and make amends.

- **Vault.** You don't share information or experiences that are not yours to share. I need to know that my confidence is kept and that you're not sharing with me any information about other people that should be confidential.

* **Integrity.** Choosing courage over comfort; choosing what's right over what's fun, fast, or easy; and practicing your values, not just professing them.

* **Nonjudgment.** I can ask for what I need, and you can ask for what you need. We can talk about how we feel without judgment.

* **Generosity.** Extending the most generous interpretation to the intentions, words, and actions of others.

A Model for Bold, Inclusive Conversations

Mary-Frances Winters identified six steps necessary to engage in having effective conversations across lines of difference in *We Can't Talk about That at Work! How to Talk about Race, Religion, Politics, and Other Polarizing Topics.* The following model, Bold, Inclusive Conversations, equips folks with the critical skills to foster equity in conversations (Figure 11.2). The model is broken down into phases while also encouraging ongoing learning and reflection.[4]

Step 1. Focus on Self- and Other-Understanding

As spiritual teacher Matt Kahn wrote: "People can only meet you as deeply as they've met themselves." This quote shakes me to my core and rings true in all my interactions—mundane, challenging, contentious, loving, you-name-it. This dynamic is always present: we can only be met as deeply as someone can meet themselves. In other words, I have no chance of *authentically* connecting with you if you do not have a basic awareness of your own identities, privileges, and positional power. And vice versa. This is especially true when it comes to interacting across differences.

Allow me to demonstrate. These are some of the identities I currently hold. I invite you to reflect on your own identities in each of these categories nonjudgmentally.

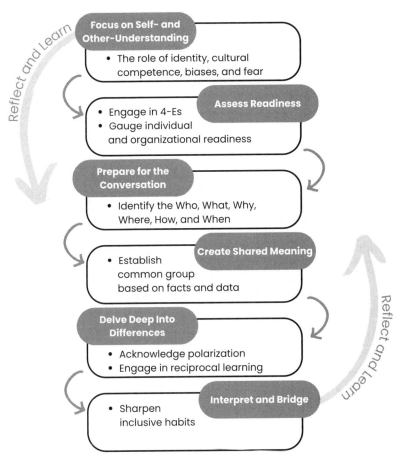

FIGURE 11.2.
Bold, Inclusive Conversations Reflect and Learn Model
SOURCE: The Winters Group

Race: Light-skinned, dark-haired, mixed race, white and SWANA (South West Asian/North African). Racially ambiguous with features deemed "attractive" by Eurocentric standards of beauty

Ethnicity: Egyptian, Irish, French, English, Dutch, German

Gender: Cisgender woman, she/her/hers, femme

Sexuality: Queer, in a long-term relationship with a cis white male

Ability: Temporarily able-bodied, no known invisible disabilities

Age: 36

Size: Curvy, 5'2"

Religion/Faith: Spiritual seeker, most closely aligned with Unitarian Universalist, raised Evangelical Christian

Class: Middle class

Language: English, with a college-educated white American vernacular

Immigration: Father immigrated to the United States from Cairo, Egypt, in the '70s by choice

Our identities influence what we interpret as right or wrong. Have you ever considered *why* you believe what you believe? The first step is to unpack your own identities intentionally. We need to know *why we disagree with those things we disagree with* if we are to be effective in engaging in dialogue about polarizing topics. This begins by asking questions like:

- *What are my identities, and which of these grants me unearned power and privilege?*

- *Who are my "cultural others"? What perspectives are missing from my worldview?*

Step 2. Assess Readiness

The 4-E model breaks down key components to developing cross-cultural trust and can be a helpful tool for determining readiness for challenging conversations (Figure 11.3).

Any one of these elements in isolation will not get us to a place of cross-cultural understanding. When we simultaneously invest in a cross-cultural experience, education, and exposure, we can begin to deepen our understanding of our "cultural others" and grow our empathetic capacity.

Developing Understanding for Our Cultural Others

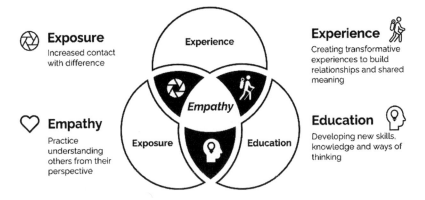

Exposure
Increased contact with difference

Empathy
Practice understanding others from their perspective

Experience
Creating transformative experiences to build relationships and shared meaning

Education
Developing new skills, knowledge and ways of thinking

FIGURE 11.3.
The 4-E Model for Cultural Competence
SOURCE: The Winters Group

Step 3. Prepare for the Conversation

Preparing for the conversation is about identifying who, what, why, where, how, and when you will have the conversation. This may feel unnecessary and logistical, but it is a critical step. Take time to get clear on these questions:

- *Why are we having the conversation?*
- *Who should be part of the dialogue, and why?*
- *What is the desired outcome?*
- *How should the conversation be conducted?*
- *Where should the conversation be held?*
- *When will the conversation take place?*

Step 4. Create Shared Meaning

The goal of these difficult conversations is not to get someone to change their fundamental belief system. Try to engage in a spirit of dialogue, not debate. It can be incredibly helpful to reach a point of mutual understanding that softens the discussion and regrounds you into the reality of what "is." You could name an uncomfortable truth you both can agree on or ground into a shared value. You might even reflect on an aspect of their perspective that resonates with you.

As Jovida Ross and Weyam Ghadbian write in their *Turning Towards Each Other: A Conflict Workbook*, "It can be helpful to remember that there are always multiple truths present in a conflict: We each experience a situation differently, and interpret what is going on from a different vantage point. Making space for our feelings and experiences to be acknowledged can help us surface deeper insights hidden in the tension and uncover new solutions."

Step 5. Delve Deep into Differences

Now that you have established shared meaning, it's time to dig into the core issue. Share specifics of what activated the pain points and underlying needs. Share concrete actions and requests kindly, without demanding. Here are some helpful phrases from Ross and Ghadbian that can serve as a starting point:

- *When I (see, hear)…I feel (a real emotion)…because I need/value…*
- *And that impacted me/the group/our goals in this way…*
- *Is there something going on?*
- *The story I'm telling myself is…. Is there any truth in that?*
- *Would you be willing to… or, What would make it possible for you to…*

At this point in the conversation, we are creating space for reciprocal understanding. Be gentle with yourself. What you just shared likely took a lot of emotional labor.

Step 6. Interpret and Bridge

At this point, invite the opportunity to continue the conversation. The discussion likely created new awareness and opportunities for both people to reflect. Most importantly, continue to practice having these conversations and intentionally build habits in each of these areas:

- **Acknowledging.** You don't know everything; there is always something to learn.

- **Legitimizing.** Other perspectives are just as valid as yours and should be listened to for understanding, not necessarily agreement.

- **Listening.** Listen to understand. Listen for your own cultural assumptions, perceptions, and expectations.

- **Reflecting.** Spend more time reflecting on your own values and beliefs.

- **Describing.** Learn to describe the behavior before providing your interpretation, and expand the number of interpretations you consider.

- **Contextualizing.** Consider the circumstances, conditions, and history of the topic about which you are having a Bold, Inclusive Conversation.

- **Pausing.** Take a deep breath. Think about what you are going to say. Pause to be more patient as well. Be patient with mistakes.

- **Accepting.** Accepting does not mean agreeing. You are accepting that there are myriad worldviews, and it is important to learn more about them.

- **Questioning.** Be curious, not judgmental about differences.

- **Respecting.** Respect the dignity of every person even when you disagree with them.

- **Apologizing.** If you say something that offends someone else, genuinely apologize.

- **Connecting.** Making meaningful connections across differences is one sure way of breaking down barriers and enhancing our capacity for empathy and shared understanding.

- **Empathizing.** Sympathy leads to patronization and pity. Empathy allows you to see the situation from the perspective of the other person.

Ongoing: Reflect and Learn

There will be many conversations that may not result in resolution. Instead, reflect after those conversations and be intentional about uncovering what you learned, heard, and its impact on you.

Liberate Yourself

I am inspired by the words of J. Miakoda Taylor, Founder and Lead Steward at Fierce Allies: "The goal is for people with privilege to engage in the struggle of equity and justice from positions other than shame, blame, and hero, as oppressed people reclaim the power and responsibility for their own liberation."[5] We cannot actualize justice without holding ourselves and each other accountable. As we are invited to move toward growth, honesty, and healing, we also necessarily decenter white comfort. These conversations can be messy, awkward, and difficult—but this is the only way we grow our capacity to own our mistakes and cultivate healing. When done with care, skillfulness, and humility, we increase our chances of staying engaged for the long haul.

What is *just one* tricky conversation you've been meaning to have? Consider this your gentle nudge to reveal your needs and uncomfortable truths, so you can finally liberate yourself to show up more fully in your work. Chances are, you'll liberate others in the process.

SUMMARY

- We must always center those who are most impacted by racism and white supremacy within an organization and be accountable for our missteps.

- Restorative dialogue holds the key to actualizing interpersonal accountability.

- If we are committed to the work of racial justice, we need to get comfortable owning our mistakes.

- Slow down and get curious about your emotions. Take time to just "be" with what is coming up for you. Don't rush the process.

- Consider using a conversation tool to guide the discussion, especially when it is emotionally charged.

- Try to elicit a healthy dose of self-compassion and a whole lot of grace and patience. Accepting imperfection and nonresolution is crucial.

DISCUSSION/REFLECTION QUESTIONS

1. Notice how it feels to hear the term accountability. What sensations come up for you? Invite a gentle curiosity in response to the term and begin to uncover your own history with accountability, nonjudgmentally.

2. If you happen to be in a white body, how might you grow your capacity to stay engaged in difficult conversations across lines of race? If you haven't already, jot down the things that help you ground yourself and come back to this when needed. Consider what settles your nervous system— singing, humming, moving your body, deep breathing, snuggling a pet or loved one. Whatever you do, *do not* expect a Black, Indigenous or person of color to comfort you in the midst of your racial awakening.

3. Recall a time you had a difficult conversation. What racial and other power dynamics were at play? How might that have influenced the outcome? Consider the radical candor framework—were there elements of ruinous empathy, manipulative insincerity, or obnoxious aggression?

4. What is *just one next step* you plan to take as a result of reading this chapter?

CHAPTER TWELVE

The Problem with "Professionalism"

TAMI JACKSON
Instructional Designer
The Winters Group, Inc.
(she/her/hers)

> It is a peculiar sensation, this double-consciousness, this sense
> of always looking at one's self through the eyes of others, of
> measuring one's soul by the tape of a world that looks on in
> amused contempt and pity. One ever feels his two-ness, an
> American, a Negro; two souls, two thoughts, two unreconciled
> strivings; two warring ideals in one dark body, whose
> dogged strength alone keeps it from being torn asunder.
>
> —W. E. B. DU BOIS

Entering the workforce, I was taught by those before me that in order to survive and succeed, I'd need to sacrifice everything about myself—no speaking in my natural voice or speech patterns, no wearing my natural hair in the styles that represented me, no bright colors or bold prints in my dress, and certainly no acknowledgment of how my race, gender, ethnicity, or size had a very real impact on my lived experiences. It was then, and only then, that when I committed to these rules of slow and steady self-erasure, I would master "professionalism." I was mentored to mask my personhood and humanity into a small, shallow, tight box that was intentionally designed to suffocate me with white norms, through the white gaze, for the comfort of whiteness and white people. If I conquered that tightrope, if I became the most revered and beloved acrobat of white comfort and obedience, then surely I would be rewarded with "success."

However, it turned out that no matter how much I worked to change myself in the name of "professionalism," no matter how many times I straightened my hair, wore black or navy pantsuits, spoke with perfect grammar and enunciation of American Standard English, changed the register of my voice to be perky, airy, and "approachable," it never was enough. *I* was never enough. Something was always wrong, both when I played the game and when I didn't. My hair was too messy, my clothes too big or too short, my makeup too much or too little, my voice too deep or too aggressive, or I was not speaking up enough or too often. My efforts in either direction were moot because it was a system that was not designed for me to exist within or be considered. I liken the experience to playing a wicked game of whack-a-mole; as soon as I adjusted and accounted for one critique, another popped up in an unexpected area that I hadn't been aware was to be considered "unprofessional."

In an effort to master this "corporate double consciousness"—this two-ness that warred between who I really was and who I was told I needed to be in order to succeed—my spirit, energy, and focus became casualties of workplace warfare on my Blackness. So many of us in the workplace, but especially Black folx, have learned this same hard lesson: it's difficult winning at "professionalism." Many find themselves having to choose between competence or likeability. Those who are marginalized are seen as one or the other, but not both. This is especially true for Black women.

According to a study[1] by Coqual (formerly the Center for Talent Innovation), Black employees are more likely than any other group to experience racialized prejudices at work at an alarming rate of 58 percent. Non-Black employees of color are not too far behind at 41 percent and 38 percent for Latine and Asian employees, respectively. This raises the question: why is such harm permitted to persist even when organizations claim to have a diverse and inclusive culture? DEIJ work is more than the simple act of "just add water"; you can't just recruit more non-white employees into your organization or onto your team without taking an intentional look at how your current structure and policies create real-life barriers to inclusion, equity, and justice. One way to foster such a critical mindset is to carefully consider how the white supremacist ideal of "professionalism" has contributed, and continues to contribute, to these problematic statistics.

While many are effective at playing the "professionalism Olympics," I've found this to be taxing on my mental health. In an effort to relieve myself of the stress, I have decided to challenge these norms up front. After a while, in an effort to prioritize my mental health, I made a conscious choice to stop trying to win at the "professionalism Olympics" and instead began showing up in the workplace as myself. And by doing so, I started the healing process. But there were also unspoken (and sometimes spoken) consequences. A fat, tall, plus-size Black woman whose laugh is as loud and rich as the colors in her wardrobe disrupted the sensibilities of a white-centric workspace—despite the organizations begging employees to "show up as their authentic selves" in their DEIJ campaigns and emails. As my truest self, I was still a workplace contradiction; still competent, but not the image of a leader nor worthy of being included or even considered as one.

As a first-generation Black girl, born in one of the Blackest cities in the nation, whose parents graduated from poor to working class at just the right time, whose voice sounds more like a gumbo of soul, hip-hop, and blues rather than a perfect soup of quirky pop-music, I was still not enough, and, perhaps even unironically, too much at the same time. It would be okay if I were Black but not *that* type of Black. That type of Black was *too* Black. Too "hood." Too "urban." Unsafe, unrefined, and unprofessional—the antithesis of a "culture fit." And to be honest, I still struggle because I, too, have been conditioned by white supremacy to constantly remember that I, just as I am, am not the right type of Black to be worthy of protection and inclusion in the workplace. I'm doing too much and not enough all at the same time.

The neuroses it all induces are exhausting. No matter the degrees and accolades from the shiny schools, the proven competency, the perfect attendance, or the expertise that evidenced the contrary, I was still not considered a "professional."

From there, I began challenging these norms and sharing my concerns during the intake stages of my interviews and all interactions moving forward. I decided to question the systems and policies in place that allow harassment and microaggressions to go unchecked and claims of workplace inclusion to simply be stated without any action out the gate. I began "managing up" by teaching my managers and supervisors, from the very beginning of our relationship, the concerns I had with professionalism and how the blind adherence to it was a barrier for those like me. I challenged them to use their proximity to whiteness and power to make a concerted and concentrated effort to create change.

For example, it is important that those who are in subordinate positions feel empowered to ask their managers and leadership direct questions about their experience with managing and leading those who have a historically marginalized identity. For me, I asked questions like:

What is your experience managing a Black person in a workplace that has a very small Black population? What did you learn from that experience, and what did it teach you?

Additionally, it's important to get an idea of exactly how management and leaders are educating themselves on the unique experiences Black people, especially Black women and Black queer people, have in the workplace. To note, doing so, and asking such questions has not come without risk. These are very uncomfortable and nontraditional questions to ask in the interview stages. But that is the point—it's imperative that you start the relationship with this manner of disruption so that the tone can be set to get the support you may need. And by doing so, I learned that every manager and workplace leader is not always willing to do such important justice-centered work and holster such a responsibility. Thus this practice increased my chances of working with a manager who I was in alignment with from the very beginning of our working relationship.

Managers must be responsible for fostering an environment where everyone can be safe to show up as themselves without the threat of being seen as "unprofessional." As you seek to create a supportive climate for Black and other historically excluded people, it's crucial to reflect on how written and unwritten standards of professionalism can be getting in your own way. The construct of professionalism is less about the people and more about control over the "other." Striving to reshape a world where cultural and racial markers of subordinated identities are no longer considered a liability to career goals is of utmost importance when working toward operationalizing justice in the workplace. Managers and supervisors who are entrusted to lead and develop Black talent are on the frontlines of this mission. Understanding diversity is easy; however, inclusion and belonging are challenging and require you to dig past deeply ingrained biases, but it can be done.

Because your employees and team members are professionals at their work, their full expression of self and their cultural identities are also professional. Full stop. If you build it, they will come. If it's inclusive, they will stay. As you strive toward operationalizing justice, I offer the following points of reflection:

Professionalism comes in different shapes, sizes, and colors. How are you and the organization defining professional? Think about what you have been taught to perceive as "professional" in terms of an individual's name, appearance, speech, and attire. Consider the way in which white supremacy has influenced how individuals and organizations have come to define what is and is not considered to be professional. Also, ask yourself what are the shared characteristics of those promoted within your organization and those who aren't, and work to change that. For example, does everyone on your leadership team wear a similar style of clothing, such as black and blue suits and natural colors in their dress style? Do they all share the same body size, complexion, and hair texture? How do those in positions of power wear their hair? Are those who are Black in your organization expected to or encouraged to change their appearance in any way as a means of securing leadership opportunities within your organization?

What have you learned about Black hair and hairstyles as they relate to professionalism? Consider policies such as the CROWN Act, which stands for "Creating a Respectful and Open World for Natural Hair." The CROWN Act is a law that prohibits race-based hair discrimination, which is the denial of employment and educational opportunities because of hair texture or protective hairstyles, including braids, locs, twists, or Bantu knots.[2] The legislation passed by the US House of Representatives in 2022 made it illegal to discriminate against "Black" hairstyles. Ask yourself how you can support and implement similar policies for your employees who may be most affected by a lack of protective policies in your workplace.

If your workplace enforces a dress code, in what ways does this dress code enforce harmful restrictions that leave Black employees vulnerable and excluded? Give thought to the cultural-specific styles of dress that are most likely to be targeted by such dress codes when worn by Black people, and think of the best ways in which you personally might mitigate any potential harm in this regard. Ask yourself whether or not the dress code is vital to the larger success of the organization and take steps to eradicate harmful dress codes.

Who in your organization is allowed space to speak directly and be seen as assertive versus who is seen as aggressive and criticized when they bring up matters of concern or offer critiques? Make it a practice to actively observe the dynamics of who is genuinely permitted the most license to "speak freely" within your organization. Note whether it is the actual content of the criticism that is repeatedly seen as a problem or if it is simply the source of the critique. To ensure that other voices are heard, consider implementing some of the following actionable strategies:

- Utilize an agenda for every meeting and send it to attendees in advance so that internal processors are given ample time to prepare for the meeting.
- Create meeting agreements that set the tone for each meeting. Such as:

  - One mic, one speaker.
  - Pass the mic: remain mindful of how long and how often you speak.
  - Own your impact despite your intent.
  - Disrupt interruptions immediately.
  - Address microaggression publicly and in real-time as they happen.

Who on your team is receiving critique on their clothing choices, and who is not? Seek to identify when there are discrepancies in the critiques based on the target of said critiques. Pay close attention to who is most frequently making complaints of this nature and be prepared to step in and speak out against criticism that comes from a place of prejudice and bias.

SUMMARY

- Professionalism that requires individuals to model their behavior after archaic cishet white male norms has a real-life detrimental impact on the lived experiences of Black and historically excluded people, forcing them into self-erasure and erasing one's humanity.
- DEIJ work is more than the simple act of "just add water." You can't just recruit more non-white employees into your organization or onto your team without taking a critical look at how your current structure and policies create real-life barriers to inclusion, equity, and justice.

- Managers must be responsible for fostering an environment where everyone can be safe to show up as themselves without the threat of being seen as "unprofessional."

DISCUSSION/REFLECTION QUESTIONS

1. How does your organization define professionalism? What needs to change in order to make this definition more inclusive?

2. Does your organization have any policies related to hairstyle or dress that could potentially perpetuate harm onto Black and other historically excluded people?

3. Who feels safe to speak up in your organization, and who does not? What actions can your leadership take to ensure all voices are heard?

CHAPTER THIRTEEN

Allyship Is for All

SCOTT FERRY

Lead Instructional Designer

The Winters Group, Inc.

(he/him/his)

> Allyship is not self-defined—our work and our efforts must
> be recognized by the people we seek to ally ourselves with.
>
> —LAYLA SAAD

Allyship is a fraught term. For years in the social justice and activist spaces, *ally* was a prime signifier of someone from a dominant group who "gets it." Calling oneself an ally was convenient shorthand for saying, in effect, "I recognize that I have power and privileges that others do not, and this status quo should not stand." It was, for all intents and purposes, a meaningful show of solidarity at a time when recognition of harmful and oppressive systems and practices was terribly uncommon among dominant group members.

As with language, though, the connotation shifted, even while the denotation remained the same. As the public has become more aware of social justice issues, and the terminology has become ever more embedded in our day-to-day discourse, what used to be a useful label has been co-opted and watered down to the point of near meaninglessness. As a result, calling oneself an *ally* now more closely means,

"I'm not racist or sexist or homophobic or any of that ugly stuff!" It is, in essence, virtue signaling—an oft-empty show of sympathy.

The idea itself, however, is still hugely important to the advancement of equity and justice. If, as the African concept of *ubuntu* has it, we are people only through other people—if our individual and collective humanity is inextricably bound to the humanity of others—then the *practice* of allyship is as critical as it has ever been. That is, in a country and world overloaded with physically and emotionally repressive and oppressive systems that are designed to diminish—if not outright destroy—the humanity of marginalized groups, the only path to justice lies in the collective. Therefore, it's important to reset the definition, if not the concept, of "allyship" so that we can unify and move forward together.

There Is No Allyship Without Action

Those who aspire to be allies need to understand and fully internalize this basic fact: Allyship is *active*. Rather than a state of mind, a belief, or a self-reassuring label, it is fundamentally the manifested actions of a deep commitment to justice. Allyship requires that one understands, recognizes, and *consistently uses* their power and privilege to center the needs of marginalized people and advance equity and justice for everyone. Allyship also means decentering yourself and listening to the needs of the people and communities you seek to stand alongside.

An ally is one who can be counted on to show up, stand up, and speak up in the face of injustice.

What Allyship *Is* and Is *Not*

Before unpacking the ways we can be allies, it's important to be clear about what allyship is and is not. Often *ally* is a term that people give themselves to signal their support for any number of social justice causes (antiracism, LGBTQIA+ rights, etc.). True allyship, however, isn't a label—it's a way of being, of showing up day-in and day-out for those whose voices and needs are silenced, ignored, and made invisible.

To put a finer point on it, *allyship* is a commitment, a habit, an occupation. It is:

- **Substantive, not performative.** There is certainly power in symbolism, but allyship is more than putting a black box in a social media profile, sharing an Angela Davis quote, or starting meetings and seminars with a perfunctory land acknowledgment. While none of these things are *bad*, they do not in and of themselves constitute allyship. They are all symbolic gestures grounded in good intention but without the necessary weight of change behind them. They look nice, but they don't create any real movement. Consider, instead, the conversations that these gestures are theoretically meant to spark and find or make the spaces to *actually have them* with others who do not yet agree.

- **Egalitarian, not exclusive.** Anyone can be an ally, so long as they put in the work. The work begins with understanding yourself— your power, your privileges, and the ways your intersecting identities have shaped you and influenced your worldviews. The next crucial step is understanding how your own experiences and identities complement and contrast with others. Finally, allyship requires knowledge and understanding of the world and the systems of power that undergird the current sociopolitical order. Without this understanding, *allyship* is an empty label devoid of real meaning, signifying only a vague self-concept of one's own general goodness. To understand others, we must understand the world. To understand the world, we must understand ourselves. To understand ourselves, we must work really, really hard.

- **A lifestyle, not an achievement.** Allyship is acting in accordance with a commitment to equity and justice, a commitment to recognize the humanity of all people. And recognizing the humanity of all people, regardless of power or privilege, is basic. Wearing the label *ally* as a badge of honor is an implicit recognition that treating those in marginalized groups as humans with the same inviolable rights as the dominant groups is a challenge. Instead of *saying* you're an ally, *show* it.

- **Dynamic, not static.** Since allyship is incumbent upon listening to and centering the needs of marginalized communities, and communities' needs change over time, the day-to-day mechanics of allyship may shift over time. Maintain your allyship's relevance by continuously listening to and engaging with those you seek to walk alongside.

- **A learning process, not perfection.** Understand that in your journey toward true allyship, you will make mistakes. The stakes feel, and are, higher when discussing issues of justice and equity, which can intimidate an aspiring ally into silence or inaction. Remember, though, that listening and learning are crucial to being an effective ally; therefore, receiving and productively processing feedback arising from the inevitable misstep is a concrete chance to *improve* how you show up for others. In your allyship, strive for effectiveness and evolution, not perfection.

What Might Allyship Look Like?

An active, continuous version of allyship looks fairly straightforward in our personal lives: challenging bigoted statements, jokes, and people; supporting protests; voting in the interests of others; and so on. In a workplace, however, the ally-in-training may find it more difficult to act in service of justice continuously. The key to remember here is that in a system that is built to reinforce traditional hierarchies and power structures, acts of allyship may be received as resistance or even insubordination.

This dynamic is exactly why the distinction between *ally* as a label and *allyship* as an action is so crucial. Allyship in the workplace comes with risks, and it's taking those risks that earn one the label of ally. When finding ways to practice allyship at work, consider your sphere of influence—what do you have full or some control over?

Within that sphere, what changes can you make *now* that will increase equity?

In practice, this may look like:

- Directly calling it out when the voices being centered in a conversation or meeting are primarily from dominant group members.
- Lifting up and giving appropriate credit for the ideas, insights, and contributions of BIPOC colleagues.
- Restructuring meetings to allow for more equitable sharing and valuing of ideas.
- Building new hiring processes and job descriptions that increase the diversity of the applicant pool.
- Shifting the organizational structure to a flat or completely nonhierarchical org chart.
- Using equity-centered processes that center the voices and needs of those most impacted when making significant changes or decisions.

This list is nonexhaustive, as the specific actions that you can take will arise from critical self-reflection and interrogation of organizational practices, but they offer possible models for how an ally can show up in the workplace. The key is that allies must push for change themselves if they wish to turn "allyship" from a label into action.

SUMMARY

- Allyship is always *active*—it is what one does and how one shows up for others, not just a frame of mind.
- Effective allyship necessitates a deep understanding of power structures and the dynamics within them in order to challenge and change the status quo.

- True allies listen to the needs of those who are most impacted and take actions that reflect and advance those causes.

- An aspiring ally will make mistakes and missteps; these are opportunities to listen, learn, and become a stronger, better ally in the future.

- In the workplace, allyship means being willing to take personal risks to uplift and stand alongside others, as acts of allyship can be seen as resistance and insubordination.

DISCUSSION/REFLECTION QUESTIONS

1. Do you consider yourself an ally? Why or why not?

2. Think about your workplace over the last six to twelve months. What opportunities did you miss to be an active ally?

3. How does your organization react to acts of allyship? What does this suggest about the organization's culture of inclusion?

4. What are three actions you can take this week to become an active ally?

CHAPTER FOURTEEN

The Problem
with DEIJ Data

MARY-FRANCES WINTERS
Founder and CEO
The Winters Group, Inc.
(she/her/hers)

Facts can obscure the truth.

—MAYA ANGELOU

Data has become the powerful engine that drives decisions in every organization. With the rapid advances in technology, the ways in which data can be used to provide insights and intelligence has grown exponentially. Such capabilities give us better tools to uncover systemic inequities embedded in organizational systems.

Data scientists who specialize in DEIJ are emerging to support organizations in more robust analysis. Most of the commercial analytical frameworks on the market focus on quantitative reporting. We continue to live in a world that believes if it cannot be counted, it does not count. These tools may assess pay equity and reveal correlations between race and upward mobility or the rate of voluntary to involuntary terminations by ethnicity. They have the capability of devising inclusion indices and predictive analytics.

If organizations are really going to hold themselves accountable to data-driven standards to correct racial inequities, we need both qualitative and quantitative methods. In Chapter 18, Thamara Subramanian explains two frameworks that she has advanced at The Winters Group that include both approaches. Thamara says that "to root out injustices, we need to give just as much credence to the stories and lived experiences of BIPOC that might not fit neatly into a statistical algorithm." In addition to our overreliance on "the numbers," there are other problems with the traditional ways that DEIJ data has been collected and analyzed.

Compliance-Driven Approaches

In the US, diversity data collection has often been a compliance-driven exercise to meet Equal Employment Opportunity Commission (EEOC) regulations. Companies with over fifty employees who do more than $50,000 in business with the government are required to take affirmative action and report hiring, promotion, and termination data by "protected groups," including race, gender, and ethnicity. These reports provide an annual snapshot of utilization in government-designated job categories. Companies are required to set goals to correct underutilization based on the labor market availability of the protected groups. The Office of Federal Contract Compliance Programs (OFCCP) can decide to audit companies to ensure compliance. The EEOC uses these statistics to determine prima facie cases of discrimination.

While this data offers some high-level insights, it does not easily provide evidence of patterns over time, nor does it provide correlations between and among variables. For example, the reporting will reveal how many African Americans were hired into leadership roles. It will report the number that terminated from these roles. This gives you a quantitative measure of retention. However, it does not tell you why you are not retaining African American leaders. The EEOC does not require organizations to collect performance data. Therefore, you would not be able to correlate performance to termination rates. Even if you could, it would beg the question, "why are more African American leaders rated lower than their white counterparts?"

A common justification for high termination rates among Black executives is the "speculation" that there are so few in the pool—that they are recruited away by other companies. Often companies do not collect accurate or detailed exit data, so all they have are assumptions.

Analysis without Interrogation

We can enhance the traditional EEOC data driven by affirmative action with a more justice-centered approach by beginning to interrogate our data and not just analyze it. Analysis can uncover some of these inequities, but interrogation reveals the systems that perpetuate them. Here are some examples of how to interrogate data that the government requires an organization to collect, such as applicant flow, hiring, termination (both voluntary and involuntary), promotion, and performance appraisals.

Applicant Flow

Where do you source? How have your sourcing patterns changed to achieve equitable representation? Who manages the sourcing? What is their level of cultural competence? Who applies? Who does not apply? Where do you recruit? How has that changed over the years? How much do you rely on employee referrals? Are the referrals largely from dominant groups? What is your applicant flow-to-hire ratio? These are all questions to begin interrogating your hiring processes. If your answers do not include Black talent pools or take into account Black cultural patterns or experiences, then your system might be perpetuating racism. Chapter 17 provides advice on taking a justice-centered approach to recruiting and hiring.

The Winters Group conducted a cultural audit for a client a few years ago. This client had a goal of improving women of color in leadership. During our analysis period, they had one hundred openings that they filled with external candidates. Women of color had applied at the same rate as white women. However, only one woman of color was hired out of the one hundred open positions. Twenty white women were hired. This is where the interrogation begins. Why was that the outcome if there was a stated goal to improve the representation of women of color? We recommended that the company review every résumé received, as well as interview notes, to understand this outcome. It is reverse engineering of sorts—backtrack to understand what happened in the system that caused that result.

Hires

Who did you hire? Why? In what ways did your hiring profile align more with cultural patterns and characteristics associated with whiteness? For example, how often do hiring managers use "good fit" for the final decision?

Lauren Rivera, a professor at the Kellogg School of Management, conducted research that revealed that hiring is as much about *cultural matching* between candidates, evaluators, and firms as it is about skills. In her study, employers hired candidates who were not only competent but also culturally similar to themselves in terms of leisure pursuits, experiences, and self-presentation styles.[1] Leveraging a justice lens means organizations should dismantle these subjective criteria by interrogating what hiring managers really mean by "fit" and disrupting processes that allow for those biases to be used.

The Winters Group also looks at five-year projections for the hiring of BIPOC and other historically underrepresented groups to allow for matching of stated goals and the likelihood of achieving those goals at current and historical rates, which Thamara Subramanian speaks to in the next chapter. HR business partners often lament that they bring candidates of color to hiring managers, but often they are not the selected candidate. HR needs more power in the final decisions as they may see biases that the ultimate hiring manager does not.

Promotions

Some very large Fortune 500 companies that we have conducted audits for do not maintain reliable data on promotions. They change job codes or have inconsistent titling of jobs, making it difficult to identify

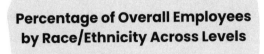

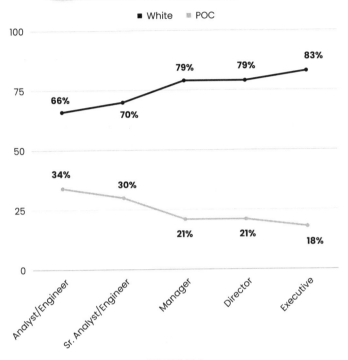

FIGURE 14.1.

A Client Example Showing Disparities in the Upward Mobility of Employees
Based on Race/Ethnicity

SOURCE: The Winters Group

actual upward mobility. Organizations need to maintain reliable promotion data. The excuse that "our data is not in order" is a form of injustice in and of itself.

For those organizations where we can examine promotion history and projections, it often reveals concrete ceilings and sticky floors. Figure 14.1 is a client example that shows that white people's trajectory for leadership increases from the entry-level analyst position, while the opposite is true for BIPOC. Interrogation should include examining every single promotion, who was considered, and the rationale for the decision. In addition, companies that have "ready now" (those individuals ready for a promotion) practices to manage career advancement should examine the diversity of those who are deemed "ready" for promotion and, importantly, who is not ready and why not.

What criteria is used to assess leadership readiness? Black people are more often passed over for leadership positions and find themselves midcareer without having had supervisory roles. Black people make up 12 percent of the workforce and only 3 percent of executive positions. Studies show that Black people more often than whites hold leadership positions in the community, at their churches or in civic organizations. To correct the harm from disproportionately being overlooked, leadership experiences gained outside of the workplace should be given consideration.

Performance Reviews

BIPOC often are disproportionately rated lower than their white counterparts. Studies show that Black employees are overscrutinized and penalized more severely for mistakes. People managers should be required to defend these disparities based on unbiased criteria. In addition, correlations between performance and promotions should be analyzed. We have found that there is not always a correlation. BIPOC often express that they do not receive straightforward feedback and thus are unable to adjust performance. BIPOC should be more diligent in requiring specific feedback from leaders with questions like, "Can you give me a specific example of that?" Or, "Specifically, what behaviors would draw you to that conclusion?"

Terminations

Many organizations that we have conducted audits for are woefully lacking in the data that they collect on why people terminate voluntarily. Multiple choice categories such as "return to school," "a better opportunity," or "family reasons" are common. Applying a justice approach should include a qualitative exit interview that probes in

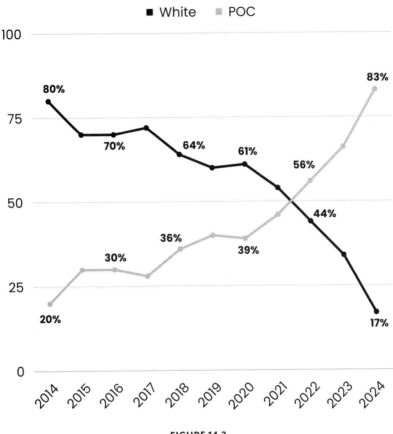

FIGURE 14.2.
Five-Year Forecasting Analysis of Involuntary Terminations by Race
SOURCE: The Winters Group

depth about the leaving employee's experience around issues of equity and justice. In our audits, we often find that BIPOC are terminated involuntarily at disproportionate rates. Again, the reason codes do not provide the whole story—"poor performance," "violation of the rules," and "misconduct" are popular categories. To understand the disparities, we need to interrogate what is happening in the system that creates this outcome. Figure 14.2 is an example of a five-year projection for involuntary terminations at this company. How will they stem the tide if they do not get to the root of the issue?

Intersectional Data Analysis

It is important to recognize intersectionality in our interrogation. How do the experiences of Black women differ from those of white women, for example? Research shows that the experiences are very different. Black women receive less support and mentoring than other groups.[2] How do the experiences of millennials of color differ from their white counterparts? How do the experiences of Black engineers differ from Black maintenance workers? These deeper analyses are not always possible because the numbers are just too small. This is also where conducting qualitative data analysis can provide robust insights where quantitative analysis may be limited.

Analyzing data brings potential inequities and injustices to the surface. Interrogation uncovers practices and policies that cause unintentional harm and disadvantage BIPOC and other historically marginalized groups.

BIPOC Fear

Organizations may supplement the quantitative data with qualitative focus groups or listening sessions organized by different identities in an attempt to uncover the "why." While this can be useful, The Winters Group has found that it is difficult to encourage employees to volunteer for focus groups. There are many reasons, including the time commitment and fear of being honest in a culture that may not be "safe" for BIPOC employees. We have conducted focus groups where employees look to see if there are hidden cameras in the room before they are willing to share.

In addition, employees often lament that they never hear the results of the focus groups, and their day-to-day lived experiences do not change as a result of their participation.

Hiding and "Sugarcoating" the Results

DEIJ data is often viewed as "eye-opening" or "disturbing" at best and deemed "unactionable" at worst. The Winters Group has conducted audits for clients that never see the light of day, as the saying goes. There are gatekeepers who may insist on putting a more positive spin on the findings as a means of prioritizing the comfort of leadership who are most often white and male. We have actually heard: "We cannot share this report as is with top leadership."

When we "push back" and refuse to allow the client to modify our interpretation, we have actually been "fired," and the fallout is the proverbial "shoot the messenger" outcome. We conducted an audit for a large manufacturing company. The HR leader sat on the results for months. The meeting to present the findings to the CEO was canceled a number of times and ended up never happening. We were told our services were no longer needed because they could not really understand the findings and make them actionable, even though there were many actionable recommendations such as hiring a full-time DEIJ leader, conducting leadership training, and forming an executive diversity council.

In many instances, the people analyzing the data or making decisions on the action steps are from dominant cultures and have few insights into the experiences of historically marginalized groups. They lack the cultural competence to take the perspective of those different from them. Decisions about next steps usually focus on the comfort of the white dominant culture. Conclusions are based on worldviews and mindsets that uphold dominant cultural values. Gatekeepers knowingly "spin" the results so they are "palatable" for leadership.

Mitigating the Problems with DEIJ Auditing

These core tenets are key to alleviating the problems associated with DEIJ data collection, analysis, and reporting.

1. The highest level of leadership should commission the audit, be intimately involved in all of the stages of data collection, and receive regular updates throughout the process. The external organization selected to conduct the audit should report directly

to the most senior leaders so that there will be no intermediaries who can "reinterpret" the results.

2. Prior to the data collection phase, there needs to be alignment on the purpose of the project, the level of transparency with which the findings will be shared, how to handle defensiveness and resistance, and what actions the organization will be willing to take on the results.

3. A justice-centered approach is designed to discover: Who is most harmed by our systems? Who benefits from our systems? How do we repair harm and change our systems so that everybody benefits?

4. There needs to be an understanding of the organizational culture and the projected willingness of employees to participate in surveys and focus groups. Is it a toxic work culture where people do not feel safe to share their perspectives openly? Is it a culture of fear? If so, culture change work may need to precede the audit.

5. Who is going to interpret the findings? To what extent will those most impacted by systemic inequities be involved? Consider leveraging employee resource group members to support the external consultant in their analysis and also include their presence in the presentation of findings.

6. How will we handle resistance or defensiveness? We encourage clients to anticipate opposition, as Kevin A. Carter points out in Chapter 6. You should set norms for the meetings where the results are shared, such as (1) showing curiosity over judgment; (2) being mindful of the limitation of your own lens; (3) centering the experiences of those most impacted (e.g., do not be defensive).

7. What action is the organization prepared to take? This question should be agreed upon in advance of the audit. Leadership should make a commitment that any inequities uncovered will be corrected. Sometimes after the results are revealed, clients argue

that it would be too costly to undertake the actions. It has not been budgeted.

8. With what frequency are you going to repeat the audit? What does success look like? The results of the audit should lead to metrics that will measure progress over time, including qualitative.

SUMMARY

- In our high-tech world of "big data," we give more credence to quantitative than qualitative data. Justice-centered approaches require us to include qualitative methods to uncover systemic racism.

- Learn to interrogate and not just analyze your data.

- DEIJ data collection methods have often been limited to compliance reporting with little advanced statistical analysis to understand correlations and the reasons for results.

- Even when approaches are used to uncover the "why," such as focus groups or listening sessions, an employee may be reluctant to share, fearing reprisal.

- Too often, the results of DEIJ queries are not shared broadly and transparently to those who provided input.

- There is a tendency to "spin" the data in a more positive light.

- Often the internal team tasked with interpreting the data lack the cultural competency to do so with fidelity.

- Senior leaders should be intimately involved in the entire audit process to mitigate any issues with DEIJ data—agreeing on the purpose, how resistance and defensiveness will be handled, and how and with what transparency the results will be shared.

- Those most impacted by the results should be involved in the analysis, interpretation, and reporting phases.

DISCUSSION/REFLECTION QUESTIONS

1. How robust is your DEI data analysis? To what extent does it go beyond compliance-driven approaches?

2. To what extent does your organization value qualitative insights?

3. How confident are you that you know the "whys" of your results?

4. How transparent is your organization in sharing both the quantitative and qualitative results?

5. How do you ensure that those most impacted by inequities are involved in deciding the actions that will be taken? To what extent do you center those most impacted by inequities by including them in the decisions about the actions that will be taken?

6. What approaches do you use to increase the safety for BIPOC, so they feel safe in being open about their experiences?

CHAPTER FIFTEEN

Make a Difference with Your DEIJ Data: A Four-Step Process

THAMARA SUBRAMANIAN
Equity Audit and Strategy Manager
The Winters Group, Inc.
(she/her/hers)

Not everything that can be counted counts,
and not everything that counts can be counted.

—WILLIAM BRUCE CAMERON

A justice-centered approach to data analysis, often conducted as equity or civil rights audits, requires us to acknowledge and address the impact of culture and power within organizations. As Kevin A. Carter mentioned in Chapter 6, culture change is imperative to implementing and creating systemic change at the micro-, meso-, and macro-levels.

We use two justice-centered analytical frameworks, racial equity and dominant culture, to uncover and amplify the nuances and intricacies of inequities that have been embedded in behaviors, actions, and systems. Historically, organizational audits and data collection often rely too heavily on quantitative findings and thus miss important insights that can only be gained from listening to the lived experiences of those most impacted in the organization by inequities. Therefore, these frameworks are intended for use as a mixed method approach for valuing and amplifying qualitative data *and* improving the collection and analysis of quantitative data. Ultimately, the justice-centered framework helps answer these questions:

- Who is benefitting from our current systems, and how can we ensure the benefit is accessible to all?

- Who has been and continues to be harmed by our systems, and how can we reduce this harm?

- How can we shift our workplace culture to redistribute power and create equity?

Racial Equity Analysis

The Racial Equity Analysis Framework serves as a tool to help interpret qualitative and quantitative data to reveal attitudes and practices regarding racial justice in the workplace. Many clients have questioned why only racial equity and not other inequities? Historically, we have seen racism, racial justice, and racial equity be neglected in favor of other dimensions of diversity, such as diversity of thought. We have also seen racial equity be diluted or touched upon without interrogating the systems that uphold the status quo. Intentionally amplifying and examining racial equity may reveal other larger organizational cultural patterns that negatively impact all employees. In other words, if we fix racial disparities, everyone benefits.

How may these measures of racial equity manifest in the workplace?

- **Acknowledgment and awareness.** This can show up at varying levels across micro-, meso-, and macro-levels of our society. For example, at the micro-level, when people share what diversity means to them, is race avoided or seen as less important than another dimension? From the macro-level, is racism mentioned as an area of opportunity or an integral part of an organization's strategic plan?

- **Self-understanding.** Although many organizations may talk about race or racism in the abstract, do employees across all levels of the organization have an understanding of their own racial identity?

For example, when talking about challenges in the workplace, do leaders mention themselves as "a Black man" or a "white woman," or are leaders dissociating from their racial identity? Do white employees feel that they think DEI work isn't relatable to them because of their race? As pointed out in Chapter 2, Pew Research conducts an annual race perceptions study. In 2019, they asked, "to what extent is race core to your identity." Seventy-four percent of Black respondents, 59 percent of Hispanic participants, and 56 percent of Asians say that it is very or extremely important. Only 15 percent of white respondents feel that race is core to their identity.[1] Not recognizing the role that one's race plays in how they see themselves and how others see them inhibits progress toward racial justice. It is necessary for white people to recognize their place at the top of the racial hierarchy and the impact, intentional or not, on their lived experiences.

- **Priority.** When assessing an organization's commitment to DEIJ, to what extent are race and racism a prime concern for the organization? For example, has your organization allocated funding specifically for BIPOC organizations to address racial injustices? Would all employees be aware of the organization's commitment to racial justice? Is it communicated both internally and externally?

Applying this analytical framework, we can determine the extent to which these measures are prevalent in the organization and the specific areas of opportunity to improve in each of these areas.

Dominant Culture Analysis

The Dominant Culture Analysis Framework serves as a tool to uncover and interrogate dominant culture patterns that create barriers to achieving equity and disproportionately impact historically marginalized employees in the workplace. Dominant groups are those with systemic power, privileges, and social status within a society, most often white people, especially white men. Dominant groups are considered the norm, and by default, subordinated groups are "abnormal" or "othered" in the workplace.[2] *White dominant culture* or *white supremacy culture* is the "water that we all swim in." We are all impacted by it, live within the culture, and uphold the cultural patterns, but BIPOC are affected in more detrimental and even violent ways by these cultural patterns.

White Dominant Culture Characteristics

As discussed in Chapter 2, scholar Tema Okun and other social scientists have identified some key characteristics and manifestations of dominant cultural patterns in the context of organizations as impediments to organizational success.[3] When these characteristics manifest in excess in our attitudes, behaviors, and actions, they disproportionately impact BIPOC and other marginalized groups. These characteristics, such as perfectionism and individualism, are Western American values that we often strive for or are even considered "success" in the workplace. However, while continuous improvement is laudable, the patterns, when in excess, described below, perpetuate injustice in the workplace.

- **Perfectionism.** An excess of seeking perfection from the worldview of the dominant culture. Mistakes are punished rather than used as learning opportunities. This characteristic in excess manifests as "only one right way" and either-or thinking. One study showed that when a Black leader made the identical mistake that the white leader had made, the Black leader was rated more harshly.[4] Another study showed that Black workers in a manufacturing setting were watched more and had their work scrutinized more than white workers. This resulted in more errors being detected which led to lower performance reviews, often leading to more terminations.[5]

- **Concentration of power.** Most organizational structures are very hierarchical, with authority at the executive and board levels. Hierarchy fuels paternalistic norms where those in power believe they are capable of making decisions for and in the best interest of those without power. Even as organizations begin to see the wisdom of transparency and power sharing, this does not correct the fact that it is more likely that there will be disproportionately more BIPOC in the lowest job categories with no decision-making power. *Concentration of power* can also show up as leadership defensiveness, such as creating channels for input but not acting upon the feedback or preserving the current power structures to maintain the status quo, such as saying, "that's not how we do things here."

- **Right to comfort.** We routinely hear from our clients, "We don't want to make our leaders too uncomfortable," or "Race is too uncomfortable to talk about." The *right to comfort* is intolerance for conflict, especially open conflict. Those in power, mainly white people, have the right to comfort, and those without power often do not.

- **Individualism.** The US has been called the most individualistic society on the planet. It is the belief that we are independent and not interdependent. "I pull myself up by my own bootstraps." We saw this excess of individualism play out during the COVID-19 pandemic where people were advocating only for themselves, "I want to make my own decision about wearing a mask," without regard for how that decision would impact other people.

- **Progress is bigger/more.** This value is embedded immensely in the capitalist economy, where more is always the goal. This worldview in excess prioritizes quantity over quality, neglecting, for example, the emotional, social, ethical, or other costs of growth.

- **Forget the past.** White dominant culture focuses on the present and the future. We often hear: "That happened a long time ago. Why are we still talking about slavery?" We see it manifest with laws being passed to ban certain books in schools that provide an accurate account of the US's racist history.

These dominant cultural patterns are often difficult to accept and understand because they represent an excess of Anglo-Saxon cultural values established in the 1600s and 1700s with origins in colonization, slavery, war, and political shifts.[6] The characteristics originated and were used as a method of creating explicit divides between white and BIPOC and have manifested into a value set that is dominant across organizations without being explicitly named. Despite being so normalized, it is imperative to understand that an excess of these cultural patterns is harmful to *all* employees *and,* explicitly or implicitly, oppresses and creates more barriers to marginalized groups.

A Justice-Centered Model for Data Collection and Interrogation

Applying the racial equity and dominant culture frameworks to our assessment process reveals the extent to which characteristics of the dominant culture are implicitly or explicitly present in the workplace. The Winters Group Justice-Centered Equity Audit is comprised of the following components.

Step 1. Organizational Alignment

As Mary-Frances Winters pointed out in Chapter 4, "The Leadership Imperative," leadership commitment and engagement are required for a successful audit process. Therefore, to begin our data collection process, we conduct leadership alignment sessions and ask:

- *What does leadership commitment look like to you?*
- *How does DEIJ align with your organization's mission and vision?*
- *What is my role in the justice-centered audit process as a leader?*
- *How can we disrupt dominant cultural patterns in our ways of thinking and acting upon data?*

It is imperative to create shared understanding and advocacy for the process and outcomes. Without alignment, we have experienced increased resistance throughout the entire process and inaction when key findings are revealed. This resistance has shown up in the form of leaders being reluctant to participate, confusion, and distrust resulting in the lack of participation in both qualitative and quantitative data collection from employees, as well as a lack of follow-through and defensiveness toward findings and recommendations. For example, some groups such as Native Americans may not be represented well numerically in the organization and may be overlooked or combined in a category called "other people of color." A justice-centered approach requires us to amplify the voices of such groups, even though challenging, as they may not want to share if the environment is viewed as toxic. Thus, the alignment learning sessions can help leaders build transparency in the data collection process through invitation, not expectation.

The alignment educational sessions are held with a core group of stakeholders and internal change agents, including but not limited to executives, BIPOC leaders, and aspiring allies. The purpose of the alignment sessions is to introduce and affirm the impact and goals of the equity audit process, explore what justice means in the context of organizational values, increase self-understanding of leadership identity in the workplace, and get a better understanding of the components of the assessment that will lead to a DEIJ strategy.

Step 2. Discovery—Uncovering Overlooked Insights

After alignment, the data collection and subsequent analysis process can begin. Each component of data is designed to uncover organizational insights using mixed methods to find and interrogate often overlooked, unknown, and undervalued qualitative and quantitative data to inform DEIJ strategy. Throughout the analysis and development of recommendations, centering justice requires us to reflect on:

- *How do we define "data-driven"?*
- *Whose experiences are represented in existing data; whose voices are not being represented because they don't have a "category"?*

- *How do we move beyond "numbers" as the only form of data to amplify the stories and experiences of marginalized employees?*

A. Assessing Cultural Readiness

If the purpose of the audit is to uncover inequities and disparities, it is necessary to understand the capabilities of leadership to develop a systemic, strategic approach to correcting them. These are the key questions:

- *How culturally competent is the organization? What is the organization's worldview toward racial differences? What is the organization's level of readiness to engage in conversations about racial injustice?*

- *What work and education are needed to maximize the effectiveness of a DEIJ strategy? How does this look different for people across various identities?*

We assess individual and organizational cultural competence and readiness with a quantitative, psychometric assessment, the Intercultural Development Inventory (IDI). The IDI is an online assessment that provides individual and organization-wide insights into the capability of the organization to bridge cultural differences effectively.[7] A developmental model—the tool theorizes that the more experience an individual has with cultural difference, the greater their potential to understand differences in their own and other cultures and be able to develop culturally relevant adaptive strategies. Terrence Harewood, PhD, provides a comprehensive overview in Chapter 5 of how people move through the different IDI orientations from denial to adaptation. Sharing the individual and organizational results early in the audit process provides stakeholders with the opportunity to work on their Individual Development Plans, an integral part of the IDI process.

B. Key Stakeholder Interviews

After assessing cultural competence with key stakeholders, one-on-one interviews help us gain a better understanding of the opportunities, challenges, and understanding of DEIJ from organizational leaders and BIPOC employees. To get robust data and an understanding of company leadership, power, and influence, we must ask:

- *To what extent is racial equity understood in the organization? To what extent is it a priority?*

- *In what ways is leadership perpetuating dominant cultural patterns, and to what extent?*

- *How may these patterns show up in how the organization operates?*

Each leader gets dedicated time to share their challenges, areas of opportunity, and their own views and definitions of DEIJ. After collecting the raw sentiments of our respondents, we conduct an inductive and deductive thematic analysis. The first step is deductive thematic analysis, in which we summarize key themes that come up in the data on their own. For example, one of the questions we ask in interviews is: *How would you describe your organization's external commitments in the communities that you serve? What are some strengths and areas of opportunity in your external social responsibility initiatives?* This question aims to learn more about the external DEIJ initiatives so we can assess who benefits, who is harmed, and how power is distributed from the perspectives of the various interviewees. From this, we are able to find key strengths in their external DEIJ initiatives and opportunities that serve as a starting point for creating new external DEIJ goals.

C. Internal HR Data Analysis

The goal of this part of the discovery is to determine if there are significant differences that may promote or impede organizational equity by demographic group. To achieve this goal, we must ask:

- *What data does our organization NOT collect? In what ways is this impeding our DEIJ efforts?*

- *What are the significant differences and gaps in hiring, promotions, termination, and performance by intersectional identity groups? How is this impacting the retention of historically underrepresented employees?*

- *How will our past and current hiring, promotion, and termination practices influence our capability to meet our goals in the future?*

First, we begin by collecting raw data on hires, promotions, terminations, and performance ratings for a three- to five-year period. Just in this collection process, we have found that many organizations do not even collect data by groups beyond compliance requirements. For instance, a healthcare organization we partnered with had received many complaints from LGBTQIA+ employees and patients about the lack of inclusivity and empathy toward nonbinary patients. When trying to address if this was impacting LGBTQIA+ employee retention, we noticed that only "male" and "female" gender categories were collected. Thus, one of the findings from this part of our analysis was expanding their categories of data to include gender nonbinary employees for those who do not fit into a traditional data category.

With the data available from the client, we then assess the historical data to find correlations and significant differences in hiring, promotions, terminations, and performance, including but not limited to race, gender, generation, job level, and department. We look beyond statistical significance to uncover patterns where the numbers of employees are too small to drive a mathematically significant finding. Predictive analytics based on historical trends helps clients to envision how long it might take to reach hiring and promotion goals. For example, after George Floyd's murder, many companies set aggressive goals to increase the representation of Black people, especially in leadership roles. How realistic are such goals based on projections driven from past demographics and practices?

D. Listening Sessions

We conduct listening sessions with a randomized selection of employees to get a better sense of the "day-to-day" employee experience and recommendations to gain a better understanding of the opportunities, challenges, and daily experiences of various employees.

* *In what ways can we create groups that highlight the voice of underrepresented identity groups?*

* *In what ways can we ensure that confidentiality and trust are fostered with those with less power in the organization?*

* *How do employees perceive their organization's efforts? How do they describe their culture?*

* *How do the employee experiences differ based on employees' social identities? In what ways is race acknowledged or understood at the employee level?*

As Mary-Frances Winters points out in Chapter 14, one of the biggest barriers to collecting employee qualitative data has been a lack of participation, attributed to factors such as lack of time or ability to participate outside of daily duties, as well as fear of retaliation or repercussions for sharing anything negative about the organization. To better foster trust, we began shifting away from the "focus group" lexicon as some employees felt it was more like market research and less about their employee experience. Second, we created listening sessions based on demographic groups determined by organizational priorities. For example, participants might comprise different groups by race, gender, regional difference, or job type (i.e., clinical, service, client-facing, administrative). Having one or more commonalities among listening group sessions is one way to create a sense of trust and security, as well as a space for camaraderie and conversation—creating much richer raw data.

Listening session questions are aimed toward answering the questions above as well as supporting understanding of the differences in

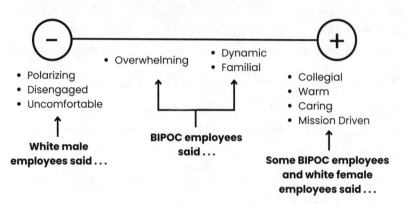

FIGURE 15.1.
A Sampling of How Different Groups Describe Their Organization in One Word
SOURCE: The Winters Group

employee experience across demographic groups. For example, one of the simplest yet most powerful questions we ask is, *what is it like to be [your demographic group] at your organization*? Often, we can see differences in the sentiment of response across listening sessions and are able to parse out why an employee experience may be negative for two groups of people, but for very different reasons. Another example is when we ask participants to describe their organization in one word (Figure 15.1). As shown, the responses varied widely in sentiment. With sessions based on demographics, we were able to capture who specifically in the organization was sharing that sentiment. This, in turn, helped the organization better understand its own employee engagement data.

E. Equity and Justice Insights Survey

An integral part of the discovery process is to conduct a quantitative survey. The Winters Group Equity Justice Insights Survey (EJIS) allows organizations to gain a quantitative understanding of the significant differences and patterns in the perception of equity across the organizational culture. The Likert-style survey (rating from *strongly disagree* to *strongly agree*) asks questions related to the dominant culture and racial equity, such as:

* *My immediate manager is comfortable having conversations about race and racism (referring to right to comfort).*

* *We set goals and measure success based on the achievement of numerical outcomes (referring to progress is bigger/more, specifically relating to notions of quantity over quality).*

* *Our organization's commitment to antiracism is evident in my day-to-day work experience (referring to racial equity, specifically acknowledgment, and awareness).*

Coding for the racial equity dimensions and disaggregating the data by multiple demographic groups such as race, gender, sexual orientation, disability, and job location, we are able to find significant associations and differences in how various groups perceive equity in the workplace. Figures 15.2 and 15.3 show examples of how differences in responses varied by race and ethnicity across question groups (questions related to racial equity) as well as single items on the survey. The percentages represent how many respondents answered "strongly agree" or "agree."

F. Policies, Practices, and Procedures Review

Historically, policy reviews from a DEIJ perspective have been compliance oriented. Are we meeting industry regulations? Requirements for nonprofit status? Yet, many times in interviews and listening sessions, employees have shared various levels in which company policies or interpretation of those policies have been a barrier to actualizing DEIJ change. In lieu of analyzing policies from a compliance lens, we apply the equity justice theory to our analysis to determine strengths and opportunities for embedding diversity, equity, and inclusion into policy language. Any available organizational policies, practices, and procedure documents are analyzed by applying the five question

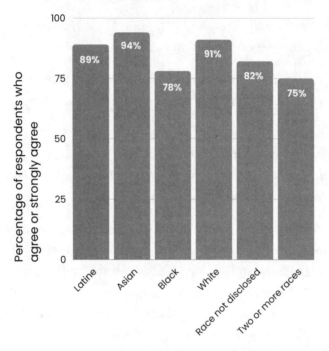

FIGURE 15.2.
Key Findings on How Different Groups Perceive Equity in the Workplace
SOURCE: The Winters Group

areas below to every policy and procedure. This lens can also be applied to communication documents, corporate social responsibility guidelines, supplier diversity commitments, and more.

- **History.** *What are the goals/objectives of this policy? What is the history of the problem/circumstance it addresses and the typical practices? How do the goals/objectives of this policy align with organization values and intended outcomes?*

- **Language.** *To what extent is there clarity on who is taking ownership of the consequences/actions of this policy?*

- **Voice.** *Whose perspectives have been sought out to create this policy, and whose views have not? How can we ensure all employees and customers are included?*

- **Implication.** *How do resources and services need to be redistributed to ensure the policy can be translated with equity into practice?*

- **Reimagining.** *How could an alternative policy or change better align with intended outcomes? In what ways can we ensure that implications of power are shifted to reduce burdens on communities most impacted by systemic injustices specific to your industry and organization?*

Going through each policy, practice, and procedure, and asking these questions, we are able to provide recommendations and considerations for policy change that centers on the most impacted. For example, after reviewing a partner organization's listening sessions and termination data, we found that maternity leave policies were a barrier to equity and a reason for termination. Upon analyzing this policy, we saw areas of opportunity in all of the five areas above. Some examples of recommendations included shifting the language from *maternity* to *parental* policy, expanding the definition of medical restriction to include mental health implications of parental needs, and interviewing employees who have been impacted by this policy to understand what barriers they faced in qualifying for the leave benefits.

Step 3. Applying the Racial Equity and Dominant Culture Analysis to the Data

After gathering all of the quantitative and qualitative data aforementioned, we use the Dominant Cultural Analysis and Racial Equity Analysis as inductive frameworks in analyzing all of the data types outlined above to provide a deeper look at inequities and injustices seen in the data.

The following table shows an example of dominant culture (perfectionism) and the extent to which we captured sentiments relating to

The Dominant Culture of Perfectionism

Overall level: Minimal in Leadership, Moderate in Staff	Either/Or Thinking: Minimal to Moderate

Overall level: Minimal in Leadership, Moderate in Staff

"I am starting to see more of the Brown people (Indian, Black, Hispanic) and in higher positions. Some of the patients when they hear an accent, they minimize their perspective or skills. We (the Brown people) all have to work twice as hard. That is the one thing that is a little rough."

"When I first started, my first few days, I felt that I had to prove myself. When they look at me, and see that I look Hispanic Latino, they would look to me as if questioning if I knew what I was doing."

Either/Or Thinking: Minimal to Moderate

Employee sentiments related to being overworked and stretched, feeling a strong pressure to perform in the way most accepted by the dominant culture at the organization.

Only the Right Way: Moderate to High

Mistakes seen as burdensome, BIPOC held to higher standards to prove their worth. Leaders shared little room for self-direction and flexibility (e.g., precise meeting times and procedures).

Worship of the Written Word: Minimal

Stakeholders did not specify or value written word more or less than embodiment of and commitment to DEI initiatives. Strong desire for the organization to show more action toward creating equity and more about how policies are implemented.

Source: The Winters Group

those characteristics. For the organization in the table, we uncovered sentiments related to perfectionism minimally shared in key stakeholder interviews with leadership but at a moderate level in the listening sessions. We also induced that within perfectionism, the cultural pattern that showed up the most was related to "only one right way," with many listening session members mentioning the cost of mistakes and BIPOC listening session members feeling held to higher standards.

Where perfectionism is high in an organization, we suggest deeper interrogation of HR data. In other words, how does this excess of perfectionism "show up" in our practices and policies? For example, do Black employees disproportionately receive lower performance reviews? Why is this? To what extent are they being scrutinized more and being held to higher standards? One performance analysis we

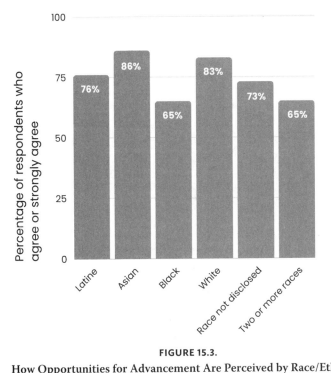

FIGURE 15.3.
How Opportunities for Advancement Are Perceived by Race/Ethnicity
SOURCE: The Winters Group

conducted for a client revealed 81 percent of white employees received the top ratings (four or five). It begs the question; how can we disrupt perfectionism culture in our promotion and performance review processes.

The following table shows insights from an organization's racial equity analysis. From listening sessions and the EJIS, race and racism were considered a high priority at the organization. This provided a firm rationale for focusing on racial equity in their strategy. As part of the strategy, the client prioritized developmental racial justice education for leaders.

Insights from Racial Equity Analysis

PRIORITY

Level: High	
"The fact that we're going through this process, it's really important and it gives me hope that we can do something about the equity issue. There's clearly a racial component to it; race, definitely race and class, play a big role in that."	• Many mentions of racial disparities in representation, inclusion of employees, and access of the organization as opportunities to act upon internally.
	• Many sentiments regarding embedding equity through having more staff and community voice in decision making, looking at pay inequities by race.
	• Frequent mentions of the external racial injustices being addressed by the organization, particularly police brutality.

Source: The Winters Group

Step 4. Reveal—Dissemination and Exploration of Our Data and Recommendations

Once all the components of the assessment are completed, we convene leaders and encourage participants of the process as well as other organizational stakeholders to be part of dialogue and conversation around the findings and recommendations.

Data should tell a story. Through weaving the data components together, we are able to capture and create tailored recommendations that tell a unique and authentic story of the organization. We recommend transparent sharing of the findings widely across the organization and work with clients to share the findings in a digestible format without diluting the information.

The next step is to develop a long-term sustainable implementation strategy based on the findings. For that purpose, The Winters Group conducts three to four strategy sessions with clients, as outlined in Chapter 7.

SUMMARY

- We should prioritize and amplify qualitative insights and improve quantitative data collection in assessing racial justice in organizations. The Dominant Culture Analysis and Racial Equity Analysis Framework can be applied to both data collection and analysis to ask questions that address the root causes of injustices in our workplace.

- Disrupting our dominant cultural patterns, such as *perfectionism* and *quantity-over-quality*, enables us to understand better and find and repair root causes of harm in our policies, communications, and partnerships.

- Applying a justice lens to all aspects of your organization increases benefits to all at the workplace by improving methods of collecting and utilizing quantitative data while uplifting narrative and qualitative data.

DISCUSSION/REFLECTION QUESTIONS

1. How is your identity and power as a leader or as a data collector influencing the responses and findings from your organization?

2. How might the company culture as a whole, or your individual relationships with interviewees, impact their forthrightness?

3. What are some of the dominant cultural patterns or root causes of injustice that impede your progress toward implementing change?

CHAPTER SIXTEEN

How to Make Reparations
a Reality Now

LEIGH MORRISON
Learning and Innovation Manager
The Winters Group, Inc.
(she/her/hers)

TAMI JACKSON
Instructional Designer
The Winters Group, Inc.
(she/her/hers)

A country curious about how reparations might actually
work has an easy solution in [HR 40]. We would support
this bill, submit the question to study, and then assess the
possible solutions. But we are not interested. That HR 40 has
never—under either Democrats or Republicans—made it to
the House floor suggests our concerns are rooted not in the
impracticality of reparations but in something more existential.

—TA-NEHISI COATES

Author Leigh Morrison's note: *There are many scholars on the topic of
reparations, of which I am not one. Also, as we build on shifting public
opinion and seek to build critical capacity in the understanding of and
support for reparations, I fundamentally believe in the importance of
white Americans learning about, discussing, and acting upon tangible*

ways to realize reparations in our country and communities. I am not, to my knowledge, personally descended from enslavers; my ancestors were white immigrants to Canada and the United States. My ancestors enjoyed access to rights and opportunities unavailable to many other immigrants and people born in the United States in the broader context of white supremacy. I believe it is critical for white people to shift from a posture of guilt and defensiveness to humility and action as it relates to our inheritance of intersectional, identity-based privileges. The first-person narratives presented here represent my voice and experience. I also acknowledge my ongoing learning and areas of limited perspective and therefore collaborated in authoring this chapter with my colleague Tami Jackson, both a scholar in Black Studies and a person with lived experience as an American descendant of chattel slavery. I am deeply grateful for her contributions.

Reparations is a term that can broadly refer to making amends for wrongdoing through financial or other means. This chapter focuses on reparations to address racialized harm and disparities tracing back to American chattel slavery. In the United States, the HR 40 bill to study reparations for slavery has been languishing in Congress since 1989. To be certain, many people and communities experience harm at the hands of systems of white supremacy, and this chapter's focus is not to discourage championing the repair of other iterations of racist harm.

There is also some debate[1] over who should qualify for receiving reparations for slavery, as the continued impact of white supremacy and anti-Black racism harms many people who are not descendants of people enslaved in the United States. We acknowledge this truth and also, in our continuous efforts to center those most impacted by unjust systems, note that economic barriers[2] and embodied trauma experienced[3] by American descendants of slavery contribute to disparate outcomes for this group as compared to Black immigrants to the US.

These inequities highlight a need for specific responses to make equity a reality—such that identity is no longer a predictor of outcome. The possibilities outlined here may be applied more broadly (and for logistical or legal reasons, may need to be, particularly within the context of organizational policy). Regardless, we always support centering the experiences and input of those most directly impacted in policy-building for a more just future—an approach from which everyone can benefit.

Legacies of Anti-Black Racism in US Class Mobility

Following the abolition of slavery, the US government failed to deliver on its promise of 40 acres of land to formerly enslaved Black people while allotting significant amounts of land to white people. These (in)actions set the trajectory for a staggering racial wealth gap that would only be exacerbated by white terrorism against prosperous Black communities and decades of discriminatory policies in housing, banking, education, law enforcement, and voting rights.[4] Today, the impact of many of these policies and events has yet to be corrected.

In 1964, Malcolm X offered in an interview: "If you stick a knife in my back nine inches and pull it out six inches, there's no progress. If you pull it all the way out that's not progress. Progress is healing the wound that the blow made. And they haven't even pulled the knife out much less heal the wound. They won't even admit the knife is there."[5] Despite the passage of the Civil Rights Act that same year, the racial wealth gap has barely shifted in sixty years.[6] Black families in the US are more likely to experience poverty and have less access to upward mobility than white families.[7] Black families are less likely to own a home. On average, the net wealth of white families is ten times that of Black families,[8] illustrating clearly the compounded effects of generational wealth and opportunity, or lack thereof.

Education, often cited as a solution to the wealth gap, has left Black students (particularly Black women) disproportionately shouldering student debt, compounded by race- and gender-based pay gaps many encounter upon entering the workforce.[9] Race-based disparities in student debt increased significantly between 2001 and 2013 as a result of predatory lending,[10] and today white college graduates possess seven times more wealth than Black graduates.[11] The Biden Administration's Student Debt Relief plan provides a much-needed first step in addressing this problem, but more significant policy shifts will be essential in closing the racial wealth gap.[12]

The passage of HR 40 would establish a commission to study the impact of slavery and anti-Black racism in the United States and explore the distribution of monetary reparations to address the enduring consequences of these atrocities. The bill was first introduced in 1989 and was reintroduced *every year* by Rep. John Conyers Jr. (Democrat of Michigan) until his retirement, never advancing past the committee's vote until 2021, when Rep. Sheila Jackson Lee (Democrat of Texas) led its sponsorship.[13] As of this writing over a year later, HR 40 has yet to pass the House.[14] If it advances to the Senate, it will likely fail due to the polarization that characterizes our current political system—and, more foundationally, an egregious lack of true representation of the US populace in our legislature.

While money should never need to motivate civil rights policy, it is worth noting that failure to address the Black–white wealth gap has cost the US economy $16 trillion in the past twenty years alone[15]—illustrating the lengths to which white supremacy is valued above justice-centered approaches that truly could benefit everyone. Research has found that reparations could *eliminate the racial wealth gap in ten years.*[16] Yet, in 2019, current Senate Minority Leader Mitch McConnell (Republican of Kentucky)—whose great-great grandparents enslaved at least fourteen people on cotton farms in Alabama—stated that he didn't "think that reparations for something that happened 150 years ago, for whom none of us currently living are responsible, is a good idea. We tried to deal with our original sin of slavery by fighting a Civil War, by passing landmark civil rights legislation, by electing an African American president."[17] ("Tried" all but acknowledges that none of these events "dealt with" this sin after all.)

We hear similar sentiments often from other white folks.

I'm not responsible for my ancestors' mistakes. It was a long time ago. We've come so far since then. I've worked hard for my accomplishments. They shouldn't be discounted because I'm white.

Each of these misses key points. US slavery was not an individual mistake but an intentionally violent system created to generate immense wealth for white people through the dehumanization of stolen Black people and exploitation of their unpaid labor. This is the harm—with ongoing consequences to this day—that reparations for slavery would seek to address.

Furthermore, it is less about white people not having worked hard for our accomplishments and more that others have not had access to the same opportunities. Even when they work as hard or harder, they may be unable to advance to the same degree because of how racism and other forms of oppression persist at all levels of our systems. Justice requires that we acknowledge the impact of historical and current-day harm. While white folks may not support the actions of our ancestors, we must acknowledge that we live under and benefit from their legacies in the context of white supremacy.

Guilt, Scarcity, and Individualism as Barriers to Reparations

Rhetoric about reparations from white people is frequently laden with guilt. Guilt functions as a distancing tactic to shut down a conversation, and I generally believe those who raise the topic of guilt project this accusation. (*People are telling me I should feel guilty for who I am!*) While it is critical to recognize and reflect on discomfort that may arise for us in conversations about privilege, I rarely hear sentiments from racial justice activists or educators instructing white people to feel guilty for "who they are."

It is worth interrogating where feelings of guilt surrounding complicity come from and what purpose they serve. While guilt is a normal response to learning about injustices in which we may be complicit, it also can easily lead to shutting down—and failing to continue reflection and learning that can support us in changing our actions.

It is imperative that we build skills around sitting with and working through discomfort if we are to make progress. Misguided narratives about guilt and right to comfort have also been weaponized by those opposed to racial justice as reasoning for censorship of curriculum and workplace trainings—a dangerous and desperate use of power to uphold the status quo.

Supporting reparations requires circumventing these "distancing" barriers by unlearning capitalist, individualist mindsets into which most of us in the US have been deeply socialized. *Individualism*, an element of white supremacy culture, is defined as the belief "that we make it on our own (or should), without help, while pulling ourselves up by our own bootstraps."[18] A *scarcity mindset* is one driven by the "zero-sum" assumption—whether conscious or unconscious—that progress for one person or group necessarily means less access to resources for others.[19] Underlying this mindset is a sense of fear and potential loss. By contrast, Living Cities defines an *abundance mindset* as one that "allows space for opportunities and scenarios that outweigh the limitations placed by fear."[20]

Spaces that are driven by capitalism, including many of our organizations and institutions, embrace and instill scarcity and individualist mindsets as assumed norms. We do not need to accept them as such, and there is much value in reflecting on how these assumptions show up in our thoughts and behaviors and asking ourselves what more can be possible. Scholars and activists devoted to racial justice have long argued that scarcity functions to divide us and prevent progress, harming everyone. Abundance framing, which can benefit everyone, is the path forward.[21]

Unlearning Scarcity and Individualism: Leigh's Experiences

As an attendee of a historically women's college, I absorbed knowledge from peers and faculty about employers lowballing women's salary offers, negotiating compensation, and self-advocacy to set myself up for compounded financial gains over the course of my lifetime. I learned quite a bit from my community and felt better equipped to navigate a world that I knew was largely biased against me as a woman.

The next step that I failed to make in my thought process for several years was "and because I have had access to this wealth of knowledge—an opportunity unavailable to many people—I can redistribute my own resources to others." I was still approaching this from a scarcity mindset. I recall, during graduate school, being asked for money by someone on a street corner. "Sorry," I said, walking past and thinking to myself, "I am $20,000 in educational debt. I can't afford that." Now when I consider how much closer I was to financial security than this person by mere virtue of attending graduate school, I would respond differently. Since then, I have learned to recognize scarcity-centered thinking and have engaged in an ongoing, intentional practice to replace it with abundance-focused thinking.

Today, I actively seek out ways to learn about barriers faced by historically marginalized groups in my communities and contribute to mutual aid efforts to address injustices. I advocate for pay equity in organizations I am involved in. If I am carrying cash and asked for assistance, I give what I feel I can, or consider if I can purchase food for the person in need. I don't wait to hear someone's full story before deciding if it is believable or "worthy" of help, instead trusting that one way or another, systems that work (better) for me have failed them, and continue to fail all of us.

Practicality of Reparations

Another barrier to reparations becoming a reality has been the label that has been routinely attached to its execution as "impractical." Even those who claim to see the benefit in theory often argue that it is logistically "too complex" to pursue. Just after Ta-Nehisi Coates published "The Case for Reparations" in *The Atlantic*, *Atlantic* contributor David Frum published a rebuttal titled "The Impossibility of Reparations."[22] Rhetoric like this also operates as a harmful distancing narrative—halting conversation, imagination, problem-solving, and progress. This approach should disturb us, particularly coming from those who have personally benefitted from the harmful systems under discussion. Coates responds to Frum's arguments in a third article, "The Radical Practicality of Reparations."[23]

Shifting to informed possibility models: The National African American Reparations Commission (NAARC) has identified a ten-point reparations plan "for review, revision, and adoption as a platform."[24] William A. Darity and A. Kirsten Mullen's 2020 book *From Here to Equality* lays out a plan for realizing reparations for American descendants of slavery. Legal experts have outlined specific tax code policies that could support reparations payments through a variety of forward-thinking channels.[25] While descendants of slavery should qualify for reparations regardless of their current economic status, payments could be distributed through a cohort model in order to prioritize those with the greatest need.

Importantly, there are historical precedents for the US government paying reparations to communities it has harmed. It allocated the equivalent of multiple billions of today's dollars to survivors of Japanese internment camps from World War II between the Japanese-American Claims Act of 1948 and the Civil Liberties Act of 1988. US and state governments have also paid reparations to survivors of egregious government-sponsored human rights violations, including forced sterilization and the Tuskegee syphilis experiment.[26] After World War II, Congress established the Indian Claims Commission, which paid out small amounts to Native Americans for land stolen from them before dissolving in 1978.[27] While these precedents each proved inadequate, they provide case studies to learn from and improve upon in the continuous fight for justice and correcting harm.

In 2020, the US collectively overcame millions of logistical challenges to transition much of our workforce to remote work. We are *absolutely capable* of overcoming logistical barriers when we want to. Often, logistical barriers are only "dealt with" when they benefit those in positions of power. Research has validated that those with access to power are less likely to empathize with or act in the interests of those without access to power.[28] Thus, it is unsurprising in the context of

white supremacy that logistical complexities to racial justice are cited
as nebulous barriers rather than solved for—a pattern we would do
well to anticipate, identify, and disrupt.

Our lawmakers remain unlikely to take action on reparations until
we vote out those who cling to racist ideals or reject measures that
would eliminate persistent disparities. We must commit to voting
(and funding!) them out. In the meantime, it is incumbent upon us to
take action as individuals and organizations to prove that reparations
are possible and to address harm in our communities where our representatives fail to do so. People continue to be harmed every day as a
result of collective inaction on reparations, and we have the power to
change this. *Reparations are as real as you make them.*

Making Reparations Real in Your Personal Life

Broadly, consider: What does "enough" mean for you, and how can
you allocate resources beyond that toward those with greater need
who are experiencing racist harm? What is your long-term life plan
to this end? Why is this important to you, and how have you educated yourself on the lived experiences of those to whom you are
contributing?

+ When you learn about injustice, seek out ways to contribute. If
  you don't know someone who personally needs support, all it
  takes is an internet search to support families and communities
  harmed by racist systems directly.

+ Identify one or more ways to contribute through recurring
  monthly payments. Mutual aid funds are devoted to connecting
  those who need support with those who can provide it. The
  Conscious Kid[29] collects funds to support rent payments
  and prevent evictions directly. NAARC[30] and Fund for
  Reparations NOW![31] are always accepting contributions. The
  Reparations4Slavery portal supports white Americans in making
  reparations to Black Americans through monetary contributions
  and other expansive possibilities.[32]

- Identify an annual budget that feels realistic to contribute to people impacted by anti-Black racism. If additional funds come your way through gifts, bonuses, stimulus money, and so on, consider allocating some or all of it to mutual aid funds or people you may know with greater need.

- Make a habit of carrying cash so you can assist people who may directly approach you with a need.

- Avoid demanding "proof" of need or projecting your own assumptions about priorities (*Funds for therapy seem less important than funds for rent…*). These are manifestations of paternalism and a system that has falsely suggested that those with more access to power and resources can understand and solve problems faced by those with less access—without consulting them. Trust that those seeking support understand their own needs best and are seeking funds because intersectional systems of oppression have harmed them.

- Avoid expectation of response or recognition. *Reparations are not a gift but an effort to correct past harm.* If you find yourself craving recognition or appreciation, interrogate why. Could it be a "savior" mindset? Or adherence to capitalist ideas suggesting we should always receive something in exchange for money? These tendencies are reflections of capitalistic-over-human-centered mindsets into which many of us have been socialized. They are also manifestations of paternalism and are contrary to justice.

- Recognize that no matter your positive intention, people may not be open to receiving reparations. Communities impacted by racism are not a monolith, and different people and cultures will naturally have varying attitudes, norms, and feelings surrounding wealth, independence, and power. In the context of a racist, individualist culture that has vilified "handouts" and interdependence, complex power dynamics between people and communities cannot be discounted or ignored. It is critical to respect individual boundaries.

Making Reparations Real in Your Organization

Broadly, consider: how can you allocate funds differently to address past and present harm or complicity caused by your organization and industry? How can you increase the quality of life among employees most harmed by oppressive systems to that which your other employees enjoy? How can you bring an understanding of the history of anti-Black racism to your organization's current policymaking and benefit structures?

- Transparently and proactively acknowledge your organization's involvement in past and present-day injustices and racialized harm.[33] Direct specific funding toward addressing this harm.

- In recognition of racialized generational cycles of wealth and poverty and unequal access to education, commit to measures like:

  - Reviewing your compensation, hiring, and promotion structures to address ways your organization may be contributing to the racial wealth gap.
  - Funding student loan repayment[34] and childcare expenses[35] for Black employees.
  - Supporting in offsetting the costs of housing for Black people in your organization.[36]
  - Providing alternate forms of compensation, like market shares in your company, to Black employees.
  - Investing in organizational initiatives that support formerly incarcerated and returning citizens who are reentering the workplace or building their own businesses.

- In recognition of the impact of unequal access to healthcare and disproportionate stress on health outcomes for Black Americans, commit to policies like:

  - Increasing access to paid time off for Black employees.
  - Increasing access to health insurance benefits for Black employees.

> ▸ Paying justice or equity "bonuses" to employees who engage in or lead DEI work in addition to other responsibilities.

- Commit to designating a portion of corporate donations to reparations quarterly or annually. Can you create or contribute to a mutual aid fund? Can you fund the creation and sustainability of Black-owned businesses and nonprofits in your community with unqualified funding? One way that anti-Blackness and paternalism show up through corporate giving is through restricted funds and "prove it again" metrics that become burdensome for organizations doing the work.

If the aforementioned suggestions don't feel practical with your organizational budget, *rearrange it.* Are your senior leaders compensated exponentially more than your lower-paid workers? Can they afford to take a small pay cut so that resources can be allocated more equitably? A 2018 study identified a salary of $105,000 as correlated with optimal life satisfaction in North America.[37] In many organizations, senior leaders are paid far more than this, while those at the lowest pay grades struggle to weather common life challenges. If your organization meets these criteria, it may be time for a frank conversation about why and how you can correct this. Increasing base pay can support individuals and organizations alike by increasing retention of employees and institutional knowledge.[38] Regressive pay adjustments, which offer larger percentage raises to those with lower income, are another practical approach.

Additionally, anticipate and come to a consensus among organizational leadership on how you will respond to accusations like "reverse racism" from various stakeholders. Affirm that racism is a system of prejudice combined with power and that as long as racial identity remains a predictor of outcome, racial equity has not been achieved. Stand strong in your commitments, which can ideally be tied to existing organizational values and priorities. Leverage statements about the organization's commitment to racial equity and justice and point to your new initiatives as part of this work to address well-documented, ongoing racial disparities tracing back to American chattel slavery and other atrocities. Organizations and their leaders must support reparations initiatives without hesitation or apology.

Despite inaction by our national representatives, organizations and even communities are increasingly taking reparations into their own hands. There are many examples emerging of organizations embarking on reparations initiatives in an effort to address past harm in which they were active or complicit. In 2020:

- Evanston, Illinois, approved the nation's first government reparations plan "to acknowledge the harm caused by discriminatory housing policies, practices, and inaction going back more than a century." The $10 million plan will create grants for homeownership and improvement and mortgage assistance for Black residents descended from those who were victims of housing discrimination in the city.[39]

- Asheville, North Carolina, followed suit, apologizing for its role in slavery, discrimination, and denial of civil liberties to Black residents and committing $2.1 million toward reparations.[40]

- The Jesuit order of Catholic priests vowed to raise $100 million for reparations to support racial reconciliation in the US and to benefit descendants of people it once enslaved. While the order has thus far failed to deliver on the anticipated timeline for raising these funds,[41] other religious groups and organizations both large and small have since begun developing reparations programs of their own.[42]

- JPMorgan Chase allocated $30 billion toward addressing structural barriers to racial equity perpetuated by the banking industry.[43]

A common distancing statement we encounter in justice work is, *Progress takes time. Think about how much progress we have made in recent decades!* This language very literally suggests to those harmed by racial injustices that they remain perpetually patient in waiting for rights, access, safety, and resources that white people not only enjoy now but have for generations. As James Baldwin once said: "You always told me it takes time. It's taken my father's time, my mother's time, my uncles' time, my brothers' and my sisters' time, my nieces' and my nephews' time. How much time do you want for your progress?"[44]

Time has a real, human price, and that is why we must commit on both personal and organizational levels to making reparations real to address past and compounded harm that continues to impact Black communities today.

SUMMARY

- Despite clear evidence of the persistence of anti-Black racism impacting wealth across generations and research identifying reparations as an expedient solution to this problem, the United States government has failed to prioritize reparations initiatives.

- Individualistic "scarcity" mindsets embraced by US cultural norms are closely tied to many people's approaches to accruing wealth. Reflecting on these narratives to unlearn them can help us to overcome personal and organizational barriers to realizing reparations.

- Organizations can operationalize reparations through adjusting pay and benefit structures, in addition to external philanthropic giving.

- Reparations are not a gift, and it is important to reflect on and address internalized paternalism that may show up in your approaches to financial and other contributions. Center the needs of those most impacted by injustices and trust their assessments of their own need.

DISCUSSION/REFLECTION QUESTIONS

1. How have you seen guilt, scarcity mindsets, or paternalism prevent progress toward racial justice? As you reflect, do you think any of these dynamics show up for you personally?

2. What harm has your organization or industry been involved or complicit in? What potential exists to reallocate budgets within your organization to realize reparations?

3. What resistance might be likely to arise in your organization as it relates to reparations initiatives? How can you tie these initiatives to your organizational values or racial justice commitments and prepare various stakeholders to affirm commitment and your organizational "why"?

4. How can we use "possibility models" of reparations within organizations to prove the potential for progress? What possibility models exist within your industry or areas of focus around correcting harm, and how can you amplify and modify them to fit within the context of your organization and its history?

CHAPTER SEVENTEEN

Recruiting, Hiring, and Other HR Practices for Racial Justice

GABRIELLE GAYAGOY GONZALEZ

Marketing and PR Strategist

The Winters Group, Inc.

(she/her/hers)

You're working against years and years of disenfranchisement, so you need to think in terms of this is what we can offer as far as training, here is where we can give you support. It's a journey and a relationship, not just a one-and-done transaction.

—DONNA LENNON

Years ago, I was tasked with piloting a recruiting program at a predominantly white company, which provided unique insight into the power of including people of color like myself as part of the process. Sourcing a diverse pool of candidates was one of my top personal priorities, so I naturally paid attention to who made the cut. After a while, I had a gut feeling that we were rejecting a disproportionate number of candidates of color early in the process, so I went back to analyze the data. What I found was even worse than I thought: We were turning away BIPOC candidates at nearly twice the rate of white candidates. Pointing this out necessitated more work on my part as an advocate for justice. I not only had to go back to investigate the roots of my hunch, but I also had to take the initiative to draft a detailed report on why we were wrong to reject these candidates prematurely and then also offer solutions. (For details on leveraging DEIJ data, refer to Chapters 14 and 15.)

Among the reasons that surfaced for the uneven outcomes was that these candidates, while demonstrating the skills needed to do the job, came to the table with slightly different work experiences compared with the white candidates who were typically hired. In other words, they had the ability to do the work but were dismissed upfront because their experiences did not exactly match those of the successful candidates. This is why justice calls for disrupting business as usual—in this case, shifting power away from the dominant group and centering recruiting efforts on the underrepresented candidates who were the most impacted, as evidenced by their higher rejection rates.

To achieve a more just and equitable workplace, those in power must intentionally broaden the hiring process beyond leaning on referrals from current employees and welcome talent from "nontraditional" backgrounds. They must provide learning opportunities so that everyone involved in the hiring process understands and addresses unconscious bias. (See Chapter 19 for more on learning and development.) Candidates with Black-sounding names are still less likely to get callbacks than candidates with white-sounding names.[1] This still occurs despite decades of research on the topic.[2] While some employers choose to address this issue by omitting details from résumés that might potentially influence hiring managers, such as the candidate's name, address, college, or graduation year, more steps need to be taken in order to achieve true equity in the workplace.

Given that the workforce has been transformed and is more competitive in the aftermath of the Great Resignation that started during the pandemic, recruiting talent is a top concern among CEOs.[3] Additionally, multicultural populations including Black, Latine, and Asian Americans have been cited as "the growth engine of the future of the United States" by the market research firm Nielsen,[4] which makes applying a justice lens to your HR practices both practical and purposedriven. Here, we take a look at several areas related to recruiting, hiring, and benefits that can help increase diversity in the workplace while also making it more equitable, inclusive, and just.

Finding and Attracting Candidates of Color

As we make strides toward openly discussing race in the workplace, we must also remember that until the passage of the Civil Rights Act of 1964, it was still legal to include "Blacks need not apply" in job ads.[5] Once outlawed, explicit discrimination in hiring morphed into implicit barriers, taking on the form of coded language that disadvantaged candidates of color, such as a minimum number of years of work experience or very specific skills that Black and other marginalized candidates would be less likely to have based on past discriminatory practices.

Rooting out such language in postings by interrogating the relevancy of certain requirements is a justice-centered approach. Screening job descriptions using software from companies such as Textio[6] or the online tool Gender Decoder[7] can surface subtle bias in job ads. Demonstrating your commitment to justice might lead you to include requirements such as:

◆ Demonstrates an understanding of institutional racism and bias.

◆ Exhibits a flexible communication style and the ability to work with diverse communities.

◆ Has experience working on diverse teams and considers how work impacts multiple communities.

◆ Approaches conflict with respect to the diverse perspectives of stakeholders and works with them to resolve differences.

Imagine seeing these criteria from the point of view of a job seeker from a historically excluded group. Would you be more inclined to apply for a position if the points listed above were part of the job description? Would you place more trust in an organization that lifted up these values?

Being explicit in your job ads about encouraging BIPOC and other historically underrepresented groups to apply can also help with casting a wider net. This is an example from the healthcare company GoodRx: "Research shows that women and other underrepresented groups apply only if they meet 100% of the criteria. GoodRx is committed to leveling the playing field, and we encourage women, people of color, those in the LGBTQ+ communities, and Veterans to apply for positions even if they don't necessarily check every box outlined in the job description. Please still get in touch—we'd love to connect and see if you could be good for the role!"[8]

The US Equal Employment Opportunity Commission (EEOC) specifically protects against workplace discrimination based on race, color, religion, sex (including pregnancy and sexual orientation), national origin, age, disability, and genetic information such as family medical history.[9] In addition to that list, workplace hiring policies may proactively expand protections to cover other factors that disproportionately affect candidates of color,[10] including:

- **Credit history.** Generations of discrimination in employment, as well as the fallout from past racist economic policies that persist, such as redlining, puts Black Americans at a higher risk for predatory lending practices that result in more debt.[11] Additionally, data from nonprofit research group the Urban Institute show that communities that are majority Black, Native American, and Latine experience at least 1.5 times higher rates of subprime credit scores, debt, and high-cost borrowing than communities that are majority white.[12] "Employers need to think about the relevance of the questions they are asking," says Donna Lennon, deputy director at the Center for Law and Social Justice at Medgar Evers College CUNY. "Why do you need information on credit history? Do you need to have this, and does it tell you anything about the strength of an applicant and how they'll do in the role you need to fill?"

- **Unemployment status.** The unemployment rates for both Black and Latine Americans were disproportionately affected by the pandemic, and the unemployment rate of Black Americans has historically been around double that of white people.[13] Adding to this, 70 percent of employers link unemployment status with poor productivity,[14] heaping on yet another bias against hiring unemployed Black workers who already face longer lag times between jobs than unemployed white workers. To combat this phenomenon—known as "last hired, first fired," according to the Center for American Progress[15]—ensure your hiring team accounts for unemployment bias and its disproportionate impact on BIPOC job seekers in their decisions.

- **Drug testing.** Research from Yale School of Medicine found that 63 percent of Black employees work for organizations that perform drug testing. The same is true for only 46 percent of white workers.[16] (Being Latine was also associated with increased employment for organizations that perform drug testing.) That disparity matters, especially given that Black Americans who test positive report being fired or reprimanded at twice the rate of white employees who also test positive, according to survey results from the American Addiction Centers' Detox.net.[17] Today, thousands of companies, including Amazon,[18] have pledged to relax or do away with drug screening policies in order to attract talent.[19]

- **Arrest or conviction records.** Black and Latine Americans are incarcerated at a disproportionate rate in comparison with white Americans, according to the nonprofit The Sentencing Project.[20] Black people are imprisoned at nearly five times the rate of whites and account for more than half of the defendants who are wrongfully convicted and later exonerated. At the same time, Latine people are 1.3 times as likely to be incarcerated and make up almost 12 percent of exonerations per The National Registry of Exonerations.[21] Meanwhile, research from the American Civil Liberties Union shows that formerly incarcerated job seekers demonstrate higher loyalty to employers and lower turnover rates.[22] This, in turn, reduces overall training and recruitment costs, making the "ban the box" movement to remove criminal history questions from employment applications a win across the board.

In addition to rethinking what goes into your job ads, *where* you post your openings also has an influence on making progress toward racial justice. Reaching out to Historically Black Colleges and Universities (HBCUs), Tribal Colleges and Universities (TCUs), and Hispanic-Serving Institutions (HSIs)—as well as two-year community colleges, where students of color and first-generation students report a greater sense of belonging than at four-year universities[23]—provides alternatives to the typical top colleges and Ivy League institutions that most organizations look to when seeking to fill entry-level and executive roles.[24] Hiring for a remote position? Consider advertising on online job boards targeted to job seekers in the southern United States, where nearly 60 percent of the Black labor force lives, according to research from McKinsey & Company.[25]

Adapting Your Interview Process

Unconscious bias can result in favoring candidates based on highly subjective factors, such as likability or the fact that the person being interviewed reminds the hiring manager of themselves. With nearly one-third of new hires quitting within the first six months, according to survey data from BambooHR,[26] clearly going with one's gut isn't the answer when it comes to sustainable staffing. In order to make better hires and achieve equity in the workplace, consider standardizing your interview process so that more candidates have the opportunity to prove themselves outside of just first impressions.

Before beginning, hiring managers should be made aware of their own biases through education by using online assessment tools, such as the ones provided by the nonprofit organization Project Implicit, to help them see instances where preferences might cloud judgment.[27] Next, come up with a standard list of questions that all candidates must answer in the same order. This will help keep the focus on skills and knowledge needed to do the job and establish a consistent baseline among the candidates.

Additionally, ask questions that elicit the interviewee's commitment to promoting diversity, equity, inclusion, and justice. Such questions are particularly important for people manager roles. For example:

- What is your understanding of diversity, equity, inclusion, and justice? Why do you think they're important to this position?

- What kinds of experiences have you had in relating to people whose backgrounds differ from your own? What did you learn from these experiences?

- What actions have you taken to further your knowledge about diversity, equity, inclusion, and justice? How has your thinking about DEIJ-related issues changed over time?

- Discuss a time when you demonstrated a commitment to equity in your work. How would you do that here?

- What challenges do you anticipate when working with diverse populations? How do you plan to address them?

- How would you handle a situation in which a colleague made a racist, sexist, or otherwise prejudiced remark?

Have multiple people, including colleagues of color and members of your employee resource groups (ERGs), sit in on the discussion or have them meet with the interviewees individually to go over the same questions so that you have input from a variety of perspectives. Asking candidates to demonstrate their skills in a format that they choose is another equitable way to assess them based on factors other than their personalities or connections.

Ensuring Fair Compensation

As one of the final steps in the hiring process, compensation negotiation is another area where racial inequity thrives. Exposure to instances of bias, exclusion, and microaggressions has made so-called imposter syndrome, where one experiences self-doubt to the point that they feel like a fraud at work, rampant among marginalized groups. (I say "so-called" because calling it a "syndrome" makes it sound as if something is wrong with the individual rather than the racist systems that create the condition.[28]) According to research published by the American Psychological Association, Black job candidates are more likely to be offered lower salaries even when they *do* negotiate the terms. In fact, they are penalized and offered less than their white counterparts when they ask for more than the person negotiating with them believes they deserve due to racial bias.[29]

These consequences are dire and compound over time: According to Pew Research Center, college-educated Black and Latine men earn about 20 percent less than college-educated white men, with college-educated Black and Latine women earning around 30 percent less.[30] Women, in general, have long faced a backlash when it comes to taking the initiative to negotiate higher pay due to deeply ingrained sexist views of women as being passive and accommodating. This has resulted in the perception that women who assert themselves are less likable and less likely to be promoted, according to research from Harvard Kennedy School.[31] All of this points to the importance of considering intersectionality, or the interconnected nature of race, gender, class, and other social categorizations that can result in overlapping systems of discrimination. (For more on intersectionality, read Tami Jackson's Chapter 12 on the problem with the concept of "professionalism.")

Clearly, the equitable answer does not lie with putting the onus on BIPOC candidates to be better negotiators. The justice-centered solution is to offer people what they deserve. This is why pay equity—compensating employees the same amount for executing the same or similar work regardless of race, gender, or other protected status, while also accounting for factors such as education and work experience—must be part of any plan to reimagine HR with a justice lens. Typically, this involves conducting a pay audit to help you understand where and how big the gaps are among different groups of employees, from the C-suite all the way to internships (which should always be paid to make the opportunity racially equitable.)[32]

Using that data, your organization can then begin forming a strategy and timeline for addressing inequities, including determining the root causes and whether pay bumps are warranted. Insight from the audit can also help with developing policies with an equity lens, such as uniform starting pay, promotion increases, and incentives. For example, in 2022, The Winters Group rolled out tiered pay increases that were adjusted to reflect inflation at the time, with a bump of up to 7 percent for those on the lowest tier and incrementally smaller increases for those on higher tiers.

Rethinking Your HR Practices

Recruiting and hiring aren't the only HR functions that benefit from a justice lens. Here are a few other examples that can be reimagined by centering those most harmed by racism:

- **Tuition reimbursement.** Policies that require employees to pay for courses and be reimbursed after successful completion may prove difficult for those from historically marginalized backgrounds. If the company pays in advance, employees of color may be more able to take advantage of this benefit. To wit: In 2021, the Starbucks College Achievement Plan, which has been in place since 2014, modified its tuition reimbursement policy to cover 100 percent of fees upfront and now has more than twenty thousand employees in the program, with more than 20 percent identifying as first-generation college students.[33] Retail giants such as Walmart and Target also tout debt-free degrees that do not require out-of-pocket costs, making this benefit accessible to any employee who needs it.

- **Performance reviews.** Mentioned in both Chapters 14 and 15, which are related to data analysis, performance reviews are another area that HR leaders can reframe around justice. Research from the National Bureau of Economic Research found that Black employees face more scrutiny in the workplace when compared with other workers, which can lead to poorer performance reviews, less pay, and even termination. As the study authors put it, employers are more likely to let go of Black employees than their white counterparts for making similar errors. In other words, Black workers are less likely to get a second chance when they make a mistake.[34] Additional research has shown that those with certain intersecting identities, such as Black and Latine women, receive less actionable feedback. This can be a barrier to promotions and higher pay because employees do not receive the specific examples and advice that lead to learning and growth that are more commonly afforded to white and Asian men.[35]

In light of such discrepancies, some companies including Adobe, Deloitte, and General Electric have moved away from annual performance reviews in favor of more frequent check-ins focused on actionable feedback. Other employers looking to revamp their approach to performance reviews might consider making the assessed competencies transparent, requiring managers to include specific evidence and action steps for each rating.[36] Providing ongoing learning and development, such as taking the Intercultural Conflict Style Inventory, can also help bridge across varying cultural norms.[37] For instance, understanding the way different cultures perceive direct eye contact or delivering constructive feedback in a manner that takes the recipient's cultural communication style into account can help make performance reviews more effective and just.

- **Retirement benefits.** Disparities in retirement savings also require a justice lens. As it stands, white retirees have seven times the retirement savings of Black Americans and five times that of Latine Americans, according to the Center for Retirement Research at Boston College.[38] In addition, white 401(k) plan participants invest an average of 23 percent more per month toward their retirement savings versus Black plan participants, who are also twice as likely to borrow from their retirement accounts as they often start at a disadvantage due to lack of inherited wealth. To offset this, Ariel Investments, which launched in 1983 as the first Black-owned mutual fund firm in the United States, has taken the step to pay 100 percent of employees' health insurance premiums to free up their funds for other allocations.[39] Providing access to financial planners attuned to racial savings disparities can also help, along with practices such as automatic enrollment, providing matching incentives, and offering lifetime annuities or lifetime income. Transparency around these efforts and why they have been put into place can go a long way toward building trust—and are sure to draw a diverse pool of candidates when advertised as part of your justice-centered recruiting and hiring campaigns.

SUMMARY

- Moving toward equity starts with self-awareness. Invest in learning opportunities that empower everyone involved in the recruiting and hiring process to identify and address their own biases.

- Race matters. Track data on candidate demographics to root out bias early in the process and make sure your recruiting and hiring team includes colleagues of color who can use their perspectives and lived experiences to inform your practices.

- Review job descriptions for barriers that exclude candidates from historically marginalized groups, such as education requirements, credit checks, employment status, and arrest records.

- Expand your interviewing process to include more objective criteria and include colleagues of color, perhaps tapped from employee resource groups, on interview panels.

- Conduct a pay equity audit and use the findings to update policies on starting pay, raises, and promotion increases.

- Rethink company benefits and practices such as tuition reimbursement, performance reviews, and retirement planning using a justice lens that takes racial disparities into account.
- Communicate your organization's policy commitments to racial justice as part of your organization's strategy to attract more candidates of color.

DISCUSSION/REFLECTION QUESTIONS

1. How does bias show up in recruiting and hiring in your organization? What is currently being done to address this?

2. Are BIPOC colleagues involved in your hiring process? What kinds of input do you find valuable from them, and why are they important?

3. What data are you tracking to ensure your hiring practices are fair and equitable? How did your organization determine the criteria?

4. What are some changes your organization can make to diversify the hiring pool? How can you get started?

5. What are some ways your organization can benefit from a pay equity audit? How would you apply the findings?

6. What benefits or policies would you need to update or add to make access more equitable?

CHAPTER EIGHTEEN

Disrupting What It Means to Be a Productive and Healthy Workplace

THAMARA SUBRAMANIAN

Equity Audit and Strategy Manager

The Winters Group, Inc.

(she/her/hers)

> If you buy into grind culture, you actually are aligning
> yourself with the concept that you're not a divine human
> being and that your worth has already been given to you
> by the fact that you're alive. Your birth is your worth.
>
> —TRICIA HERSEY

"Hustle Harder."

"Work Hard Play Hard."

"The Grind."

You've heard it everywhere, from products and celebrities, social media and television, to corporate training and K–12 education. Throughout American history, from the origins of slavery to "welcoming" immigrants to this country, the expectation was and continues to be "a productive member of society," meaning the more you work, the more you are worthy.

We are experiencing unprecedented levels of daily stress and sadness: Gallup's State of the Workplace 2022 poll showed that across the globe, 44 percent of people expressed feeling stress, 23 percent experienced sadness, and 21 percent experienced anger in the previous day of work.[1] We have internalized this "grind culture" by upholding the white dominant values such as individualism, and meritocracy, lauding individuals prevailing through adversity, trauma, systemic oppression, and mental health challenges while downplaying or completely ignoring the effects that these "obstacles" have on our bodies.

We have tied so many knots of our own self-worth, our communities' worth, our company's worth to quantifiable accomplishments, achievements, and awards—the more you "do," the greater the reward. But at what cost, and at *whose* cost? Hue's 2022 study, Racial Equity in the Workplace,[2] surveyed professionals across multiple industries and found one in two BIPOC employees report feeling increased burnout year after year and are at least twice as likely to share that it's due to workplace issues than their white counterparts. Additionally, nearly one in three Black employees, and one in four Asian employees, left their previous roles due to concerns for their mental health. These racial health disparities exist and persist outside of the workplace— Latine adults are more likely to be diagnosed with diabetes;[3] Black Americans have been at higher risk of heart disease than white Americans for thirty years and are 30 percent more likely to die from it.[4]

A justice-centered workplace prioritizes the mental and physical health of its employees, especially those most impacted by the aforementioned health inequities. Ultimately, the employees most impacted often overlap with the burden of disease. Thus, we must answer these difficult, but necessary questions through our policies, practices, and procedures:

- In what ways are we perpetuating the numerous racial, gender, and socioeconomic health disparities that already exist outside of the workplace, within our company culture?

- What can we do to correct this vicious cycle and repair the harm to the health and wellness industry that our workplaces continue to perpetuate?

- How can we redistribute power, in this case, to ensure that everyone can live and achieve what they want without the expense of their mental and physical well-being?

It is time we unravel these knots—these notions of productivity, grind, urgency, the adrenaline rush of cramming to meet a deadline, the need to have more deliverables, publications, billable hours—whatever "it" is to you in your work. To create sustainable solutions, we must fundamentally reorient our understanding of self-worth, work, and productivity to truly understand what it means to have a culture of abundant health and prioritize rest in our strides to create more just cultures.

In this chapter, I will discuss how to create sustainable solutions for health equity in the workplace—starting by addressing the barriers in current health and wellness approaches, why we continue to exacerbate health disparities in the workplace, and offering some actionable shifts toward embedding health equity in policies, practices, and procedures.

Current Health and Wellness Policies Are Not Enough

The truth is, emerging workplace trends such as offering wellness benefits like fitness memberships, mental health awareness events, flexible work environments, unlimited PTO, and better work-life balance have the right intent…but minimal impact. People are still tired, still working overtime, and burnout is rampant—especially for historically underrepresented employees. According to the Study of Women's Health Across the Nation, "Black women are 7.5 years biologically 'older' than white women." Most of this difference is due to social determinants of health—stress, fatigue, and poverty.[5]

So why are our current approaches to wellness ineffective, and why are BIPOC employees disproportionally affected? Who is benefiting and who is harmed by our workplaces goes beyond workplace politics to our culture of health.

In general, institutions approach health and wellness as individual behavior modification, something you should be able to learn once given the "tools" such as healthcare access, health education materials, classes, and wellness programs. However, these "tools" often don't consider the conditions, policies, practices, and history that affects how we ultimately cope with stresses that are within and beyond our job description. Ultimately, these "benefits" uphold a superficial culture of health for the white and wealthy. Rest has become a commodity, something you can buy or have if you "earn" it. BIPOC employees, in particular, must earn it by not just doing their job "well" but by bearing the day-to-day stressors of racism, microaggressions, and having to be held to higher standards of dominant culture than their white peers. Analysis across American professionals in many fields such as marketing, communication, finance, and engineering, shows that BIPOC employees reported three times as many microaggressions as their white counterparts and were three times as likely to leave their job due to the mental burden of dealing with race-related issues at work.[6]

This pattern of inequity goes beyond microaggressions, as discussed by Katelyn Peterson in Chapter 10. It is ingrained in our systems. As of 2020, global health and wellness has become a $4.4 trillion industry and growing,[7] run by and primarily accessible to those who possess the economic privileges to partake. Additionally, many of these benefits are geared toward white, non-disabled, and thin-bodied employees. For example, there are very few mental health programs and practitioners who specialize in the unique challenges BIPOC endure in the workplace. In Hue's study of workplace culture in 2021, 90 percent of American surveyors reported that their employers did not address the mental and emotional impact of discrimination on employees of color.[8]

Meanwhile, low-wage and hourly workers who are likely to encounter more challenges in their day-to-day lives may not even have these benefits. If they do, they seldom use these benefits due to barriers such as odd work hours, transportation, or childcare duties. This results in impounding fatigue and stress while further exacerbating the stereotype that those who do not "choose" to partake in the health and wellness industry are "lazy" and "don't care."

Our hospital and healthcare systems were also created to exclude certain communities and define health from the perspective of the dominant group: white colonizers and their descendants. The US health system has created regulations and restrictions that are often posed as benefits to Indigenous people. For example, the Indian Health System was created as a free healthcare system—which sounds great in theory, but in practice ultimately receives limited federal funding and is dictated by Western allopathic medicine practices without taking into consideration indigenous healing practices.

Shifting from a Deficit to an Abundance Culture of Health and Wellness

As an American culture, we have put tremendous value on productivity and define achievement as "more is better" (whether it is monetized or not). This has led to a public health crisis. Day-to-day fears, compounded by external responsibilities, are slowly but surely chipping away, deteriorating our social, emotional, and spiritual health. It is imperative that organizations begin taking radical shifts toward embedding rest into their policies, practices, and procedures. Instead of thinking of our time as scarce and rest as a luxury, what would workplaces look like if we saw time as sacred and rest as a necessity? This requires organizations to think *beyond* the "individual agency" approach to health and instead embrace community health accountability. We must shift the current rhetoric of rest being considered a waste of time and resources to being an act of *preserving* our time and resources. By doing so, we will actualize workplace cultures that are equitable and just. We have the power to repair the harm done and increase benefit for all. To start, here are some shifts to create a culture of health where *all* your employees can thrive.

- **From flexible and unlimited PTO to mandatory PTO.** America is the only country of its economic caliber to have no nationally mandated paid time off, leaving almost a quarter of workers with no paid time off, often for jobs that historically have paid less but are considered essential.[9] Even if you offer PTO or unlimited PTO, we have internalized productivity as a part of our worth, so much so that more than half of American employees feel guilty about taking those days off; 55 percent of Americans didn't even use their PTO in 2019.[10]

Additionally, unlimited or flexible PTO policies actually serve the employer more than the employee, as these policies often remove the organization's financial accountability for unused days. Instead, make your paid time off mandatory. Research shows that forced time off increases productivity in the workplace.[11] Some companies have even seen success in offering a vacation stipend to help reduce the guilt and create equity for employees with various incomes. Another approach is a "PTO bank," combining sick and vacation time into a bank of days so that people utilize their allotted time off to their maximum.

This has been shown to not only be better utilized than separate sick time on its own but has been seen to reduce unscheduled absences,[12] helping facilitate a more accurate understanding of team availability and capacity at the workplace. If you are a leader, practice "leaving loudly," ensuring you take time off yourself and communicating with your team and clients *why* you are prioritizing rest. Ask yourself what incentives may still be in place encouraging your team to work too hard—which facilitate burnout—rather than prioritizing rest. The culture change starts with you.

- **From reactive current event emails to responsive team shutdowns.** The email acknowledging civil unrest or any traumatic national occurrence is necessary but not nearly enough to shift your culture. Instead of responding driven primarily by a "sense of urgency," respond swiftly but intentionally by shutting down your team's work for the day after a traumatic event. Consider canceling mandatory meetings and financially compensating your employees for their time of rest. For example, having Election Day be paid time off gives people the option to do what fulfills them—working the polls, catching up on errands, and following the news. Let's be real: there's nothing "productive" about a company meeting on Zoom with everyone watching news updates on another tab or second monitor. Practicing slowing down during big events is not only dismantling our own sense of urgency but is also an act of justice.

- **From maternity leaves to parental sabbaticals.** The United States is only one of four countries in the world with no federally mandated parental leave[13] and the only high-income country without it. How can we better honor the demands of parenting and the health of future generations? Create a parental "sabbatical"—a longer-term (six months or more) time off *plus* funds for early childhood development or parental career development. With these supports in place, parents won't feel like they are stifling their careers and can stay connected to the organization and improve their skillset while also encouraging secure parent-child attachment (the most development occurs from birth to age three).

  In return, companies can benefit from sabbaticals by being able to create a strong long-term-succession plan, reducing hiring costs, and improving retention, as companies don't need to plan for the financial costs of a long-term replacement (companies often spend 12–20% of payroll budget on voluntary turnover due to burnout alone, a $322 billion cost annually).[14] Also, companies are not only increasing the *length* of leave but also *who* gets parental leave. In a study across corporations, the median number of weeks of paid leave for non-birthing parents went up from 2018 to 2021 to five weeks; as of 2021, 55 percent of companies also provide paid adoption leave, up from 38% in 2018.[15] Increasing paid leave for non-birthing parents creates equity for those who are in adoption or fostering relationships as well as eases the burden of caretaking on the birthing parent.

- **From benefits at the expense of base pay, to an increase of pay and benefits for all.** Benefits should not have to come at the expense of base pay. Many leaders may ask, how can we provide the best pay and benefits with a limited budget? The answer lies in being critical of how resources at your company are allocated and shifting from a deficit or cost-preserving mindset. For example, think about lowering the salary gap between C-Suite and an entry-level worker. On average in 2021, in the US, a CEO makes 254 times more than their average employee.[16]

Thus we must embrace a both/and mindset by reallocating resources in an innovative way that serves everyone's well-being. An organization may have "excellent" health and wellness benefits, but many of these benefits foster further consumption of products that profit from trends and fads. They typically prioritize one type of wellness (physical or mental), and many times employees don't have the time or are not encouraged to utilize these benefits during their workday.

Additionally, these benefits are only "benefitting" certain groups. Only about half of Black employees have employee-sponsored healthcare coverage.[17] Latine (38%) and Black and Asian (54%) are significantly less likely than white workers to have an employer sponsored retirement plan.[18] Because of this, many Black and underrepresented employees have to pay increased out-of-pocket costs that, in combination with low base pay, deter from their ability to build or sustain generational wealth. Increasing base pay equitably *and* mandating health and retirement benefits for both hourly and salaried employees is not only a sound strategy for improving retention but also a form of supporting employee financial wellness for generations to come. Whether through retention bonuses or guaranteed wage increases, ensure employees feel supported across all areas of life and have the ability to invest in their families' futures through a combination of both flexible and structured financial support.

- **From individual resiliency to culturally specific care.** As much as someone can harness the strategies for resilience, it is important to not only recognize but also act upon the social and environmental factors that influence our ability to manage stress and overall health. National Institute on Minority Health and Health Disparities (NIMHD) reports that less than 50 percent of Americans, and even lower for Black Americans, with a mental health condition are able to access necessary treatment due to cultural stigma, insurance coverage, and other socioeconomic factors.[19] Yet, 70 percent of Americans, and even higher for BIPOC (75 percent), report having no mental health professionals accessible at work.[20]

Consider bolstering your healthcare plan and health service access to better suit the needs of marginalized employees. For example, are BIPOC and LGBTQIA+ mental health professionals covered in your insurance plans? Another example of culturally specific care is implementing a community garden at the workplace. Nearly one in five African American households and one in six Latine households are food insecure[21]—meaning they have little access to food, little to no financial ability to buy fresh food, or live in urban or rural communities with limited access to grocery stores. Community gardens are a great way not only to create food security for your employees but also to honor and learn about the native language and food-sovereign communities near your workplace.[22] Gardens also create an opportunity for employees to reduce stress and sedentary time during the workday.[23] To ensure sustainability, create complementary policies to support and encourage employees to use these services during work hours.

These changes may require drastically rethinking organizational approaches to work and rest and require significant adjustments to financial and people resources. Yet, if there is one thing we know, it's that current approaches to health and wellness are not conducive to retention and sustainability and are decidedly inequitable, failing historically marginalized and underrepresented employees. Promoting a culture that prioritizes community health, rest, and resource reallocation for those most impacted represents a critical shift toward actualizing justice.

SUMMARY

- Workplace health and wellness are at the nexus of racial justice and public health.

- Workplace burnout, fatigue, and exhaustion continue to rise and disproportionately affect communities of color, further exacerbating racial health disparities beyond the workplace.

- Typical health and wellness benefits are not as effective because they serve to uphold the wellness industry, driven by and for those with race and socioeconomic privileges, while further stigmatizing those who do not engage in the industry as "lazy."

- To truly create change and achieve a just workplace, we must address and repair the harm caused by centuries of focusing on meritocracy, productivity, and quantifiable achievement. To do this, we need to enact policy and procedural changes that offer culturally specific, community-focused, and rest-embedded resources.

- To ensure that these shifts in health and wellness are actualized, adequate financial and people resources will be needed to sustain and create an equitable and just culture of health in the workplace.

DISCUSSION/REFLECTION QUESTIONS

1. Consider how your employees' diverse life experiences and identities influence how they show up at the workplace, what difficulties they may have, and how comfortable they feel even talking about their health and well-being. For example, could a suspension have differential impacts on white students versus students of color, who have been historically discriminated against in the educational space?

2. Reassess what policies may put certain people at a disadvantage over others. For example: How might your parental leave policies not be sufficient for single parents or parents seeking adoption? What qualifies as a "sick day"?

3. What are some culturally specific challenges that have not been addressed by your organization's healthcare benefits?

CHAPTER NINETEEN

A Racial Justice–Centered Approach to Learning and Development

LEIGH MORRISON

Learning and Innovation Manager
The Winters Group, Inc.
(she/her/hers)

I would like to see more consideration for those who may be burnt out over the years with equity trainings after investing so much personally and professionally. There was a burden placed on individuals with more experience with the topic to act as facilitators.

—BLACK WOMAN PARTICIPANT IN AN ANTIRACISM SESSION

I recall the first time I heard a client succinctly explaining who would be attending a mixed-audience learning session on anti-Black racism: "It's an A, B, C audience—Allies, Black folks, and those who are largely Clueless." At the time, I remember puzzling over how best to design a learning experience on this topic that could resonate with each of these distinct groups. Since the racial reckoning of 2020, this has become a constant challenge. At the same time, less than a year after George Floyd's murder—when individuals and organizations alike committed themselves to racial justice—we watched this critical work backslide as it inevitably got uncomfortable, challenging, or "messy," and momentum waned.

Organizations began reverting to requests for "one and done" learning sessions that could not possibly support strategic culture changes they claimed to be committed to accomplishing. Learning journeys were shortened or canceled, often before they were rolled out to the mid-level managers to whom many BIPOC staff report. Other times, "all staff" learning journeys continued as "proof of commitment" while board members and leaders (whose own levels of understanding, in combination with their access to power, regularly prove to be "ceilings" for what change is possible) remained largely uninvolved. Antiracism strategy work was postponed as other priorities arose, and the urgency white leaders felt to "do something" faded. The drop-off was particularly evident in the corporate world,[1] no doubt due to "the bottom line" and leaders' "right to comfort" resurfacing as top priorities.

Simultaneously, a global pandemic that disproportionately impacted BIPOC communities raged on, cases of police murders of Black and brown people continued to emerge, and we witnessed the rise of hate crimes against Asian communities. It was, and remains, a frightening and fatiguing time for everyone. Critically, that burden has not been borne equally.

As our team introduced racial justice–centered learning experiences in organizations across many sectors, we lost count of the thousands of stories we heard from Black and brown employees about the ways they have been harmed by colleagues and policies in their organizations. A common refrain rose to the surface: *"It is not my responsibility to educate my white colleagues about my experiences with racism."*

As millions of white people began to reckon with the realization that racism is still very much alive—and that they had been blissfully ignorant of this fact—they began seeking to remedy this. Many turned to antiracist book lists or documentaries. For some, their employers contracted antiracism learning sessions. Others turned to another source of information: people of color in their lives. While their intent was positive—an effort to understand the race-based injustices that play out across our society and institutions—many did not recognize the impact. As addressed in *Black Fatigue: How Racism Erodes the Mind, Body, and Spirit* by Mary-Frances Winters, for people of color who live these encounters daily and experience the associated burden and fatigue, this "ask" by white people who benefit from the same systems that harm them may be anything but benign.[2]

Further compounding this issue is the fact that, by and large, organizations approach training with a "one size fits all" approach: learning is contracted for all staff. This is one thing when the learning topics relate to new policies or general skill-building. It is quite another when the topics are—like racial justice—deeply connected to the lived experiences of *some* folks in the room and largely abstract or unfamiliar to others.

Like any type of learning, antiracism education must be approached developmentally in order to be successful. Just as a student in beginning algebra could not succeed if suddenly transferred to an advanced calculus course, those learning to understand the systemic nature of racism and other isms for perhaps the first time will likely not get much—if anything—from a seminar on white supremacy culture without appropriate "scaffolding" and buildup. This is why we begin our learning journeys with *self-understanding*, then move to *other understanding* before *bridging across differences*, and finally, *interrogating systems*—always emphasizing that each of these is ongoing, and we are never "finished." (Terrence Harewood, PhD, outlines in detail in Chapter 5 a developmental approach to antiracism education using the Intercultural Development Continuum.)

Importantly, as mentioned in Chapter 2, many white people have never been challenged to engage in cultural self-understanding reflection at all; a Pew Research study[3] conducted in 2019 on the salience of racial identity found that:

- 74 percent of Black Americans
- 59 percent of Hispanic Americans
- 56 percent of Asian Americans and
- 15 percent of white Americans

see their race or ethnicity as central to their identity.

This illustrates the ways that Black and brown people who exist within cultures where whiteness has been falsely assumed as neutral are much farther along in their understanding of themselves and their cultural others—because they have had no choice. Increasingly, we began challenging the efficacy of "ABC" audiences, recognizing that these groups generally have distinct needs. At times, grouping them all into one cohort has the potential to not only fall flat but to cause real harm. A transparent comment from a session participant illustrated this clearly:

As a Black person, I find it triggering to be in these meetings. I'm not learning anything new and find it emotionally taxing hearing my non-Black colleagues' thoughts and feelings on the matter.

These sentiments have become increasingly common in comments shared in sessions or afterward in session evaluations. As practitioners, we are working through how best to handle these challenges, and we do not have all the answers. However, we must commit ourselves to thinking them through and seeking ways to minimize harm. This is precisely the "messiness" that has scared some organizations off from their initial commitments; working through it is critical to progress. Here are a few practical considerations for minimizing harm and fatigue for employees personally impacted by racism as your organization continues on its racial justice learning journey:

- **Consider when it may be appropriate to differentiate learner audiences.** White employees may need education about microaggressions, perspective-taking,[4] or the history of racism. BIPOC employees may need opportunities for a "safer space" to process their experiences and be in community with one another. These are two very critical—and very different—pieces of antiracism work. The demand for antiracism learning may require rethinking organizational training models significantly. Caucus groups[5]—which group employees according to their race and ethnicity for differentiated learning and discussion—are one practical approach.

This inevitably invites questions of "how much to differentiate" caucus groups—and the answer will likely depend on the demographics of your organization. Generally, it is important to acknowledge both the nuances of different lived experiences and the practical limitations of discussion groups. Furthermore, affirm that building trust and psychological safety are central goals (see Scott Ferry's Chapter 9 on psychological safety) with the end goal of progress toward justice. Caucus groups should be framed with attention to these details and as part of a broader, collectively driven racial justice strategy. Establish a system for sharing insights between caucus groups without violating confidentiality agreements, and bring groups together for collaboration or to close a discussion journey with summaries and action steps.

- **Be mindful of nuances related to hosting "listening sessions."** We have seen countless organizations host these sessions, which purportedly offer BIPOC employees the opportunity to voice challenges and hardships they have encountered. Yet when little or nothing is done in response, the question must be posed: *who did this serve?* Particularly if the main outcome of these sessions is white employees leaving educated by the stories of pain that were shared, this quickly becomes invasive and tokenizing, in addition to the trauma and fatigue that BIPOC employees may experience when they share very personal experiences of harm. (See Chapter 15 for guidance on conducting listening sessions.)

- **Do not assume you know what BIPOC folks in your organization need.** Instead, center those most impacted and *ask them directly.* Ensure that the initiatives you are sponsoring resonate with those personally impacted by racism in your organization. Perhaps what is most urgently needed is not additional training or work but instead an opportunity for rest and self-care—or something else entirely.

- **Value racial equity and justice work appropriately by paying people for their additional labor.** Many organizations, with good intent, have established new diversity councils and employee resource groups. It is critical to understand that these initiatives represent additional work that often falls disproportionately on BIPOC employees who are already overburdened. If asking employee resource groups or diversity council members to take on work outside of their job descriptions, compensate them accordingly. Prior to Elon Musk's purchase of Twitter in 2022, the company was lauded for announcing that it would compensate its resource group leaders. LinkedIn followed suit, sharing it will pay employee resource group leaders $10,000 for each year they serve the organization in this capacity.[6] Compensation might come in various forms, including time off and other benefits.

- **Offer the choice to those personally impacted by racism to opt out of potentially triggering content.** This approach may look different depending on the context but could include offering BIPOC employees the option to attend racial justice learning sessions or to step away for parts of the session if they choose. Of course, organizations are made up of individuals, and introducing the same information to everyone can be valuable. However, recognizing lived experiences as significant, valid sources of knowledge is essential to justice.[7] Retraumatizing those who have personal experiences with racism in the name of "consistency" will only erode trust and psychological safety.

- **Always respect people's boundaries in sharing their experiences surrounding race and racism.** Invitation to share should never be equated with expectation, and this should be communicated explicitly. There are countless resources available on the internet and elsewhere where people have voluntarily shared their experiences with racism in support of others' learning journeys. Rather than requesting emotional labor from Black and brown people in their personal and professional circles, white people can commit to educating themselves and others with the support of these accessible resources.

In early 2020, the predominantly white faith organization in which I was raised hired its first woman of color into the position of senior minister. Members of the congregation proudly posted the news on social media and looked forward to meeting her. (Often, white people's areas of limited perspective leave us thinking that "firsts" like these are something to be proud of, rather than a historical failure to see our own identities as anything but neutral.)[8]

Less than a year later, our minister announced her resignation in a letter to the congregation. She explained in the letter that she experiences the impact of racism daily, that this institution has a lot of work to do, and that "this is not my work." She is right. The burden of addressing systemic racism should not fall on those who are most harmed by this unjust system. As many organizations work through similar challenges, it is critical that we not minimize differences in people's needs or violate their boundaries as it relates to this essential work.

SUMMARY

- BIPOC employees, who already navigate fatigue associated with racism, should not be burdened with educating white colleagues about racism. Invitations to share one's experiences with colleagues and others should be just that—not expectations.

- Be mindful of approaches to "listening sessions" where BIPOC staff are asked to share their experiences, which can be retraumatizing. Ask BIPOC employees whether an event like this would be helpful before scheduling and what they would need to come out of it. Actions to support those personally impacted by racism should be a key outcome; if the main goal is educating white staff, consider what else could accomplish this outcome.

- Contracting undifferentiated racial justice learning for "all staff" groups may not be the best approach. Race-based caucus group learning is a practical alternative. Otherwise, offer BIPOC employees the choice to opt into or step away from potentially triggering content.

- Never assume you know what BIPOC employees need without asking them. Also, recognize that employee resource groups and diversity councils are often tasked with extra, uncompensated work to support racial justice initiatives. Extend invitation, not expectation, for involvement, and demonstrate the value of this work by compensating employees for their labor and insights.

- Black and brown people's experiences within racist systems are not only a valid source of knowledge but also inherently more complex than a learning session can offer and should be recognized as such.

DISCUSSION/REFLECTION QUESTIONS

1. How might antiracism initiatives in organizations reinforce existing power dynamics and harm? Have you seen this play out in your organization? What alternatives can you imagine?

2. What may underlie white people's sense of entitlement to education from BIPOC in their personal and professional circles? How can this be disrupted?

3. What benefits may come from caucus group learning, in which white staff learn about and discuss racism together, and BIPOC staff have a "safer space" to share in community with one another?

4. What do you see as the role of white people in racial justice work?

CHAPTER TWENTY

Justice in Procurement

MAREISHA N. REESE
President and Chief Operating Officer
The Winters Group, Inc.
(she/her/hers)

The ends you serve that are selfish will take you no
further than yourself, but the ends you serve that are
for all, in common, will take you into eternity.

—MARCUS GARVEY

"I am committed to working with a Black, woman-owned company. I have already decided we want to work with you!" These were words shared by a prospective client during an introductory call to discuss a potential partnership. I was thrilled. I had not heard any company be so bold and transparent, proclaiming their intent to work *only* with a Black, woman-owned firm as a part of their goal to be an antiracist organization. More organizations recognize that firms owned by BIPOC are more often undercapitalized and underutilized due to systemic racism.[1]

Operationalizing justice in the procurement process warrants attention. There are "rules" (policies and practices) that create undue barriers for BIPOC companies. What does it mean to develop justice-centered policies and processes that address past barriers for BIPOC companies?

Supplier diversity is not a new approach to ensuring fairness in awarding business to BIPOC- and women-owned businesses.[2] As a matter of fact, many large companies set aggressive goals (e.g., 10 percent of total spending) to seek out and source from such businesses. Operationalizing justice requires moving beyond the check-the-box performative exercise of meeting spending goals and quotas. When was the last time you examined your procurement policies and practices to ensure that they work for *everyone*? When did you last ask, *Who are we harming by these requirements? Who do they benefit?* Procurement departments often devise policies and practices only with a lens of how it benefits the institution without consideration of the potential detrimental impact on the supplier partner.

As chief operating officer of The Winters Group, I have managed the team responsible for client engagement, which includes responding to requests for proposals (RFPs) and contract negotiations once we are the selected partner. This team is responsible for the entire onboarding process of new clients, starting with the initial prospective client call (or receipt of an RFP) to formulating proposals, reading through (and often redlining) master service agreements, and getting to a signed firm agreement.

I want to share in this chapter examples of barriers and harm some current practices cause small BIPOC-owned firms. I hope to encourage leaders to examine existing policies and practices with a justice-centered lens with the intent of changing those that continue to present barriers and cause harm.

RFP Process

Formal RFPs are often written to benefit the requesting organization. I understand that a standard RFP process is more convenient, but it often does not take into consideration the potential supplier. Many times, the turnaround time is unrealistic, with deadlines for submission within a week or two of receipt. Small suppliers may not have the capacity to respond within that short window. The timeline often includes in-person or virtual interviews with preset dates and times.

These restrictions often lead to scrambling to rearrange schedules, or sometimes, unfortunately, declining the interview and removing ourselves from consideration, and there is often no flexibility on the requestor's end.

While many requestors allow the submission of questions to gain clarity on the proposal, I find it more beneficial to have a conversation with the organization to understand their desired outcomes fully. Often the information included in the RFP is minimal and left for interpretation. Even before issuing a final RFP, consider discussing the elements of the engagement with the finalists for a more equity-centered design. In other words, rather than "telling" us what you want, engage in a partnership model earlier in the process and pay the supplier for their time during this stage.

Consider the number of times you ask to meet with potential suppliers prior to selection. It is not unusual to meet three to four times with various stakeholders before a formal contract is in place. During these conversations, we are sharing our thought leadership (e.g., potential solutions, intellectual property, advice on specific situations), usually without compensation. This is unjust.

"Do You Have the Capacity?"

This is a common question. Large companies may have assumptions and biases about the ability of small BIPOC businesses to serve them well. Big companies have a tendency to select "big," mainstream, and white-led consulting companies for their DEIJ solutions rather than boutique firms, such as The Winters Group, citing capacity concerns. Small does not translate into incapable or inferior. Think about how you and your leadership can support smaller firms to ensure they are successful throughout the engagement. Remove barriers and road-blocks that are in place due to policies and biases. Do not place unrealistic expectations on suppliers. Also, consider some of the benefits that come with working with smaller firms that you may not enjoy with their larger competitor, such as a more customized and personal approach.

Do not conflate capacity with convenience. As an example, one of our clients regularly says, "We do not do it that way here," or "This is the software that we use, and we expect it in this format because it is easier for us when we don't have to edit what you submit." Who does such inflexibility benefit, and who is potentially harmed?

Payment Terms

The Winters Group's standard payment term is net thirty. However, more clients are extending their payment policies to forty-five, sixty, ninety, or even 120 days with no negotiation allowed. *Who do these terms benefit? Who do they harm?* BIPOC-owned suppliers may not have access to lines of credit because of historical discrimination in access to capital. Waiting 120 days to be paid could put smaller firms out of business.

Small businesses are said to be the "heart and soul" of the US economy, accounting for two-thirds of all new jobs created.[3] Historically, many businesses owned by marginalized groups have struggled to secure bank loans, being denied at higher rates, and therefore have weaker banking relationships. According to the Stanford Institute for Economic Policy Research, only 1 percent of Black business owners secured loans within their first year of business, compared to 7 percent of white business owners.[4] Some BIPOC business owners have avoided dealing with banks completely and relied on family and friends to raise funds to get their businesses off the ground. Furthermore, the median white family has nearly ten times the amount of wealth as the median Black family,[5] meaning Black business owners generally have less cushion to deal with economic shocks than white business owners.

Some organizations also include language within contracting documents that state if they pay early, then they are entitled to a discount. Again, these terms are often non-negotiable. This type of payment policy harms the supplier and benefits the organization.

Many large organizations use procurement tools like Ariba Sourcing to manage invoicing and payment. They require suppliers to use these systems, and in order to do so, the suppliers may be required to pay transaction fees. Some of these fees can be pretty hefty, depending on the size of the contract and how many transactions are processed. *Who does this benefit? Who does this harm?* I feel that these fees should be absorbed by the organization.

An example of a justice- and equity-centered approach is Facebook's Receivables Financing Program. Facebook launched the program in 2021 and stated that it "gives our diverse suppliers exclusive access to affordable cash flow through their unpaid invoices. Instead of waiting 60 or 90 days for your customers to pay, you can sell those invoices to Facebook for immediate payment."[6] *Who benefits?* Both Facebook and the supplier benefit, as Facebook does charge a nominal 0.5 percent interest. *Who is harmed?* No one. While this is pretty innovative and very justice centered, it would not be needed if large companies would set more reasonable payment terms and be more flexible with small businesses that need to be paid promptly (e.g., net ten days).

Intellectual Property/Work for Hire

Maintaining ownership of one's intellectual property (IP) and copyrights is important. One of The Winters Group's core offerings is education. We develop content that is customized to our client, and this content contains our existing IP.

When reviewing agreements from organizations, one of the areas I flag the most is related to "intellectual property" and "work for hire" language. Organizations want to benefit most from their partnerships, so there is often language that states the vendor assigns all rights and title to all intellectual property. We usually can redline this clause and negotiate such terms out of the agreement, replacing it with language that protects our intellectual property—and I wonder, why do organizations make the supplier go through this? It takes time as it often requires several rounds of conversations and even consultations with our lawyer to agree on terms. It can become costly. A justice-centered approach would be to eliminate such language and not attempt to take ownership of others' intellectual property, especially without paying for it.

Third-Party Risk Assessments

With the increase in cyber security threats, many organizations have become stricter when it comes to IT and risk compliance. Organizations may require vendors to complete a risk assessment questionnaire as part of the onboarding process. Some of our clients have sent questionnaires with over three hundred questions. Not only is it time-consuming to complete, but it also often contains jargon that a layperson may not understand. These questionnaires are written from the lens of a large organization—not considering a small supplier. Many of the questions are not even applicable to the work to be done. Smaller BIPOC vendors may not have an actual IT department to support them in responding to such requirements.

Consider creating risk assessments based on the type of work to be performed or omitting questions that are not applicable to the vendor type or work. It benefits the organization requesting our services to be able to issue a "one size fits all" questionnaire and harms smaller organizations for whom many of the requirements are NA (not applicable). Also, consider providing IT support to smaller supplier companies to ensure that they are in compliance. This might even include purchasing the needed software and training the staff.

Flexibility

Larger organizations often have standard contracting agreements or master service agreements. These are sometimes sent where a client indicated "note this document is non-negotiable," while another stated, "we will not be able to accept any redlines to this document." In both instances, we had issues with various sections of the agreement, including payment terms, intellectual property rights, and insurance requirements. Such a lack of flexibility obviously benefits the organization and can harm the supplier. Develop policies that recognize one size does not fit all.

SUMMARY

- When espousing to be an antiracist organization, include the procurement process.

- Examine your procurement policies and practices to understand the barriers and be intentional in removing them and correcting past harm.

- Barriers such as long payment terms, intellectual property rights, and inflexible master agreements are more likely to harm BIPOC suppliers. Justice calls for removing such barriers.

- Learn more about your suppliers. Conduct listening sessions, surveys, and other qualitative and quantitative data gathering methods to better understand their challenges and concerns.

- The "that's just how we do things here" and "one size fits all" approaches must go.

DISCUSSION/REFLECTION QUESTIONS

1. When was the last time you examined your procurement policies and procedures? Have you done so with a justice- and equity-centered lens/approach?

2. Continually ask yourself: *Does this benefit only us? Does this harm who we seek to work with?*

3. Whose perspectives have been sought out to create our procurement policies, and whose have been excluded? How can we ensure all organizational stakeholders and customers are included?

4. Are there alternative policies or changes to existing ones that could better benefit those most harmed/impacted and still align with intended outcomes?

CHAPTER TWENTY-ONE

How Algorithms Automate Bias

MEGAN ELLINGHAUSEN

Marketing and Branding Specialist

The Winters Group, Inc.

(she/her/hers)

> Whether AI will help us reach our aspirations or reinforce
> the unjust inequalities is ultimately up to us.
>
> —JOY BUOLAMWINI, PHD

What was the first thing you did this morning? What about the last thing you did before going to bed? Or on your lunch break? Waiting in line? In between meetings?

My guess is, like most of us, you were on your smartphone. All of those times you innocently pick up your phone, you leave a digital footprint and bits of data that are analyzed and dictated by algorithms. Algorithms are a form of artificial intelligence (AI) that are step-by-step instructions a computer follows to perform a task. The computer can begin to learn on its own and teach itself, which is called *machine learning.* The algorithm combs through data to make correlations and predictions, which is how Netflix offers you suggestions on what to watch and how you get ads on Facebook for that product you were just thinking about buying.

These algorithms have a dark side, though. As Ruha Benjamin, PhD, wrote in her book *Race after Technology,*[1] power is relational, and if we are experiencing the upside of algorithms, then someone is experiencing the underside. Called *algorithms of oppression* by Safiya Umoja Noble, PhD,[2] or the *New Jim Code* by Benjamin,[3] these algorithms reinforce oppressive social relations and even install new modes of racism and discrimination.

While they determine what media we watch and what purchases we make, they also decide whose résumé gets pushed to the next round, what level of creditworthiness someone has, what neighborhoods police are sent to, and even how long a prison sentence should be. The issue with this, among many, is that by allowing our thinking to merge with the technology's, we end up giving a pass to these more subtle forms of discrimination.

To put it simply, we are automating our bias.

So, what can we do about it? How can we actualize justice when it comes to technology? There are three main areas we need to look at: the people designing technology, the organizations producing and using it, and the individuals impacted by it.

Systemic Structures Exclude Women and BIPOC from Entering Technology Fields

When thinking about these oppressive algorithms, we often want to place blame on the people designing the technology. Our digital world, for the most part, has been created by and for cis, straight, white men. At five large US tech companies, fewer than one in four of the technical workforce in each were women as of 2021.[4] A 2021 AnitaB.org report found that 12.6 percent of the tech workforce in the US are white women, 9.3 percent are Asian women, 1.7 percent are Black women, and 1.5 percent are Latine women.[5] When white men are the only ones writing the algorithms, they embed their biases into the programs and overlook how it impacts marginalized communities.

That doesn't mean that the solution is to fill every tech position with a Black coder because that places the onus for change back on Black people, asking them to solve their own oppression. Simply placing BIPOC in these roles is what Benjamin calls "cosmetic diversity,"[6] which does not take into account or address the marginalization that continues to happen in tech workplaces. Even if a Black woman is hired as a programmer and is aware of the racist ways the code is working, will she be able to exercise power to say something, or would she be silenced, ignored, or fired?

Women make up about 27 percent of tech workers in the US,[7] and the quit rate for women in high tech jobs is 41 percent, which is more than twice that of men.[8] A 2019 study led by Accenture and Girls Who Code showed that only 21 percent of women in the US said they believed the tech industry was somewhere they could thrive, and that number dropped to 8 percent for women of color.[9] The reason these women leave at such high rates: company culture. Women named their biggest challenges in tech as lack of opportunity for advancement, lack of female role models, and lack of mentorship.[10] The result is that even when women and BIPOC do get in the door, "they often find themselves looking for the exit before long," as Sam Dean and Johana Bhuiyan wrote in an *LA Times* article on June 24, 2020.[11]

The problem is not that there are no women and BIPOC communities for tech to hire and invest in; it is that there are systemic and corporate structures excluding them from entering the field.

In fact, BIPOC students are being excluded and steered away from STEM fields of study before they even reach the career level. The Markup, a nonprofit newsroom that examines how institutions are using technology to change society, found through public records requests that some universities are using software to determine students' success, and race is often considered in these algorithms as a "high-impact predictor."[12] For example, at the University of Massachusetts Amherst, Black women were 2.8 times as likely to be labeled a high risk as white women, and Black men 3.9 times as likely as white men. Latine students were also assigned high-risk scores at much higher rates than their white peers.

These scores, which are often assigned before a student has even taken a class, tell professors and administrators at these schools whether they should push a student to another major where the risk score is lower. The idea is that these students can switch to less "risky" majors to increase the institution's enrollment and graduation rates, which are important numbers with the increasing financial pressure put on public universities. So, rather than use these scores to find students who may need additional support to succeed, they weaponize them to push potential students out of STEM fields, with BIPOC students being impacted the most on the basis of their race.

If these students do achieve their STEM degrees, there are still hurdles to success. Tech companies are reluctant to recruit from schools where they might find more BIPOC candidates. The focus on Stanford and MIT overlooks HBCUs, and even at the colleges they do recruit from, BIPOC students are often not in the networks to know about these opportunities. Many tech companies rely on referrals, which means they tend to hire the same types of people from the same schools.[13] This reliance on personal relationships perpetuates gatekeeping in the tech world. A lack of women and BIPOC representation at the top permeates throughout the entire organization and industry, making it more and more difficult for marginalized students and graduates even to enter the door.

Along with the lack of recruitment, hiring, and support for BIPOC in tech, engineers, in general, are not given training or education on systemic oppression, humanities, or social justice. Most engineering programs have a one-semester ethics course at best. A 16-week course is not enough for a career that can dictate the future of people's lives, jobs, credit, housing, and even prison sentencing.[14] The people being hired to design and code technology should be given a better education in these areas so that they are not designing without an understanding of the people and communities being impacted. They should also partner with people or organizations who have training in social sciences to help eliminate or rectify the gaps and biases currently in tech.

This education can start in universities while students earn their degrees. For example, the University of Washington began implementing an Engineering for Social Justice curriculum through their Department of Human Centered Design and Engineering.[15] They acknowledged the engineering students' lack of exposure to social justice in their framework, so this curriculum attempts to fill in those gaps. Students examine how engineers' cultural ideas about race, gender, disability, and sexuality influence science and engineering knowledge and practice and, conversely, how science and engineering influence our cultural ideas. They also look at how they can use science and engineering to promote social justice for all people, how to design solutions for diverse user groups, how engineers can handle implicit bias during the research and design process, and how the identity of the engineer affects what engineering is and can be.

Social justice and humanities education should be included for all individuals involved in algorithms, from the students aspiring to enter the tech world to the employees using the tech. The necessary changes do not end with education, however. We need more marginalized identities and voices in tech, and for the organizations and leaders who are struggling to increase this representation, find new candidate sources. If women and BIPOC candidates are not coming to you, go to them. Expand recruiting efforts outside of the go-to tech schools, attend or organize events specifically for women or BIPOC students, or work within communities and with nonprofits to help develop the talent yourself. For example, Code2040, Black Girls CODE, Ada Developers Academy, Hack the Hood, The Hidden Genius Project, and Year Up all do the work of increasing representation in tech. Once you have recruited candidates, provide a support system to develop their talent and career success. Make paths for diversity in the leadership team to show that women and BIPOC are not limited to technical roles but can rise to leadership positions with the support of the organization behind them.

Algorithms are trained to think more like humans, so who those humans are that train them matters greatly.

Holding Tech Companies Accountable

As important as it is to consider who is coding the technology, the job of "algorithmic accountability," as Cathy O'Neil, PhD, calls it in her book *Weapons of Math Destruction: How Big Data Increases Inequality and Threatens Democracy,*[16] should start with the organizations developing and deploying the algorithms. Over the past few years, the tech world has proudly touted its commitment to human-centered design as the new buzzword, but which humans are being centered? The answer is usually the white male executives running Silicon Valley. Thus, these organizations are mass producing inequity and streamlining marginalization.[17]

Tech organizations need to take on a socially conscious design that centers those most impacted, that puts justice ahead of profit, and that prioritizes equity over efficiency.[18] This sounds far-reaching for the fast-paced tech world, but they have proven before that the capacity is there. For example, in Noble's *Algorithms of Oppression*, she details how when "Black girls" was Googled, the results were almost entirely of pornographic content.[19] When this was brought to the world's attention, Google quickly changed those results to display Black women leaders. Clearly Google had the technical capacity to prioritize justice over profit. They just did not have the social consciousness or the incentive to do so. The tech world has to slow down in the race to be the most efficient and most profitable and instead consider who is being impacted and how they can repair harm and shift power.

O'Neil posits that a socially conscious approach is technical just as much as it is ethical.[20] There needs to be standards in place for monitoring algorithms, rather than giving them blind trust that results in toxic feedback loops. For example, as Gabrielle Gayagoy Gonzalez points out in Chapter 17, some employers have used credit scores to evaluate job candidates, assuming that those who cannot pay their bills on time are less likely to be good, reliable workers. This creates a feedback loop where those with bad credit cannot get jobs, pushing them into poverty, which worsens their credit score and makes it even more difficult to get a job. Without a system to monitor and make changes to this algorithm, the loop will continue.

Just in the way that our understanding of diversity and inclusion has evolved to include equity and justice, our algorithms have to evolve as well.

This requires a higher level of transparency. O'Neil describes a case of an algorithm used to "weed out the low-performing teachers" in a Washington, DC, school district. One teacher who had excellent reviews from administrators and parents, even being called "one of the best teachers I've ever come into contact with," was fired for receiving a low score from the algorithm. The school district hired a consultancy to come up with this algorithm, and the scores were calculated by looking at students' test scores from year to year, and their advance or decline was attributed to their teachers.[21] But does the algorithm take into account if a student is experiencing family issues, money struggles, or bullying? How much of the students' gap in test scores can really be attributed to the teacher? How is the algorithm receiving feedback and learning from its mistakes? This should be made clear to the people impacted.

The organizations using the technology, such as the school district in this example, have a responsibility to interrogate not just the technology itself but the algorithms and data collection processes behind it. Questions for organizations to consider when interrogating their technology, algorithms, and data collection processes include:

- Do your employees have an inventory of all the algorithms being used in the company, particularly in regard to the ones that impact them?

- Do your employees understand and accept how the technology is being used?

- Do your employees have the opportunity to challenge the processes if they see harm being caused? Maybe offer a way to do this anonymously.

- Were the communities being impacted by the algorithm involved in its development?

- Are you screening what the algorithm is actually targeting versus what it is supposed to be targeting?

- Algorithms learn from a training dataset. What did that dataset look like in comparison to the population in which the algorithm is being applied? If you use a third-party organization for your algorithm, you may not have immediate access to this information, but you can ask for it.

- Do you have requirements for documenting algorithms? For example, Microsoft recommends that every component of an algorithm be documented with a data sheet describing its operating characteristics, test results, recommended usage, goals, training process, and performance.[22]

- Are there proxies in the dataset that directly identify protected classes (e.g., gender, race) and that indirectly identify them (e.g., hormone levels, zip codes)?

- Is your quantitative data supplemented with qualitative insights to add depth and context to the data?

There are many critical questions to understanding algorithms, and there are organizations available to help audit algorithms for you, such as the Data & Trust Alliance, the Algorithmic Justice League, and O'Neil Risk Consulting & Algorithmic Auditing (ORCAA).

Organizations cannot wait for society at large to actualize justice. Hahrie Han, PhD, professor of political science at Johns Hopkins University, lays out the levels of social change as systemic, organizational, and individual.[23] Organizations are the conduits in the middle that can listen to the individuals and build their capacity while also exercising influence over the systemic level. By being in the middle, organizations have a responsibility to actualize justice *themselves*.

How Technology Disproportionately
Impacts Marginalized Identities

In Han's social change levels, she argues that societal transformation begins with individual transformation.[24] This requires that we understand how differently we are affected by algorithms. Where some technology fails to see Blackness and marginalized identities, others make them hyper-visible.

For example, a 2016 ProPublica investigation[25] found that software being used in the US court system rated Black people as much "higher risk" of committing a crime than white people. These rates are used to determine everything from bond amounts to how long an individual is going to spend in prison. Because the US criminal justice system has a long history of being unjust (to say the least) to Black Americans, the algorithms are reinforcing that data. They study everything from our neighborhoods to our Facebook friends for "predictive policing." This data is used to predict which neighborhoods are more likely to have crime, drawing more police into certain neighborhoods where they are more likely to make arrests, even just for low-level crimes. Those arrests add more data to the models that send more police to the same neighborhoods—another feedback loop.

BIPOC individuals have historically faced discrimination in getting access to lines of credit and capital, so when banks use algorithms to determine the creditworthiness of individuals, they are more likely to repeat discrimination. A study by Brandeis University found that the gap between Black and white wealth quadrupled between 1984 and 2007. Noble writes, "This is not the result of moral superiority; this is directly linked to the gamification of financial markets through algorithmic decision making."[26]

BIPOC are also excluded and silenced on the internet. In 2021, The Markup investigated how Google and YouTube are blocking social justice–related content.[27] These platforms have brand safety guidelines that prevent advertisements from running on harmful content.

In theory, a neo-Nazi group cannot make money from advertisers on a YouTube video they create. The Markup found that in Google's guidelines, the terms "Black Lives Matter" and "Black power" were blocked phrases, but "white lives matter" and "white power" were not. Discrepancies like this were fixed, but Google's spokesperson declined to answer questions related to these blocks. Google later quietly blocked 32 more social and racial justice terms, including "Black excellence," "say their names," "believe Black women," "Black is beautiful," and "Black liberation."

Twitter came under investigation in 2019, as a study found tweets written by Black Americans were twice as likely to be flagged as offensive compared to others.[28] Instagram's algorithm is also guilty of privileging whiteness and discriminating against BIPOC. In 2020, Black plus-size model Nyome Nicholas-Williams had her photos removed from Instagram for nudity, even though she was clothed. She argues that "when a body is not understood, I think the algorithm goes with what it's taught as the norm, which in the media is white, slim women as the ideal."[29] These algorithms send clear messages about what kinds of bodies and identities they think are fit for consumption.

Although this may not directly impact the casual user, many people rely on social media to grow their business and make a living—artists, bloggers, musicians, and small business owners. The flagging and removal of content can be detrimental to their livelihoods. This media representation is also important for societal representation. As Noble[30] wrote, how people are represented (or misrepresented) is an important element of engaging in efforts to bring about justice in society.

What Can We Do As Individuals?

Societal transformation begins with individual transformation. It can be as simple as intentionally seeking out marginalized creators online to retrain your algorithms to recommend more of that content. Algorithms are trained on data, so introduce them to the actions you want them to perform. This may be oversimplifying it to a degree, but essentially, if you want to see more trans artists on your social media feeds, more books from Indigenous authors on your Amazon account, and more movies from Black producers on Netflix, intentionally seek out and engage with that content. The flip side to this is also to *not* engage with the content you do *not* want to see. The algorithms are trained on actions, so by clicking on an ad for a politician you do not support, you are rewarding the algorithm for bad behavior. You do have some power to retrain your algorithms; it just takes intention.

Individuals must also explore how our data is being handled so that we can demand transparency. One of the most important things we can do as individuals is to get legislation on the ballot for regulations in the tech world. There is a serious lack of industry standards or regulations that hold these companies creating and using algorithms accountable. Algorithmic audits, like the ones described in the previous section, currently have no industry standards, so approval from one auditor could look entirely different from another auditor. In 2018, New York City produced the first legislation in the country to shine a light on how government agencies are using AI to make decisions about people and policies.[31] Since then, more than forty pieces of legislation have been introduced to study or regulate government agencies' use of AI. Illinois enacted a law in 2019 requiring private employers to notify job candidates when algorithmic hiring tools are being used, and Colorado passed a law in 2021 that creates a framework for evaluating insurance underwriting algorithms and bans the use of discriminatory algorithms in the industry.[32]

Unfortunately, the majority of these bills do not make it further than a brief hearing. The Markup reported that the biggest reason for this is a lack of access to and understanding of what algorithms agencies are using, how they are designed, and how they influence decisions.[33] The big companies in tech also push to derail legislation regulating their technology, arguing that it is too broad and killing innovation. This goes back to the point in the last section: tech needs to put justice ahead of profit and equity over efficiency. As individuals, we must put pressure on our legislators to establish industry regulations. In our fight for racial justice, we cannot let these subtle but incredibly powerful forms of racism and discrimination go unnoticed and unregulated. We deserve access to the information being used to categorize us, and we deserve the ability to challenge it.

To learn more about how algorithms are being used and data is being handled, visit www.racialjusticeatwork.com for a list of resources on the topic.

Conclusion

Algorithms have the ability to comb through data to make correlations and predictions. They are able to find the people who have been marginalized and face challenges in jobs, crime, poverty, or education. What we must recognize is that although algorithms provide us with this data, it is up to *us* whether we use it to punish and further marginalize people or to reach out and uplift them.

The smartphones that we spend so much time on each day will not solve inequities. An app will not solve oppression. Technology will not solve injustice. *We* have to do that. Ruha Benjamin, PhD, posited that maybe what we need is not human-centered design or liberatory designs, that perhaps those buzzwords are just rebranding social change without actually doing anything about it.[34] Maybe what we need to focus on is just simply liberation in all forms.

SUMMARY

* Create inclusive workplaces that hire, support, and develop BIPOC talent in tech.
* Be intentional in recruiting for tech talent, expanding outside of go-to tech schools and referrals.
* Require education in social justice for people developing, managing, and using algorithms, starting in schools and continuing throughout an employee's career.

- Adopt a socially conscious design in tech that centers those most impacted, puts justice ahead of profit, and prioritizes equity over efficiency.

- Push organizations and legislators to establish industry standards and regulations on algorithms and the tech world.

- As an organization, interrogate the technology, algorithms, and data collection processes being used, and be transparent about this with employees and consumers.

- Seek out marginalized creators online to retrain your algorithms and expand your feeds.

- Learn about how algorithms are used in your life and how your data is being handled in order to demand transparency.

DISCUSSION/REFLECTION QUESTIONS

1. As you consider a socially conscious design that puts justice ahead of profit and prioritizes equity over efficiency, consider that for yourself as an individual as well. Are you willing to personally sacrifice efficiency in your life in the interest of equity and justice?

2. As you go throughout your day at work and in your personal life, take note of how many of your daily actions require, are controlled by, or are impacted by an algorithm. Do you understand how they all work? Do you know which ones are using your data and how?

3. What do your social media feeds look like? Whose identities are being represented? What about your Facebook ads, your Netflix suggestions, your Spotify or Apple Music recommendations? This could indicate whose voices are missing from your feeds and who you can intentionally seek out to engage with online and in real life.

CHAPTER TWENTY-TWO

Disrupting the Racist Narrative in Marketing and Advertising

MEGAN LARSON, EDD

Vice President, Marketing and Business Development

The Winters Group, Inc.

(she/her/hers)

Perception is reality, so if we are to change our perceptions, then we must change our reality.

—UNKNOWN

Systemic racism is perpetuated by a narrative created both deliberately and passively by cultural gatekeepers. Often these gatekeepers are driven by known prejudices, unconscious biases, and the demands of capitalism. They create stories and themes that reinforce racist and sexist ideas and fortify entrenched hierarchies of power that advantage dominant culture groups and further disadvantage marginalized people. The narratives created by cultural gatekeepers are both overt and subtle. They are easily assimilated into an individual's worldview because they are packaged as news, entertainment, and advertising. They are ubiquitous and often uncritically received because they are delivered in some form of entertainment where the recipients of the message play a passive role. Dismantling of racist systems needs to hold the cultural gatekeepers accountable for the racist and sexist narratives they create.

This chapter outlines the ways in which marketing and advertising have historically perpetuated portrayals of marginalized groups and continue to do so. The strategies that follow are intended to correct this type of systemic oppression.

Creating Perceptions

Think back to the books you read when you were little and to the movies and TV shows you watched as a child. What did the characters look like? What behaviors defined a hero or a villain? Think about the ads you saw. What was the underlying narrative being sold? The narratives impacted the way you looked at the world and assigned value to cultural norms. They impacted how you viewed yourself and the world around you. These narratives were created by powerful gatekeepers. The perceptions they created became your reality.

Remember when you were a child and saw an ad for a doll or action figure that you just *had* to have? Whether or not it was attainable didn't matter. This was a toy you dreamed about. Did it look like you? Or did it represent a distorted, unattainable standard of beauty and perfection like a Barbie doll or the overly muscled and disproportionate physique of an action figure? I grew up in the 1980s. All of my favorite dolls had blonde hair, blue eyes, tiny noses, and white skin. These were the dolls I dreamed about because the narrative of beauty I understood was that white girls with blonde hair and blue eyes were the most beautiful. Everything else was inferior. This was my perception as a child, and therefore it was my reality. This cultural narrative was reinforced by the product mix on the market, the ads I saw, and the performers on TV and in movies and was reflected by the attitudes and actions of the people around me. This perception didn't naturally evolve. This narrative was intentionally created by corporations, ad and marketing executives, entertainment studios, and magazine editors.

In 2021 when Disney's smash hit *Encanto* debuted, one of the animators intimated in a tweet that studio executives didn't want the character of Luisa to be broad-shouldered and strapping. Luisa is tall, extremely muscular, and does not fit the traditional representation of a Disney princess. Luisa was more "Gaston" than "Belle." It turns out fans loved Luisa just as she was, and she was a commercial success that the Disney marketing team didn't account for. Stores had an abundance of Isabela and Mirabel merchandise, both whom fit the more traditional "princess" archetype. When fans raced online to buy Luisa dolls and merchandise, they were disappointed to find such a dismal selection. This is an example of people rejecting an artificially enforced narrative and pushing back against the gatekeepers' definition of the idealized notion of girlhood, beauty, and worth.

Selling a Dream (or Nightmare)

Before a product is created, an advertisement is designed, or a movie goes into production, an entire team of people evaluates the return on investment and (hopefully) the impact it would have on the brand. It's rare that the project is viewed critically with an eye toward racial justice. Each of these endeavors takes an enormous amount of money to come to market, and companies want to make sure they will generate a profit. It's commonly thought that deviating from the entrenched cultural narrative would narrow the opportunities for profitability. What we find is that genuine expressions of inclusion and diversity are overwhelming successes. For example, the movie *Black Panther* broke box office records and was the highest-grossing film by a Black filmmaker as well as the thirteenth highest-grossing film of all time (at the time of this writing).[1] Though other Black-led superhero movies found success before *Black Panther*, none truly measured to the scope and scale of the Marvel franchise. It took over a decade to bring *Black Panther* to the screen as it was delayed to make room for other, white-led movies in the Marvel universe.[2]

As marketing and advertising teams create a campaign strategy, they deliberately create concepts intended to influence behavior and compel action—whether that is making a purchase, watching a show, asking (or begging) an adult to purchase something for a child, starting a conversation, or forming an opinion. There are three common tactics they use.

1. **Appealing to emotion.** One of the most popular emotional appeals in advertising is the feeling of superiority. Creating us-versus-them rhetoric plays into our core feelings of self-worth. Advertising has always been for the white gaze. Representations of Black people, particularly women, have historically had overtly racist contexts. Progress has been made in recent years. That's not to say we don't need to improve. Black women represented in advertising are objectified seven times more than white women and are more often depicted as not working and unintelligent.[3]

   In 2018, Heineken released an ad showing a bartender sliding a bottle of beer down the bar toward a white woman. On the way, it passes two elegantly dressed Black women. When the bottle comes to rest in front of the white woman, and she takes a drink, the following words appear on the screen: "Sometimes, lighter is better." The racism in that ad wasn't even subtle. But the ad was still approved and released publicly. The gatekeepers didn't even see that it was problematic. The narrative created was that even the most sophisticated, well-dressed, and beautiful Black women still aren't worthy. It created an emotional response of superiority and inferiority to create demand. This is just one example of the cultural narrative being created about the role and value of women and race and the influence of emotion in advertising.

   Another emotional appeal is to create a sense of fear. In news reports, often Black men accused of crimes are visibly depicted by a mug shot, while white men accused of similar (or worse) crimes are shown in a suit or a headshot taken in a more candid or professional context.

   It's not just the visuals. It's the *narrative*. Black Americans represent 37 percent of the criminals shown in news stories but only 26 percent of those actually arrested. White Americans are portrayed as criminals in 28 percent of news stories, while they are crime suspects in 77

percent of cases.[4] In fact, a 2011 study showed that most media portrayals of Black men from the 1930s to the early 2000s could be broken
down into four distinct conceptual themes: Black men as absent and
wandering, impotent and powerless, soulful and adaptive, or endan-
gered and in crisis.[5] The fact that this narrative has persisted for over
seventy years isn't happenstance. This reinforces a racist stereotype of
Black men as "thugs" or "felons" regardless of guilt or innocence. The
repetition and consistency of this messaging ingrains this bias into
people's conception of the world and perception of people in it.

2. **Creating a feeling of inferiority.** One of the most successful
   advertising tactics is to tell consumers they have a flaw. You can't
   sell a skin-lightening cream unless people believe their skin is
   too dark. The global market for skin-lightening products was
   projected to reach $11.8 billion by 2026.[6] You can't sell body-
   contouring shapewear if people are already comfortable with how
   their body looks. North America accounted for 38.8 percent of
   the global shapewear market in 2020, which amounted to over
   $853 million.[7] The subtle (and not so subtle) messages perpetuated
   through advertising have an overwhelming impact on how people
   view themselves and each other and what is considered desirable
   and "normal." The depiction of the ideal standard of beauty has
   long reinforced the prioritization of whiteness.

3. **Reinforcing a collective identity and cultural appropriation.**
   The ability of advertising and media to create a framework and
   value judgment for both the conception of self and the perception
   of culture means that it has the power to dictate whether
   something is "cool." Even the word *cool*, as we understand it
   in a modern context, was adopted into the cultural lexicon in
   the late 1880s from "Negro English" and was popularized from
   terminology from African American vernacular.[8] The truth is,
   in both a historical context and current reality, white cultural
   gatekeepers appropriate cultural norms of marginalized people
   and whitewash them to be positioned as aspirational. White

advertisers adopt "commercial blackface" to entice and attract consumers to a product at a superficial level by appropriating Black music, customs, vernacular, and style while still maintaining a white-centric cultural narrative.[9]

White celebrities are notorious for wearing their hair in cornrows, where their hair is tightly braided to their heads. This style originated within Black culture. In fact, Black people are often penalized or harassed for wearing their hair this way, while white people are celebrated for their style. As mentioned in previous chapters, in 2022, the US House of Representatives passed the CROWN Act (Creating a Respectful and Open World for Natural Hair) that bans race-based hair discrimination in workplaces and public accommodations. As of this writing, the legislation still needs to pass Senate approval which is not guaranteed. The Black culture is only deemed acceptable when applied to a white audience. This is the power of cultural gatekeepers and their influence over the norms, beliefs, and expectations of society. We need to actively interrogate the messages they are creating and critically examine how they are shaping the overall cultural narrative. We need to shift the power from the gatekeepers to the consumer and hold gatekeepers accountable for correcting both current and past harms to create a narrative that reflects equity and inclusion.

It's All about Capitalism

Capitalism, particularly American capitalism, was founded on racism. Scottish philosopher and economist Adam Smith is credited as the founder of modern capitalism based on a collection of books he wrote in the late 1700s called *An Inquiry into the Nature and Causes of the Wealth of Nations*.[10] In it, he argues for the supremacy of free markets and self-regulating economies. He also argues for the supremacy of white men.[11] These concepts were among the founding ideas of America. It's a system built on inequity.

This experience of capitalism is the very bedrock of the modern American economy and informs and guides the ideas and practices that define success in business. It's no great surprise then that American companies and organizations continue a tradition of unchecked exploitation in marketing and advertising. The primary motivations are driven by improving the bottom line for the Wall Street analysts and shareholders rather than correcting the harm to marginalized groups that may be perpetuated by the messaging.

Since the murder of George Floyd in 2020 and the seeming racial reckoning that followed, we witnessed many large corporations making bold statements to focus on racism inside their organizations and in the communities they serve. These pledges often included increasing advertising with BIPOC-owned media companies. For example, in 2021, twenty companies, including Uber, General Mills, Adidas, Tyson Foods, and Target, signed up to participate in GroupM's Media Inclusion Initiative, pledging to commit 2 percent or more of their annual media budget to Black-owned media. The initiative is an integrated investment strategy to grow Black-owned media companies and support creatorship.[12] Is 2 percent enough to lead to systemic change?

Progress

We have seen improvements in media advertising, with many more positive depictions of BIPOC in nonstereotypical roles. According to the Geena Davis Institute on Gender and Media, in 2019, Black women represented 5.7 percent of leading characters in family films while comprising 6.5 percent of the population, and Black women are now more likely than white women to be shown in positions of leadership or with careers in a STEM field.[13] This type of representation matters. In 2017, Paramount launched an entirely new *Star Trek* property (*Star Trek: Discovery*) that is primarily staffed by a BIPOC crew, and a Black woman leads the series. It has been tremendously successful. It was the most-watched show on Paramount+ in 2021.[14]

Brands are reassessing their logos and mascots. A number of brands changed logos and images that perpetuated racist stereotypes. Quaker Oats retired Aunt Jemima. Mars removed Uncle Ben's image from its rice packaging. Conagra foods agreed to redesign its Mrs. Butterworth's syrup bottles shaped like the stereotypical "mammy." B&G Foods agreed to review its Cream of Wheat packaging that shows a smiling Black chef holding a bowl of cereal. Land O'Lakes removed "Mia," a Native American woman, on its packaging.

Removing symbols and addressing portrayals in the media that perpetuate stereotypes are needed steps but are insufficient to root out systemic racism. It requires understanding who the gatekeepers are and appealing to them to use their power to change the systems that allow these inequities to persist. It also will mean increasing the number of BIPOC people in power positions.

Who Are the Gatekeepers?

Our gatekeepers—people in positions of profound power and influence—are overwhelmingly white and male. They are the heads of corporations, elected officials, and government appointees. These people make the decisions about what is important in the world and what ideas hold value. Those decisions trickle down to impact every facet of our lives. Historically, these men have not intentionally examined, or been forced to examine, their biases and consider how their thoughts, beliefs, and actions impact BIPOC and marginalized communities.

Government

In the hundreds of years since the United States was colonized by white settlers, the racial composition of the government has barely changed. In 2021 there was less than 24 percent BIPOC representation in Congress.[15]

- Black: 59 (11.0 percent)

- Hispanic: 46 (8.6 percent)

- Asian: 17 (3.2 percent)

- Native American: 6 (1.1 percent)

Only 3 of 115 Supreme Court justices have been non-white until Ketanji Brown Jackson was confirmed in 2022 as the first Black woman on the highest court of the land. The rest of the judiciary, including circuit and district courts, have only 20 percent BIPOC representation.[16] There have only been four Black governors in the history of the United States. Reviewing state legislators, Black lawmakers continue to hover around 10 percent.

Financial Markets

Black workers are significantly underrepresented in financial services and on Wall Street, and the number is actually dropping. A report by the *Financial Times* found that in 2017 the number of Black Americans working in top financial positions was lower than it had been in the previous decade.[17]

Corporate Boards

BIPOC representation on boards for the three thousand largest publicly traded companies in the United States has hit a high of 12.5 percent—with only 4 percent being Black.[18]

Company Leadership

As of 2022, only six of the Fortune 500 companies have a Black CEO, and throughout the entire history of naming Fortune 500 companies, there have only ever been twenty-four Black CEOs.[19]

Gatekeepers Control the Power

Whether we are looking at the government, the judiciary, financial markets, or corporate leadership, most people in positions of power are overwhelmingly white and wealthy. They control the narrative. They also control the culture and norms of our society.

The cultural gatekeepers, those who create the messages and narratives that form our perception of self and those around us, are also overwhelmingly white. Only 5.8 percent of the US advertising industry is Black.[20] The impact of this homogeneity has been felt for a long time. As the CEO of a prominent ad agency mentioned in a 2009 speech, "Like it or not, in this business, I essentially hire a bunch of white, middle-class kids, pay them enormous, enormous sums of money to do what? To create messages to the inner city, to kids who create the culture the white kids are trying like hell to emulate, but if you go into the inner city, odds are these kids aren't even going to see advertising as a possibility, as an opportunity for them."[21] White gatekeepers are not expected, at any point, to cultivate cultural awareness and truly examine the ramifications of their work.

It turns out, 75 percent of business schools don't require any courses on ethics.[22] To date, no schools require courses or curricula on diversity, equity, and inclusion. This means that people are going to stick to what they know. Any unexamined biases, prejudices, and stereotypes are going to continue to be perpetuated.

Impact over Intent

Even when professional marketers have the best of intentions and are taking every opportunity to prioritize equity and inclusion, they can still fall short. It is frustratingly easy to create a campaign that appears to go against a company's core mission and values.

Marketing has drastically changed. When I started my career, marketing channels were fairly standard. Brands would, depending on industry and audience, have a certain ratio of television, radio, print, outdoor, direct mail, event, tradeshow, and digital strategies to reach potential customers. I remember when hosting webinars was cutting edge, while today it is standard practice and almost passé.

The explosive growth of digital channels has upended traditional marketing and created new challenges for marketers. Digital marketing can feel like the Wild West. Effective digital channels change quickly, and it takes specialized knowledge and skills to use them effectively. If you have ever spent any time looking at Google Analytics or tried to add search engine optimization to a website, you will have experienced the overwhelming confusion and frustration many marketers face. (There's a good reason there are companies wholly devoted to the tiniest aspects of digital marketing and can command large fees.) It's not realistic for most brands to have a staff large enough to effectively manage digital marketing on their own, especially when technology changes so rapidly.

There is no clear answer to the size of the global digital advertising market. A quick Google search shows claims range anywhere from $176 billion to $477 billion. Most of this market is driven by tech—algorithms and programming created to automate serving digital ads to the right audience at the right time. One of the most popular ways to do this is through *ad networks*. Imagine ad networks as a giant warehouse distributor. Nearly every site on the Internet that chooses to monetize its audience through ad revenue is represented. Websites love it because all they have to do is sign up, and ad networks display ads on their site, and they get paid. Marketers love it because, in theory, they can create an ad and enter their audience parameters, and the ad network will serve their ad to the right audience at the right moment. Sounds simple. In reality, ad networks are opaque, closed networks, and marketers have no idea where their ads are placed. They are able to see metrics that show how many people clicked on a specific ad and when but often have no idea *where* it was placed.

The first ad campaign I created and ran through an ad network taught me just how closed the system was. We specified our audience: C-suite tech executives in US companies within the grocery industry and had more than five hundred employees. The only control we had over where our ad was to be shown was to select that it not be displayed on any "adult" sites, and our expectation was that since we were targeting a business audience, our ads would be shown in a business context.

The idea is that the data people generate in their daily lives—websites you visit, purchases you make, all the information you leave with your digital fingerprint—creates a digital profile. If your digital profile matches that specified by a marketer, you will see their ad. Our ad was getting seen, and people were clicking, but no one was converting to a customer. We tried troubleshooting. Was the ad unclear? Did we need to optimize the landing page? We tried every iteration we could think of to reach the right people. We were finally able to meet with a representative from the ad network, and we were stunned when he walked us through the breakdown of where our ad was displayed. This information was not available to us in our account. This was internal information he shared as part of the troubleshooting process. It turns out most of our ads were served on mobile phone games and news aggregator sites. This was not what we wanted nor envisioned when we created our campaign.

Having our ads shown on mobile games, while disappointing from a performance standpoint, wasn't the worst-case scenario. Advertisers have unwittingly found their ads on conspiracy theory sites, Russian disinformation sites, weapons forums, and racist online communities. Watchdog organizations like Check My Ads are shining a light into the hidden world of ad networks and working to hold big-tech to account for the utilization of websites that actively work to destabilize the social order.

What Can We Do?

Collectively we can work to combat the influence of cultural gate-keepers and reject racist and sexist narratives that are portrayed. How do we do it?

1. **Support brands that are BIPOC-owned or are genuine allies and use their platforms to lead the justice conversation.**
   In May 2022, Walmart released a limited-edition, store-brand "Juneteenth" ice cream. It was already selling the same flavor by a Black-owned brand. It would have been much easier (and more ethical) for Walmart to simply highlight Black-owned brands rather than performatively exploiting the labor of a Black-owned brand for profit. The Walmart marketing team missed an opportunity to center justice. Applying a justice framework to marketing and advertising isn't always easy or comfortable. Marketing is hard. Doing it well is even harder. And pushing

back against policies and practices that exploit marginalized people and cause harm can create personal and professional ramifications when marketers are expected to meet specific sales goals developed with a capitalistic mindset. The marketing team could have pivoted to suggest a campaign that lifted the products of Black-owned brands as a way to celebrate Juneteenth.

2. **We can hold tech companies accountable for the systems they create that shape and define how brands advertise.** We can support government intervention to increase transparency and competition in the ad markets so that brands are not forced to advertise in channels that are counter to equity and justice.

3. **We need to diversify the voices of the gatekeepers and redistribute power to those who have been traditionally marginalized.** We need more BIPOC voices in leadership roles in finance, government, and corporations. We also need to increase BIPOC representation throughout organizations, so those making the ad concepts, casting the movies, creating stock artwork, and deciding which products to market are diverse and de-center the narrative of whiteness.

4. **More practically, marketers should incorporate "sensitivity reviews" as standard practice when creating marketing campaigns where members of marginalized communities review pre-released ads and materials to ensure that the themes, copy, and imagery they use are not perpetuating harmful stereotypes.** At an even more granular level, marketing teams should ensure that the makeup artists and stylists on set for photo and video shoots have multicultural experience and are skilled at styling textured hair. There are numerous opportunities where marketers can create a positive impact with their work at the macro- and micro-levels.

While the recommendations above are at a global, systemic level, here are things you can do in your capacity as an individual that will also help to combat harmful narratives of cultural gatekeepers. As part of your practice of self-reflection and understanding, consider the following:

- Examine how the cultural narrative you experience is influenced by the messages you receive from media and advertising.

- Explore how those messages impact your sense of self and those around you.

- Acknowledge the messages that are harmful to BIPOC and other marginalized people and use your power as a consumer to push back to hold brands accountable.

- Watch that you aren't participating in or perpetuating cultural appropriation.

- Recognize and support brands that are intentionally disrupting the dominant culture narrative and authentically cultivating a justice focus.

The most effective way to combat the influence of cultural gatekeepers is to be aware and mindful of the messages you are exposed to and the impact they have on marginalized communities. Awareness of an unjust narrative gives you the opportunity to counter the message and recognize the influence it has on your perception. When we change our perception, we are changing our reality—for ourselves and others.

SUMMARY

- Systemic racism is perpetuated by a narrative created both deliberately and passively by cultural gatekeepers.

- The narratives the cultural gatekeepers create are both overt and subtle. They are easily assimilated into an individual's worldview because they are delivered in the guise of news, entertainment, and advertising.

- Historically, gatekeepers are white men with little incentive or desire to elevate the voices of marginalized people.

- The messages created by cultural gatekeepers are the foundation of our culture and are driven by, and feed into, the capitalist structure of the United States.

- We have the power, at the collective as well as the individual level, to disrupt the racist cultural narratives and hold gatekeepers accountable for their actions.

DISCUSSION/REFLECTION QUESTIONS

1. What are the cultural messages you are receiving through your media consumption? What type of stereotypes do they perpetuate?

2. Who are the gatekeepers within your organization? To whom are they accountable?

3. How transparent is your organization when it comes to reporting on DEIJ representation?

4. Does the messaging and branding for your organization reflect diversity and inclusivity? Does your brand perpetuate harm by depicting negative, racist stereotypes?

5. If your brand is diverse and inclusive, does it cross the line into exploitation?

6. What opportunities are there to create genuine, authentic messages of diversity and inclusion?

CHAPTER TWENTY-THREE

Justice
in Philanthropy

MARY-FRANCES WINTERS
Founder and CEO
The Winters Group, Inc.
(she/her/hers)

As token people of color working within the field of philanthropy, one of our regular watercooler conversations revolves around the analogy of a plantation. Those seeking funding are the people with the least power—the field hands, begging for scraps, given no dignity, and treated with no respect. One step up, people working in philanthropy, are the house slaves... some help those still in the fields.... But some take on the characteristics of the master and lord over the less fortunate.

—EDGAR VILLANUEVA

This chapter highlights how philanthropy has perpetuated harm and offers new ways to support BIPOC communities with justice-centered approaches.

Defining Corporate Social Responsibility and ESG

Many large organizations are committed to giving back to the communities in which they operate through structured corporate social responsibility initiatives. Such initiatives often involve financial contributions to nonprofit groups dedicated to improving the lives of the marginalized, subordinated, and oppressed. Corporate social responsibility reporting is fairly common in the US and mandatory as of 2017 in the European Union. Such reporting includes environmental, social, and financial results. Corporate social responsibility is also often accomplished through philanthropy, volunteerism, and activism.

Another term that speaks to wealth and social justice is ESG reporting, which stands for environmental, social, and governance. Environmental, social, and corporate governance is an evaluation of a firm's collective conscientiousness around social and environmental factors. "Social" refers to efforts that organizations take to contribute to positive societal outcomes for people. And both the environmental and governance aspects of ESG also relate to equity and social justice. For example, corporations like Walmart, Coca-Cola, Nestlé, and PepsiCo donated water to the largely Black community of Flint, Michigan, when it was discovered that the water was contaminated. Studies show that African Americans are three times more likely to live near landfills and industrial plants that pollute water and air and erode the quality of life.

However, as a cautionary note, ESG investing has been criticized by Bloomberg and others as not really measuring a company's impact on the earth and society but rather evaluating the opposite—the potential impact of world events on the company and its shareholders.[1] From a justice lens, it might be more impactful for organizations to ensure that they consider BIPOC-run investment firms to manage their portfolios.

Racial Justice in Philanthropy

After the murder of George Floyd in 2020, as with many other aspects of DEIJ, the philanthropic world came under scrutiny for its policies and practices. America's fifty largest public companies pledged approximately $50 billion to address racial inequities, of which just over $4 billion was allocated to grants.[2] Most of the money was earmarked for loans and investments that the investors could potentially profit from. Grants earmarked for "racial justice" have been largely awarded to white-led organizations that may have pivoted their mission in 2020 to take advantage of these funds, leaving BIPOC-led nonprofits in the same state as before the "racial reckoning," compounding existing inequities. The funds allocated to white-led organizations are often used to diversify their staff rather than directly impacting the communities in need. A racial justice approach would have the goal of building capacity and agency among communities of color to develop their own solutions. Before funding a white-led organization, the question should be, is there an organization of color doing this work? Are there other investments that would build power and self-determination directly?

When BIPOC organizations are considered for funding, their worthiness is often judged on white dominant culture standards, which large funders acknowledge can be unfair and not accomplish the desired outcome for either party.

Jumping through Hoops

I moderated a panel discussion at the Forum on Workplace Inclusion's annual DEI conference in 2022 entitled Decolonizing Philanthropy. The intent of the session was to bring together large funders to have a conversation with BIPOC-run nonprofits who seek financial support from these large grantmakers. Large funder panelists represented corporate giving, a community foundation, and a large advocacy organization. BIPOC panelists represented a civil rights organization, a local emerging nonprofit supporting fledging Black entrepreneurs, and an organization that supports Black women entrepreneurs. The desired outcome of the conversation was to understand the harm levied by colonized philanthropy and to recommend action steps.

The large funders acknowledged that their policies and practices often led grant seekers to feel like they had to "jump through hoops" to be awarded funding for their programs. Success measures are usually based on outcomes rather than impact. There may be onerous reporting requirements that only use quantitative measures to assess worthiness. Questions that measure outcomes might be: *How many people did you serve, and at what cost? What IT systems do you have in place to track progress? Who is on your board, and how much financial support do board members provide?*

One panelist representing the organization that funds local, new Black entrepreneurs related a story that illustrates how the decision-making process adds to the jumping-through-hoops phenomena. As a new nonprofit, he requested $25,000 in funding from a large funding organization. The many conversations with a decision influencer focused on questions about their viability as an organization and assumptions about their management capabilities. The potential funder was even surprised that they had a board in place. The decision influencer thought he could take a ten-thousand-dollar-ask to the final decision makers due to the lack of the organization's track record. The final decision maker "proudly" granted the organization $1,000. The funder was concerned that the organization might not be viable in the long term and therefore was only willing to invest a small amount. And with the $1,000 grant, the organization was required to submit a semi-annual report on how the money was being used. The funder did not ever review the report. This is an example of thinking from a deficit mindset rather than taking an asset-based approach. What are the strengths of this organization versus focusing on their perceived weaknesses?

Another panelist representing a small BIPOC nonprofit concurred with the story above. She said she has great conversations with the mid-tier people in funding organizations but then, in a room that you are not invited to, the final decisions are made.

The burden put on BIPOC grant seekers is fatiguing.

As an alternative approach, The New Commonwealth Racial Equity and Social Justice Fund focuses on trust-based grantmaking, meaning that the written application is less important than relational face-to-face interviews where there is an opportunity to really understand the goals and hopes for the organization.[3] The corporate foundation representative on the panel shared that they have abandoned some of their old approaches to evaluating the worthiness of fund seekers for a more justice-centered one that starts with: "Here are the outcomes that we both want. You tell us how you think we can achieve them." Rather than telling the BIPOC nonprofit what the corporate foundation wants, they are giving the power to grant seekers to set the strategies and actions to achieve the desired outcomes. The power imbalance between grantees and funders is a widely recognized dynamic that prevents the adoption of justice-centered approaches. Shifting power to those who are closest to the community requires trust, which continues to be an elusive goal.

Who Has the Power?

We continue to operate with a paternalist charity mindset that assumes those in power are capable of making decisions for and in the best interest of those without power. Sometimes this manifests as a savior mentality. Often large funders are predominately led by white people, including the boards of directors. These power brokers who make the ultimate decisions may not possess the cross-cultural competence to know what is best for the communities they want to help. Clients have admitted until the worldwide attention that the George Floyd murder garnered, they did not fully understand racial injustice. Even though these large funders were not new to the data confirming widespread racial disparities, they were unaware of their complicity in maintaining policies and practices that upheld the status quo.

As mentioned earlier, BIPOC are not usually the ultimate decision-makers—they are influencers at best. I have witnessed more than a moderate level of resistance from boards of directors to focus their strategies on racial justice. The pushback sounds like: "We cannot just focus on race and neglect other issues in the community" or "How can we guarantee that we will get a return on this investment?" Usually, the staff of large funders are more aware of the needs in BIPOC communities and want the board to be more engaged. However, staff also lack cultural competence and may exercise their power while leaving BIPOC out of the decision-making process.

This also begs the question of who is on the board. Often board members are prominent community leaders who are "big" donors. BIPOC nominated to these boards are also usually influential people in the community but may not have the capacity to donate large sums of money. Those with the financial ability to give significant gifts usually are given more power on the board than those who do not. Boards, therefore, often lack the voices of those most impacted. If we want to change this dynamic, it could look like dominant group individuals giving up their board seats to others who represent those most impacted.

Not All Money Is Good Money

"We don't want check-the-box money," lamented one panelist representing a civil rights organization. Check-the-box money may come from a place of guilt or performative action. Such grants often have numerous restrictions on how the funds can be used. For example, it might target a very specific program that the funder is interested in without knowledge of broader issues in the community. As mentioned above, the people who know the community may not be at the table when the final decisions are made. Program-focused grants usually do not address systemic issues. "We need coalitions on how to fund systems and not just programs," offered one panelist.

Grants that have too many stipulations and may only be for one year are not worth pursuing, according to the BIPOC panelists. If, in that one year, the organization is not able to achieve the targets set by the funder, there will be no additional funding. Panelists called for investing in BIPOC nonprofits as partners for long-term relationships to effect change. They likened it to R&D. A company invests in research and development for the long term.

Measuring Success

While quantitative measures of success are important, they often supplant qualitative impact measures that are told through stories and lived experiences. Justice-centered impact measures focus more on people and communities and less on programs, policies, and interventions. In a paper jointly published by Candid, the Global Fund for Community Foundations (GFCF), and Philanthropy for Social Justice and Peace (PSJP), based on conversations over a two-year period with 130 people from civil society from all over the world, the group came up with four overarching success criteria for measurement: (1) it will be useful, and it will be used; (2) it will be easily adaptable to different contexts; (3) it will provide inspiration rather than standardization; (4) it will be accountable and empowering to the people and communities we aim to serve.[4]

Measures like changes in attitudes and behaviors, how power dynamics have shifted, enhanced relationships, and increased trust may be more important indicators than those that measure cost reductions, efficiencies, and numbers of people served. These values may come from the dominant cultural view that bigger is always better. Thamara Subramanian speaks to the importance of qualitative evaluations in Chapter 15.

Shifting from linear thinking about how to evaluate impact is also important. What are the interconnections between and among programmatic initiatives? This allows for a more systemic, holistic view of assessing change. Approaches drawn from methods like outcome mapping[5] to gather evidence of change by looking back at the actions that contributed to it and Vital Signs, a tool used globally by community foundations to identify and monitor needs in the community, designed to uncover interconnections, may be useful.[6]

Measuring what matters is key to racial justice in philanthropy. It begs the question, matters to whom? Funders and grantees have been far apart in their worldview on what success looks like. Justice means that dominant group funders allow the communities most impacted by injustice to take the lead in determining how to measure success.

SUMMARY

- More large funders are acknowledging their complicity in upholding racist practices that harm the communities they are trying to help.

- Onerous and often irrelevant application criteria make it difficult for BIPOC-led organizations to receive funding.

- There are deep-seated assumptions about BIPOC nonprofits' ability in organizational management and to effectively address their community issues. White saviorism continues to be an issue.

- White-led organizations take on racial justice initiatives to take advantage of funding opportunities, which can usurp BIPOC-led organizations for these opportunities.

- BIPOC-led organizations want a real seat at the table where the decisions are made. Often they present their needs to lower-level staff without the power to ultimately decide and are not invited to the meetings where the final decisions are made.

- Program-based solutions are suboptimal. There is a need to take a systems approach to connect interrelated issues by building coalitions.

- BIPOC-led organizations want funders to invest in them for the long term rather than in one-year increments.

- Qualitative measures of success may be even more important than quantitative ones based on capitalistic dominant group notions of bigger is better.

- Boards of directors and staff need to be closely aligned on the strategies, goals, and desired outcomes.

- Boards need to have representation of the people most impacted by outcomes.

DISCUSSION/REFLECTION QUESTIONS

1. Why is it critical for those most impacted to be included in philanthropic decision-making?

2. Why are qualitative outcomes important to include in evaluations?

3. What are some examples of white saviorism in philanthropy?

4. How can white-led organizations partner with BIPOC-led organizations using racially just frameworks?

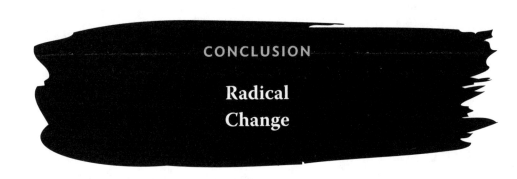

Radical Change

MARY-FRANCES WINTERS

Founder and CEO

The Winters Group, Inc.

(she/her/hers)

I know that for some of you, after reading the solutions recommended in this book, your head is spinning, or maybe it is just shaking, thinking, "These ideas will never work in my environment."

"Who is going to pay for more benefits, higher wages, more rest?"

"If we enact reparations, how do we decide who is eligible, and how do we do it fairly?"

"Don't there have to be some standards of 'professionalism'?"

"Repairing harm is such a monumental task. Where do we begin?"

Let's face it, most of the strategies and solutions to workplace racial inequities that we have tried over the past fifty or so years have not worked. Our goal of creating equitable, inclusive workplaces is stuck and in some cases regressing. After doing this work for almost forty years, I can testify that many of the same issues that we had then we have now. The incremental, programmatic approaches that are largely focused on fixing BIPOC, so they fit into existing systems, do not lead to justice. We need to change systems—to dig deep into the genesis of existing practices and policies and interrogate them by simply asking, "Why do we do it this way? Who does it serve?"

As Leigh Morrison points out in Chapter 3, we need a radical shift in consciousness. Employees and other stakeholders are demanding more than incremental change. To use a metaphor: the cauldron has been boiling for a long time, and the compounding impact of the George Floyd murder, the COVID-19 pandemic, the reversal of *Roe v. Wade*, the economy, and other sociopolitical issues have caused the pot to overflow. We must do something big and bold once and for all if we are serious about the "J" in DEIJ.

Any time you do something big and bold like we are suggesting, there will be resistance. In Chapters 6 and 7, Kevin A. Carter gives us a comprehensive roadmap for addressing the resistance in ways that consider the impact that radical change can have on people. We invite you to contemplate our recommendations to achieve justice-centered workplaces and spaces. Discuss them in your organization. Who would benefit if you implemented some of these ideas? We believe that everyone would, not just BIPOC and other historically marginalized and oppressed groups.

This work is not easy, but consider the consequences of not doing it. It has been said that change happens when the pain of staying where you are is greater than the pain of doing something different. What is your pain level? Our individual and collective pain levels should be motivation for radical change.

NOTES

Preface

1. Vanesha McGee, "Latino, Latinx, Hispanic, or Latine? Which Term Should You Use?," BestColleges, March 29, 2022, https://www.bestcolleges .com/blog/hispanic-latino-latinx-latine/#:~:text=Latino%2FLatina%20is %20how%20the,say%20they%20identify%20as%20Latinx.

2. SWANA Alliance, "About," https://swanaalliance.com/about (accessed October 28, 2022).

3. Kate Birch, "Chief Diversity Officer Appointments Continue Surge in 2022," Business Chief, March 4, 2022, https://businesschief.com /sustainability/chief-diversity-officer-appointments-continue-surge-in -2022. Brian Good, "Hiring of Chief Diversity Officers Triples over Past 16 Months but Representation in the Workforce Is Still Lagging," DiversityInc, March 15, 2021, https://www.diversityinc.com/hiring-of-chief-diversity -officers-triples-over-past-16-months-but-representation-in-the-workforce -is-still-lagging/.

4. Tina Shah Paikeday, "Positioning Your Chief Diversity Officer for Top Performance," Russell Reynolds Associates, June 1, 2021, https://www .russellreynolds.com/en/insights/articles/positioning-chief-diversity-officer -top-performance.

Introduction

1. "History of Executive Order 11246," Office of Federal Contract Compliance Programs, U.S. Department of Labor, accessed November 11, 2022, https://www.dol.gov/agencies/ofccp/about/executive-order-11246-history.

2. Meta Invoice Fast Track, https://fbinvoicefasttrack.app/login (accessed July 7, 2022).

3. Mark Guarino, "Evanston, Ill., Leads the Country with First Reparations Program for Black Residents," Washington Post, March 22, 2021, https://www.washingtonpost.com/national/evanston-illinois-reparations /2021/03/22/6b5a308c-8b2d-11eb-9423-04079921c915_story.html.

Chapter 1

Epigraph: Francis Bellamy wrote the Pledge of Allegiance in 1892, https://www.smithsonianmag.com/history/the-man-who-wrote-the
-pledge-of-allegiance-93907224/.

1. Michelle Maiese and Heidi Burgess, "Types of Justice," Beyond Intractability, July 2020, https://www.beyondintractability.org/essay/types_of
_justice#narrow-body.

2. "Make Business a Force for Good," B Lab, https://www.bcorporation
.net/en-us/ (accessed July 7, 2022).

3. "'Letter from Birmingham Jail' Reveals King's View of 'Just' and 'Unjust' Laws, and Which Can Be Disobeyed," *Wharton Journal Spectator*, January 16, 2008, https://www.journal-spectator.com/editorial/opinion
/article_5293c365-66e7-55fb-9309-04843f7f56fc.html.

4. Jessica Guynn, "George Floyd Protests Lead to Reckoning as Black Employees Speak Out on Racism and Discrimination in the Workplace," *USA Today*, June 18, 2020, https://www.usatoday.com/story/money/2020
/06/17/george-floyd-protests-black-lives-matter-employees-corporate
-america-racism/3195685001/.

Chapter 2

Epigraph: Michael Bernard Beckwith, New Thought minister, author, founder, and spiritual director of the Agape International Spiritual Center in Beverly Hills, California.

1. "Combating Race and Sex Stereotyping," Executive Office of the President, *Federal Register*, September 28, 2020, https://www.federalregister
.gov/documents/2020/09/28/2020-21534/combating-race-and-sex
-stereotyping.

2. CS/HB 7: Individual Freedom, The Florida Senate, July 1, 2022, https://
www.flsenate.gov/Session/Bill/2022/7.

3. Florida House Bill 1557: Parental Rights in Education, LegiScan, March 29, 2022, https://legiscan.com/FL/text/H1557/id/2541706?web=1&wdLOR=
c4B6F6CC2-721B-4C78-8D4A-C605D7515B9C.

4. Trip Gabriel, "A Timeline of Steve King's Racist Remarks and Divisive Actions," *New York Times*, January 15, 2019, https://www.nytimes.com/2019
/01/15/us/politics/steve-king-offensive-quotes.html.

5. Devan Cole, "Graham Denies Systemic Racism Exists in US and Says 'America's Not a Racist Country,'" CNN, April 25, 2021, https://www.cnn

.com/2021/04/25/politics/lindsey-graham-systemic-racism-america/index
.html.

6. "Commission on Race and Ethnic Disparities: The Report," Commission on Race and Ethnic Disparities, March 2021, https://assets.publishing
.service.gov.uk/government/uploads/system/uploads/attachment_data/file
/974507/20210331_-_CRED_Report_-_FINAL_-_Web_Accessible.pdf.

7. "UN Experts Condemn UK Commission on Race and Ethnic Disparities Report," United Nations Human Rights Office of the High Commissioner, April 19, 2021, https://www.ohchr.org/en/press-releases/2021/04/un
-experts-condemn-uk-commission-race-and-ethnic-disparities-report.

8. "Executive Order Number One (2022): Ending the Use of Inherently Divisive Concepts, Including Critical Race Theory, and Restoring Excellence in K-12 Public Education in the Commonwealth," Commonwealth of Virginia, Office of the Governor, January 15, 2022, https://www.governor
.virginia.gov/media/governorvirginiagov/governor-of-virginia/pdf/eo/EO
-1-Ending-the-Use-of-Inherently-Divisive-Concepts.pdf.

9. James Druckman, "The Majority of Americans Are Concerned with How American History Is Taught," Northwestern Institute for Policy Research, January 4, 2022, https://www.ipr.northwestern.edu/news/2022
/survey-majority-americans-concerned-with-how-american-history-is
-taught.html.

10. Jane Coaston, "The Intersectionality Wars," Vox, May 28, 2019, https://www.vox.com/the-highlight/2019/5/20/18542843/intersectionality
-conservatism-law-race-gender-discrimination. African American Policy Forum (AAPF), United States, 2012, Web Archive, https://www.loc.gov
/item/lcwaN0034282/.

11. Sarah Schwartz, "Map: Where Critical Race Theory Is under Attack," *Education Week*, July 15, 2022, https://www.edweek.org/policy-politics/map
-where-critical-race-theory-is-under-attack/2021/06.

12. Russell Falcon, "Texas Sen. Ted Cruz: Critical Race Theory Is as Racist as 'Klansman in White Sheets," *Valley Central Daily News*, June 21, 2021, https://www.valleycentral.com/news/state-news/texas-sen-ted-cruz
-critical-race-theory-is-as-racist-as-klansmen-in-white-sheets/.

13. Amanda Barroso, "Most Black Adults Say Race Is Central to Their Identity and Feel Connected to a Broader Black Community," Pew Research Center, February 5, 2020, https://www.pewresearch.org/fact-tank/2020
/02/05/most-black-adults-say-race-is-central-to-their-identity-and-feel
-connected-to-a-broader-black-community/.

14. Tema Okun, "(Divorcing) White Supremacy Culture," Dismantling Racism Works, May 2021, https://www.dismantlingracism.org/white -supremacy-culture.html.

15. Tema Okun, "(Divorcing) White Supremacy Culture," White Supremacy Culture, https://www.whitesupremacyculture.info/ (accessed July 7, 2022).

16. Tema Okun, "White Supremacy Culture Characteristics," White Supremacy Culture, https://www.whitesupremacyculture.info/characteristics .html (accessed July 7, 2022).

17. Roman Stubbs, "A Wrestler Was Forced to Cut His Dreadlocks Before a Match. His Town Is Still Looking for Answers," *Washington Post*, April 17, 2019, https://www.washingtonpost.com/sports/2019/04/17 /wrestler-was-forced-cut-his-dreadlocks-before-match-his-town-is-still -looking-answers/.

18. Lawrence Mishel and Jori Kandra, "CEO Pay Has Skyrocketed 1,322% Since 1978," Economic Policy Institute, August 10, 2021, https://www.epi.org /publication/ceo-pay-in-2020/. Abigail Johnson Hess, "In 2020, Top CEOs Earned 351 Times More Than the Typical Worker," CNBC, September 15, 2021, https://www.cnbc.com/2021/09/15/in-2020-top-ceos-earned-351 -times-more-than-the-typical-worker.html.

19. "The 'Great Replacement' Theory, Explained," National Immigration Forum, https://immigrationforum.org/wp-content/uploads/2021/12 /Replacement-Theory-Explainer-1122.pdf (accessed July 7, 2022).

20. "May 28, 1830 CE: Indian Removal Act," *National Geographic*, https://education.nationalgeographic.org/resource/indian-removal-act (accessed July 7, 2022).

21. https://www.nbcnews.com/news/asian-america/how-1800s-racism -birthed-chinatown-japantown-other-ethnic-enclaves-n997296.

22. Sandra Feder, "Stanford Professor's Study Finds Gentrification Disproportionately Affects Minorities," Stanford News, December 1, 2020, https://news.stanford.edu/2020/12/01/gentrification-disproportionately -affects-minorities/.

Chapter 3

Epigraph: adrienne m. brown, *We Will Not Cancel Us* (Chico, CA: AK Press, 2020), 10.

1. Kim Barker, Mike Baker, and Ali Watkins, "In City after City, Police Mishandled Black Lives Matter Protests," *New York Times*, March 20, 2021,

https://www.nytimes.com/2021/03/20/us/protests-policing-george-floyd
.html.

2. Kellie C. Jackson, "The Inaction of Capitol Police Was by Design," *The Atlantic*, January 8, 2021, https://www.theatlantic.com/culture/archive/2021
/01/inaction-capitol-police-was-design/617590/.

3. Angela Haupt, "The Rise in Book Bans Explained," *Washington Post*, June 9, 2022, https://www.washingtonpost.com/books/2022/06/09/rise
-book-bans-explained/.

4. Katie Reilly, "Florida's Governor Just Signed the 'Stop Woke Act.' Here's What It Means for Schools and Businesses," *Time*, April 22, 2022, https://time.com/6168753/florida-stop-woke-law/.

5. Tema Okun, "White Supremacy Culture Characteristics," last modified 2021, https://www.whitesupremacyculture.info/characteristics.html.

6. "JPMorgan Chase Commits $30 Billion to Advance Racial Equity," JPMorgan Chase & Co., October 8, 2020, https://www.jpmorganchase.com
/news-stories/jpmc-commits-30-billion-to-advance-racial-equity.

7. "JPMorgan Chase Provides an Update on its $30 Billion Racial Equity Commitment," JPMorgan Chase & Co., October 26, 2021, https://www
.jpmorganchase.com/ir/news/2021/jpmc-provides-update-on-30-billion
-racial-equity-commitment.

8. Rob Wile, "Bank of America Announces Zero Down Payment, Zero Closing Cost Mortgages for First-Time Homebuyers in Black and Hispanic Communities Nationwide," NBC News, August 31, 2022, https://www
.nbcnews.com/business/consumer/bank-america-zero-down-payment
-mortgage-first-time-buyers-details-rcna45662.

9. "We are deeply and profoundly sorry: For decades, The Baltimore Sun promoted policies that oppressed Black Marylanders; we are working to make amends," *Baltimore Sun*, February 18, 2022.

10. Susan Dynarski, "Why I Changed My Mind on Student Debt Forgiveness," *New York Times*, August 30, 2022, https://www.nytimes.com/2022/08
/30/opinion/student-loan-debt-relief-biden.html.

11. Lily Zheng, "We're Entering the Age of Corporate Social Justice," *Harvard Business Review*, June 15, 2020, https://hbr.org/2020/06/were-entering
-the-age-of-corporate-social-justice.

12. Rebecca Knight, "How to Hold Your Company Accountable to Its Promise of Racial Justice," *Harvard Business Review*, December 11, 2020, https://hbr.org/2020/12/how-to-hold-your-company-accountable-to-its
-promise-of-racial-justice.

13. "Consumer Activism Poses a Threat to Brands Using Damaging Ad Campaigns," Phys.org, November 24, 2021, https://phys.org/news/2021-11 -consumer-poses-threat-brands-ad.html.

14. "Glassdoor's Diversity and Inclusion Workplace Survey," Glassdoor, September 29, 2020, https://www.glassdoor.com/blog/glassdoors-diversity -and-inclusion-workplace-survey/.

15. David Leonhardt, "The NFL's Race Problem," *New York Times*, February 3, 2022, https://www.nytimes.com/2022/02/03/briefing/nfl-head-coach -brian-flores-racism.html.

16. Jeff McDonald, "San Diego Museum of Art Sued for Sexual Harassment, Racial Discrimination," *San Diego Union-Tribune*, July 15, 2021, https://www.sandiegouniontribune.com/news/watchdog/story/2021 -07-15/san-diego-museum-of-art-sued-for-sexual-harassment-racial -discrimination. "'White Art Audience' Job Listing Prompts Resignation of Indianapolis Museum Head," NBC News, February 19, 2021, https://www .nbcnews.com/news/us-news/white-art-audience-job-listing-prompts -resignation-indianapolis-museum-head-n1258322.

17. Sam Dean and Johana Bhuiyan. "Why Are Black and Latino People Still Kept out of the Tech Industry?," *Los Angeles Times*, June 24, 2020, https://www.latimes.com/business/technology/story/2020-06-24/tech -started-publicly-taking-lack-of-diversity-seriously-in-2014-why-has-so -little-changed-for-black-workers.

18. Lora Kolodny, "Tesla Must Pay $137 Million to Ex-Worker over Hostile Work Environment, Racism," CNBC, October 4, 2021, https:// www.cnbc.com/2021/10/05/tesla-must-pay-137-million-to-ex-worker-over -hostile-work-environment-racism.html.

19. Zach Fuentes, "Racial Discrimination Lawsuit Filed Against Google on Behalf of Minority Employees," ABC 7 News, March 21, 2022, https:// abc7news.com/google-racial-discrimination-lawsuit-black-employees -racism-suit-april-curley-ben-crump/11669663/.

20. Robert Burnson, "Google Agrees to Pay $118 Million to Settle Pay Equity Suit," *Bloomberg*, June 10, 2022, https://www.bloomberg.com/news /articles/2022-06-11/google-agrees-to-pay-118-million-to-settle-pay-equity -suit.

21. Kari Paul, "Judge Approves Activision Blizzard's $18m Settlement over Sexual Harassment Suit," *The Guardian*, March 29, 2022, https://www .theguardian.com/technology/2022/mar/29/activision-blizzard-sexual -harassment-lawsuit-eeoc-settlement.

22. Alex Veiga and Lynn Elber, "Chappelle Special Spurs Netflix Walkout and Counter Protests," ABC News, October 27, 2021, https://abcnews.go .com/Entertainment/wireStory/correction-netflix-chappelle-protest-story -80805598.

23. Irina Ivanova, "Wayfair Employees Walk Out after Company's Sales to Migrant Children Holding Facility," CBS News, June 26, 2019, https:// www.cbsnews.com/news/wayfair-employees-plan-walkout-after-companys -sales-to-detention-centers/.

24. Joe Hernandez, "Disney Workers Walk Out over the Company's Response to So-Called 'Don't Say Gay' Bill." National Public Radio, March 22, 2022, https://www.npr.org/2022/03/22/1088048998/disney-walkout -dont-say-gay-bill.

25. Adam Serwer, "The Amazon Union Exposes the Emptiness of 'Woke Capital,'" *The Atlantic*, April 14, 2022, https://www.theatlantic.com/ideas /archive/2022/04/amazon-labor-union/629550/.

26. Karen Weise and Noam Scheiber, "Amazon Workers on Staten Island Vote to Unionize in Landmark Win for Labor," *New York Times*, April 1, 20022, https://www.nytimes.com/2022/04/01/technology/amazon-union -staten-island.html.

27. David Molloy, "Apple Store Workers Vote to Form First US Union," BBC News, June 19, 2022, https://www.bbc.com/news/technology -61855301.

28. Jaclyn Diaz, "Starbucks Must Rehire 7 Memphis Employees Who Supported a Union, a Judge Says," National Public Radio, August 18, 2022, https://www.npr.org/2022/08/18/1118322322/starbucks-ordered-to-rehire -fired-union-employees.

29. Joshua Siler, "Strong Leaders and Strong Organizations Are Transparent," *Forbes*, June 2, 2022, https://www.forbes.com/sites/forbeshuman resourcescouncil/2022/06/02/strong-leaders-and-strong-organizations -are-transparent/?sh=6f1baf71ba94.

30. "The Best Workplaces for Millennials," Great Places to Work, last modified 2018, https://pubfiles.greatplacetowork.com/root/li/2018 _Millennials_KeyFindings_1.3.pdf?mkt_tok=NTIwLUFPTyo5ODIAAAGE -NEWfhGC-TdgOebQnDCG5cMLukBPkfW5Mroo_KoyEn87nCogQjeZEK y6KSwuZ1h7T-XmKGU2-hjI7qo_ZknA5HBh8.

31. "Racial Equity Stages," Dismantling Racism, last modified May 2021, https://www.dismantlingracism.org/analysis-tools.html.

32. Tayari Jones, "There's Nothing Virtuous About Finding Common Ground," *Time*, October 25, 2018, https://www.time.com/5434381/tayari-jones-moral-middle-myth/. A. Wiley, *Intercultural Development Inventory (IDI): Independent Review* (Las Vegas, NV: ACS Ventures, LLC, 2016).

33. Sarah Repucci and Amy Slipowitz, "The Global Expansion of Authoritarian Rule," Freedom House, https://freedomhouse.org/report/freedom-world/2022/global-expansion-authoritarian-rule (accessed July 7, 2022).

34. Elizabeth Elkind, "Americans Trust CEOs More Than Their Own Government, Survey Finds," *CBS News*, January 13, 2021, https://www.cbsnews.com/news/edelman-trust-barometer-2021-ceo-government/.

Chapter 4

Epigraph: James Baldwin, "As Much Truth as One Can Bear," *The New York Times Book Review*, January 14, 1962. https://timesmachine.nytimes.com/timesmachine/1962/01/14/118438007.pdf.

Chapter 5

Epigraph: Mitchell Hammer, *The Intercultural Development Inventory Resource Guide, 2021* (Olney, MD: IDI, LLC, 2021), 128.

1. Jennifer Garvey Berger, *Changing on the Job: Developing Leaders for a Complex World* (Stanford, CA: Stanford University Press, 2020), https://doi.org/10.1515/9780804782869.

2. A. Wiley, *Intercultural Development Inventory (IDI): Independent Review* (Las Vegas, NV: ACS Ventures, LLC, 2016).

3. Milton J. Bennett, "A Developmental Approach to Training Intercultural Sensitivity," *International Journal of Intercultural Relations* 10, no. 2 (1986): 179–86.

4. Mitchell Hammer, *The Intercultural Development Inventory* (Olney, MD: IDI, LLC, 2021).

Chapter 6

Epigraph: James Brown and Kenneth Chenault, "An Evening with Ken Chenault | The HistoryMakers," *The History Makers*, November 3, 2018, https://www.thehistorymakers.org/aneveningwithkenchenault.

1. Brian Joseph Galli, "Change Management Models: A Comparative Analysis and Concerns," *IEEE Engineering Management Review* 46, no. 3 (2018): 124–32, https://doi.org/10.1109/EMR.2018.2866860. Stephen Courtney Sistare, "Overcoming Resistance through Organizational Change

Models and Leadership Strategies," PhD dissertation, Charleston Southern University, 2022.

2. Jeff Hiatt, *ADKAR: A Model for Change in Business, Government and Our Community,* first edition (Prosci Learning Center Publications, 2006). "The Prosci ADKAR Model | Prosci," https://www.prosci.com /methodology/adkar (accessed June 18, 2022).

3. "Kübler-Ross Change Curve—EKR Foundation," https://www .ekrfoundation.org/5-stages-of-grief/change-curve/ (accessed June 18, 2022). Elisabeth Kübler-Ross, *On Death and Dying : What the Dying Have to Teach Doctors, Nurses, Clergy and Their Own Families,* 40th anniversary ed. (London: Routledge, 2009).

4. Mitchell R. Hammer, "Additional Cross-Cultural Validity Testing of the Intercultural Development Inventory," *International Journal of Intercultural Relations* 35, no. 4 (2011): 474–87, https://doi.org/10.1016/j.ijintrel .2011.02.014. Mitchell R. Hammer, Milton J. Bennett, and Richard Wiseman, "Measuring Intercultural Sensitivity: The Intercultural Development Inventory," *International Journal of Intercultural Relations* 27, no. 4 (2003): 421–43, https://doi.org/10.1016/S0147-1767(03)00032-4.

5. Jakomijn van Wijk, Charlene Zietsma, Silvia Dorado, Frank G. A. de Bakker, and Ignasi Martí, "Social Innovation: Integrating Micro, Meso, and Macro Level Insights from Institutional Theory," *Business & Society* 58, no. 5 (2019): 887–918, https://doi.org/10.1177/0007650318789104. Cortney Evans, Monica Higgins, and Jody Hoffer Gittell, "Change at the Micro, Meso, and Macro Levels: Connecting across Research in US Public Education," *Academy of Management Proceedings* 1 (2018): 18030, https://doi.org/10 .5465/AMBPP.2018.18030symposium.

6. Catrien J.A.M. Termeer and Art Dewulf, "A Small Wins Framework to Overcome the Evaluation Paradox of Governing Wicked Problems," *Policy & Society* 38, no. 2 (2019): 298–314, https://doi.org/10.1080/14494035 .2018.1497933. Karl E. Weick, "Small Wins: Redefining the Scale of Social Problems," *American Psychologist* 39, no. 1 (1984): 40–49, https://doi.org/10 .1037/0003-066X.39.1.40.

7. Anthony M. Grant, "The Efficacy of Executive Coaching in Times of Organisational Change," *Journal of Change Management* 14 no. 2 (2014): 258–80, https://doi.org/10.1080/14697017.2013.805159. Bahar Rumelili and Jennifer Todd, "Paradoxes of Identity Change: Integrating Macro, Meso, and Micro Research on Identity in Conflict Processes," *Politics* 38, no. 1 (2018): 3–18, https://doi.org/10.1177/0263395717734445.

Chapter 7

Epigraph: "Anti-racism and Criminal Justice Reform Resources," UC Santa Cruz Institute for Social Transformation, accessed November 14, 2022, https://transform.ucsc.edu/anti-racism-resources/.

1. M. E. Krause, "The Role of Personal Values in Shaping Leaders' Experiences with Employee Engagement: A Qualitative Phenomenological Study," thesis, University of Phoenix, 2015. "Taylor Protocols—About the CVI," https://www.taylorprotocols.com/about (accessed June 18, 2022).

2. E. H. Friedman, *A Failure of Nerve, Revised Edition: Leadership in the Age of the Quick Fix,* edited by M. M. Treadwell and E. W. Beal (New York: Seabury Books, 2007). Jemima Neddy Organ, "Motivational Interviewing: A Tool for Servant-Leadership," *International Journal of Servant-Leadership* 15, no. 1 (2021): 209–34. H. Patrick and G. C. Williams, "Self-Determination Theory: Its Application to Health Behavior and Complementarity with Motivational Interviewing," *International Journal of Behavioral Nutrition and Physical Activity* 9 (2012), https://doi.org/10.1186/1479-5868-9-18. Stephen Rollnick, William R. Miller, and Christopher C. Butler, *Motivational Interviewing in Health Care: Helping Patients Change Behavior* (New York: Guilford Press, 2010).

3. T. Ray, "Failure of Nerve," *Teddy Ray Blog,* July 3, 2018, https://teddyray .com/failure-of-nerve/.

Chapter 8

Epigraph: Michelle Winfrey, *Famous Mahatma Gandhi Quotes: Inspirational Mahatma Gandhi Quotes & Sayings* (Independently Published, 2020).

1. James R. Bailey and Hillary Phillips, "How Do Consumers Feel When Companies Get Political?" *Harvard Business Review,* February 17, 2020, https://hbr.org/2020/02/how-do-consumers-feel-when-companies-get -political.

2. "Neutral Policies As Discrimination," Compliance Assistance Resources, US Department of Labor, https://www.employer.gov/employment issues/Workplace-inclusion/Neutral-policies-as-discrimination/ (accessed June 21, 2022).

3. Edwin J. Nichols, *Philosophical Aspects of Cultural Differences* (Western Psychiatric Institute and Clinic, 1981).

4. Buck Gee and Denise Peck, "Asian Americans Are the Least Likely Group to Be Promoted to Management," *Harvard Business Review,* May 31,

2018, https://hbr.org/2018/05/asian-americans-are-the-least-likely-group-in
-the-u-s-to-be-promoted-to-management.

Chapter 9

Epigraph: Benjamin Disraeli, "Agricultural Distress," speech in the House
of Commons, February 11, 1851, *Selected Speeches of the Late Right Honour-
able Earl of Beaconsfield*, ed. T. E. Kebbel, vol. 1 (1882), 321.

1. M. Lance Frazier, Stav Fainshmidt, Ryan L. Klinger, Amir Pezeshkan,
and Veselina Vracheva, "Psychological Safety: A Meta-Analytic Review
and Extension," *Management Faculty Publications* 13 (2017), https://
digitalcommons.odu.edu/management_fac_pubs/13.

2. Laura Delizonna, "High-Performing Teams Need Psychological
Safety. Here's How to Create It," Center for Creative Leadership, August
24, 2017, https://www.ccl.org/articles/leading-effectively-articles/what-is
-psychological-safety-at-work/.

3. Amy Edmonson, "The Importance of Psychological Safety," *HR Magazine*, December 4, 2018, https://www.hrmagazine.co.uk/content/features
/the-importance-of-psychological-safety.

4. D. L. Hoyert, "Maternal Mortality Rates in the United States, 2020,"
NCHS Health E-Stats, 2022, https://dx.doi.org/10.15620/cdc:113967.

5. Equal Justice Initiative, "FBI Reports Hate Crimes at Highest Level in
12 Years," September 9, 2021, https://eji.org/news/fbi-reports-hate-crimes
-at-highest-level-in-12-years/.

6. Paige McGlauflin, "The number of Black Fortune 500 CEOs returns to
record high—meet the 6 chief executives," *Fortune,* May 23, 2022, https://
fortune.com/2022/05/23/meet-6-black-ceos-fortune-500-first-black
-founder-to-ever-make-list/.

7. Dina Gerdeman, "Minorities Who 'Whiten' Job Resumes Get More
Interviews," *Harvard Business School*, May 17, 2017, https://hbswk.hbs.edu
/item/minorities-who-whiten-job-resumes-get-more-interviews.

Chapter 10

Epigraph: R. O. Kwon, "Your Silence Will Not Protect You by Audre
Lorde review—prophetic and necessary," The Guardian, October 4, 2017,
https://www.theguardian.com/books/2017/oct/04/your-silence-will-not-
protect-you-by-audre-lorder-review.

1. A. Nieweler, "How to Develop an Effective (and Believable) Speak-Up Culture," Whistleblower Security, May 17, 2021, https://blog.whistleblower security.com/blog/how-to-develop-an-effective-speak-up-culture.

2. Ruchika Tulshyan "Speaking Up as a Woman of Color at Work," Forbes, February 10, 2015, https://www.forbes.com/sites/ruchikatulshyan /2015/02/10/speaking-up-as-a-woman-of-color-at-work.

3. S. Johnson and D. Hekman, "Women and Minorities Are Penalized for Promoting Diversity," Harvard Business Review, March 23, 2016, https:// hbr.org/2016/03/women-and-minorities-are-penalized-for-promoting -diversity.

4. Mary-Frances Winters, *We Can't Talk about That at Work! How to Talk about Race, Religion, Politics, and Other Polarizing Topics* (Oakland, CA: Berrett-Koehler, 2017).

5. K. P. Jones, C. I. Peddie, V. L. Gilrane, E. B. King, and A. L. Gray, "Not So Subtle: A Meta-Analytic Investigation of the Correlates of Subtle and Overt Discrimination," *Journal of Management* 42, no. 6 (2016): 1588–1613, doi:10.1177/0149206313506466.

6. A. Limbong, "Microaggressions Are a Big Deal: How to Talk Them Out and When to Walk Away," National Public Radio, June 9, 2020, https:// www.npr.org/2020/06/08/872371063/microaggressions-are-a-big-deal-how -to-talk-them-out-and-when-to-walk-away.

7. L. S. Davis, C. Whitman, and K. L. Nadal, "Microaggressions in the Workplace: Recommendations for Best Practices," in *Sexual Harassment in Educational and Work Settings: Current Research and Best Practices for Prevention*, ed. M. Paludi et al. (New York: Praeger, 2015), 135–56.

8. Z. Abrams, "How Bystanders Can Shut Down Microaggressions," *Monitor on Psychology*, September 1, 2021, https://www.apa.org/monitor /2021/09/feature-bystanders-microaggressions.

Chapter 11

Epigraph: Jovida Ross and Weyam Ghadbian, *Turning Towards Each Other: A Conflict Workbook* (Movement Strategy, 2020), 03, https:// movementstrategy.org/resources/turning-towardstoward-each-other -a-conflict-workbook/.

1. "Communication Series by SuperCamp: #1—Open the Front Door," *The Teen Mentor*, August 30, 2019, https://theteenmentor.com/2019/08/30 /communication-series-by-supercamp-1-open-the-front-door/.

2. "A New Management Philosophy," Radical Candor LLC, last modified 2022, https://www.radicalcandor.com/our-approach/.

3. Brené Brown, *The Braving Inventory* (Brené Brown LLC, 2021), 01, https://daretolead.brenebrown.com/wp-content/uploads/2021/10/DTL _BRAVING_102221.pdf.

4. Mary-Frances Winters, *We Can't Talk about That at Work! How to Talk about Race, Religion, Politics, and Other Polarizing Topics* (Oakland, CA: Berrett-Koehler, Inc., 2017), 89–99.

5. J. Miakoda Taylor, "About: Advancing JEDI 2.0: Justice, Equity, Decolonization, & Intersectionality," Fierce Allies, last modified 2021, https://www .fierceallies.com/about.

Chapter 12

Epigraph: W. E. B. DuBois, *The Souls of Black Folk* (CreateSpace Independent Platform, 2014).

1. "Being Black in Corporate America: An Intersectional Exploration," Coqual (formerly Center for Talent Innovation), December 9, 2019, https:// www.talentinnovation.org/_private/assets/BeingBlack-KeyFindings-CTI.pdf.

2. "Creating a Respectful and Open World for Natural Hair," Official Campaign of the CROWN Act, Led by the CROWN Coalition, https:// www.thecrownact.com/ (accessed July 7, 2022).

Chapter 13

Epigraph: Layla Saad, *Me and White Supremacy* (Naperville, IL: Sourcebooks, 2020).

Chapter 14

Epigraph: Maya Angelou, posted on official Twitter account, May 12, 2013, https://twitter.com/drmayaangelou/status/333609578686197760?lang=en.

1. Lauren A. Rivera, "Hiring as Cultural Matching: The Case of Elite Professional Service Firms," *American Sociological Review*, November 28, 2012, https://journals.sagepub.com/doi/10.1177/0003122412463213.

2. "Women in the Workplace 2021," McKinsey & Company, September 27, 2021, https://www.mckinsey.com/featured-insights/gender-equality /women-in-the-workplace-2019.

Chapter 15

Epigraph: William Bruce Cameron, *Informal Sociology: A Casual Introduction to Sociological Thinking* (New York: Random House, 1963).

1. Pew Research Center, "Blacks Are More Likely Than Other Groups to See Their Race or Ethnicity as Central to Their Identity," *Race in America 2019*, https://www.pewresearch.org/social-trends/psdt_03-25-19_race_up date-16/ (accessed June 21, 2022).

2. Mary-Frances Winters, *Black Fatigue* (San Francisco: Berrett-Koehler, 2020), 44.

3. Kenneth Jones and Tema Okun, "White Supremacy Culture," *Dismantling Racism: A Workbook for Social Change*, 2001, https://images-cdn.sphereis here.com/White-Supremacy-Culture_Okun.pdf (accessed June 21, 2022).

4. Jennifer L. Knight, Michelle R. Hebl, Jessica B. Foster, and Laura M. Mannix, "Out of Role? Out of Luck: The Influence of Race and Leadership Status on Performance Appraisals," *Journal of Leadership & Organizational Studies* 9, no. 3 (August 2003): 85–93, https://doi.org/10.1177/107179190300 900308.

5. Gillian B. White, "Black Workers Really Do Need to Be Twice as Good," *The Atlantic*, October 7, 2015, https://www.theatlantic.com/business /archive/2015/10/why-black-workers-really-do-need-to-be-twice-as-good /409276/.

6. Nikole Hannah-Jones, "Episode 2: The Economy That Slavery Built," *The 1619 Project* (podcast), August 30, 2019, *New York Times*, 31:55, https:// www.nytimes.com/2019/08/30/podcasts/1619-slavery-cotton-capitalism .html.

7. M. Bennett and J. Wurzel, "Toward Multiculturalism: A Reader in Multicultural Education," *Becoming Interculturally Competent* (2004): 62–77.

Chapter 16

Epigraph: Ta-Nehisi Coates, "The Case for Reparations," *The Atlantic*, June 2014, http://www.theatlantic.com/magazine/archive/2014/06/the-case -for-reparations/361631/.

1. "Who Should Receive Reparations and in What Forms?" National African-American Reparations Commission, March 25, 2022, https:// reparationscomm.org/naarc-news/press-releases/who-should-receive -reparations-and-in-what-form-032522/.

2. Christine Tamir and Monica Anderson, "One-in-Ten Black People Living in the U.S. Are Immigrants," Pew Research Center, January 20, 2022, https://www.pewresearch.org/race-ethnicity/2022/01/20/one-in-ten-black -people-living-in-the-u-s-are-immigrants/.

3. Joy DeGruy, "Post Traumatic Slave Syndrome. How Is It Different from PTSD," *Al Jazeera*, 2019, https://www.youtube.com/watch?v= Rorgjdvphek.

4. "HR-40: The National Reparations Movement," Reparations4Slavery, https://reparations4slavery.com/hr-40-the-national-reparations-move ment/ (accessed July 2022).

5. Mateo Askaripour, "Falling in Love with Malcolm X—and His Mastery of Metaphor," Literary Hub, https://lithub.com/falling-in-love-with -malcolm-x-and-his-mastery-of-metaphor/ (accessed April 10, 2019).

6. Dionissi Aliprantis and Daniel R. Carroll, "What Is Behind the Persistence of the Racial Wealth Gap?," Federal Reserve Bank of Cleveland, February 28, 2019, https://www.clevelandfed.org/newsroom-and-events /publications/economic-commentary/2019-economic-commentaries/ec -201903-what-is-behind-the-persistence-of-the-racial-wealth-gap.

7. Scott Winship, Christopher Pulliam, Ariel G. Shiro, Richard V. Reeves, and Santiago Deambrosi, "Long Shadows: The Black-White Gap in Multi-generational Poverty," Brookings, June 2021, https://www.brookings.edu/wp -content/uploads/2021/06/Long-Shadows_Final.pdf.

8. Rashawn Ray, Andre M. Perry, David Harshbarger, Samantha Eli-zondo, and Alexandra Gibbons, "Homeownership, Racial Segregation, and Policy Solutions to Racial Wealth Equity," Brookings, September 1, 2021, https://www.brookings.edu/essay/homeownership-racial-segregation-and -policies-for-racial-wealth-equity/.

9. Susan Tompor, "Black Women Bear Largest Burden in Student Debt Crisis," *Detroit Free Press*, October 10, 2019, https://www.freep.com/in -depth/money/personal-finance/susan-tompor/2019/10/10/student-debt -crisis-us-black-women/2233035001/.

10. Santul Nerkar, "Canceling Student Debt Could Help Close the Wealth Gap Between White and Black Americans," FiveThirtyEight, May 31, 2022, https://fivethirtyeight.com/features/canceling-student-debt-could-help -close-the-wealth-gap-between-white-and-black-americans/.

11. Ray et al., "Homeownership, Racial Segregation, and Policy Solutions to Racial Wealth Equity."

12. Trey Williams, "Biden's Student Debt Forgiveness Won't Close Amer-ica's Black Wealth Gap, but It's a Start," *Fortune*, August 31, 2022, https:// fortune.com/2022/08/31/student-loan-forgiveness-and-the-racial-wealth -gap/.

13. "HR-40: The National Reparations Movement," Reparations4Slavery, https://reparations4slavery.com/hr-40-the-national-reparations-movement/.

14. "H.R.40—Commission to Study and Develop Reparation Proposals for African Americans Act," https://www.congress.gov/bill/117th-congress/house-bill/40/actions.

15. "Closing the Racial Inequality Gaps: The Economic Cost of Black Inequality in the U.S.," Citi, September 2020, https://ir.citi.com/NvIUklH Pilz14Hwd3oxqZBLMn1_XPqo5FrxsZDox6hhil84ZxaxEuJUWmak51UHvY k75VKeHCMI%3D.

16. William A. Darity Jr. and A. Kirsten Mullen, *From Here to Equality: Reparations for Black Americans in the Twenty-First Century* (Chapel Hill, NC: UNC Press Books, 2020).

17. Kim Hjelmgaard, "Reparations Bill Gets New Attention amid BLM. Could Other Nations Provide a Blueprint?," *USA Today*, July 10, 2020, https://www.usatoday.com/story/news/world/2020/07/10/slavery-reparations-bill-spurs-new-debate-other-nations-model/5396340002/.

18. Tema Okun, "White Supremacy Culture Characteristics," White Supremacy Culture, https://www.whitesupremacyculture.info/characteristics.html (accessed July 2022).

19. Caroline Castrillon, "5 Ways to Go from a Scarcity to Abundance Mindset," *Forbes*, July 12, 2020, https://www.forbes.com/sites/carolinecastrillon/2020/07/12/5-ways-to-go-from-a-scarcity-to-abundance-mindset/?sh=168529651197.

20. Marlon Williams and Alyssa Smaldino, "Ending White Supremacy Culture: A Resource for Cultivating Abundance Mindset," *Living Cities*, May 14, 2020, https://livingcities.org/blog/ending-white-supremacy-culture-a-resource-for-cultivating-abundance-mindset/.

21. Heather McGhee, *The Sum of Us: What Racism Costs Everyone and How We Can Prosper Together* (New York: One World, 2022).

22. David Frum, "The Impossibility of Reparations," *The Atlantic*, June 3, 2014, https://www.theatlantic.com/business/archive/2014/06/the-impossibility-of-reparations/372041/.

23. Ta-Nehisi Coates, "The Radical Practicality of Reparations," *The Atlantic*, June 4, 2014, https://www.theatlantic.com/business/archive/2014/06/the-radical-practicality-of-reparations/372114/.

24. "Reparations Plan," National African-American Reparations Commission, https://reparationscomm.org/reparations-plan/ (accessed July 2022).

25. Laura McCamy, "A Group of Lawyers Has a Plan for How to Pay Reparations for Slavery to Black Americans, and It Could Finally Close the Racial Wealth Gap," *Business Insider,* June 23, 2022, https://www.businessinsider.com/personal-finance/lawyers-reparations-estate-tax-black-americans-2022-6.

26. Dylan Matthews, "Six Times Victims Have Received Reparations," Vox, May 23, 2014, https://www.vox.com/2014/5/23/5741352/six-times-victims-have-received-reparations-including-four-in-the-us.

27. "Indian Claims Commission Decisions," https://library.okstate.edu/search-and-find/collections/digital-collections/indian-claims-commission-decisions (accessed July 2022).

28. Jeremy Hogeveen, Michael Inzlicht, and Sukhvinder S. Obhi, "Power Changes How the Brain Responds to Others," *Journal of Experimental Psychology* 143, no. 2 (2014): 755.

29. The Conscious Kid, https://www.theconsciouskid.org/donate (accessed July 2022).

30. National African-American Reparations Commission, https://reparationscomm.org/donate/ (accessed July 2022).

31. "This Is Not a Donation," Fund for Reparations Now!, https://www.fundforreparationsnow.org/reparationscontribution (accessed July 2022).

32. "A Portal for White Americans Walking the Path of Racial Healing," Reparations4Slavery, https://reparations4slavery.com/about-the-r4s-portal/ (accessed July 2022).

33. "Business Reckoning on Reparations," Business for Social Responsibility, https://www.bsr.org/en/emerging-issues/business-reckoning-on-reparations (accessed July 2022).

34. Lydia Dishman, "This Fintech Company Says It Will Pay Off Your Student-Loan Debt If It Hires You," *Fast Company,* March 10, 2021, https://www.fastcompany.com/90612357/fintech-company-promises-to-pay-off-student-loan-debt-for-new-hires.

35. Cristina Novoa, "How Child Care Disruptions Hurt Parents of Color Most," *American Progress,* June 29, 2020, https://www.americanprogress.org/article/child-care-disruptions-hurt-parents-color/.

36. Antoinette Perry, "Housing Inequality in the Age of Remote Work," The Inclusion Solution, May 12, 2022, http://www.theinclusionsolution.me /navigating-the-vuca-world-housing-inequality-in-the-age-of-remote-work/.

37. Andrew T. Jebb, Louis Tay, Ed Diener, and Shigehiro Oishi, "Happiness, Income Satiation and Turning Points Around the World," *Nature Human Behavior* 2 (January 2018): 33–38, https://doi.org/10.1038.

38. Bridget Miller, "Pros and Cons of Increasing Your Starting Pay," *HR Daily Advisor*, April 15, 2021. https://hrdailyadvisor.blr.com/2021/04/15/pros -and-cons-of-increasing-your-starting-pay/#:~:text=Better%2Dpaid%20 employees%20may%20mean,the%20employee%20and%20the%20employer.

39. Mark Guarino, "Evanston, Ill., Leads the Country with First Reparations Program for Black Residents," *Washington Post*, March 22, 2021, https://www.washingtonpost.com/national/evanston-illinois-reparations /2021/03/22/6b5a308c-8b2d-11eb-9423-04079921c915_story.html.

40. "North Carolina City Commits $2.1M for Reparations," AP News, June 9, 2021, https://apnews.com/article/north-carolina-racial-injustice -business-race-and-ethnicity-d9190175bb260ba2882954fd731fbe92.

41. Deepa Bharath, "U.S. Jesuits Promised to Raise $100 Million for Slavery Reparations Project. Descendants Say It's Not Happening Fast Enough," *Time,* August 16, 2022, https://time.com/6206585/jesuits-reparations -descendants-slavery/.

42. Julia Duin, "A Growing Number of Religious Groups Are Developing Reparations Programs for Black Americans," *Newsweek,* July 31, 2022, https://www.newsweek.com/2022/08/05/growing-number-religious-groups -are-developing-reparations-programs-black-americans-1727276.html.

43. "JPMorgan Chase Commits $30 Billion to Advance Racial Equity," JPMorgan Chase & Co., October 8, 2020, https://www.jpmorganchase.com /news-stories/jpmc-commits-30-billion-to-advance-racial-equity.

44. Thorsen, Karen, and William Miles. *James Baldwin: The Price of the Ticket.* San Francisco, CA: California Newsreel, 1990.

Chapter 17

Epigraph: Donna Lennon, interview with author, April 7, 2022.

1. Patrick Kline, Evan K. Rose, and Christopher R. Walters, "Systemic Discrimination Among Large US Employers," *Quarterly Journal of Economics,* June 11, 2022, https://eml.berkeley.edu/~crwalters/papers/randres.pdf.

2. Payne Lubbers, "Job Applicants with 'Black Names' Still Less Likely to Get Interviews," *Bloomberg,* July 29, 2021, https://www.bloomberg.com

/news/articles/2021-07-29/job-applicants-with-black-names-still-less-likely
-to-get-the-interview.

3. "The Conference Board C-Suite Outlook 2022: Reset and Reimagine,"
The Conference Board, https://www.conference-board.org/pdfdownload
.cfm?masterProductID=38504 (accessed July 7, 2022).

4. "The Multicultural Edge: Rising Super Consumers," Nielsen, https://
www.nielsen.com/wp-content/uploads/sites/3/2019/04/the-multicultural
-edge-rising-super-consumers-march-2015.pdf (accessed July 7, 2022).

5. Title VII of the Civil Rights Act of 1964, US Equal Employment Opportunity Commission, https://www.eeoc.gov/statutes/title-vii-civil-rights
-act-1964 (accessed July 7, 2022).

6. "Inclusion Begins Here," Textio, https://textio.com/ (accessed July 7,
2022).

7. "Finding Subtle Bias in Job Ads," *Gender Decoder*, https://gender
-decoder.katmatfield.com/ (accessed July 7, 2022).

8. "Director, User Research," GoodRx, https://jobs.lever.co/goodrx
/df4353d2-28fb-437a-a91d-c867f76abfa8 (accessed September 9, 2022).

9. "Who Is Protected from Employment Discrimination?," US Equal
Employment Opportunity Commission, https://www.eeoc.gov/employers
/small-business/3-who-protected-employment-discrimination (accessed
July 7, 2022).

10. NYC Human Rights, New York City Commission on Human Rights,
April 14, 2022, https://www1.nyc.gov/assets/cchr/downloads/pdf/materials
/ProtectedClasses_Factsheet.pdf.

11. Michelle Singletary, "Credit Scores Are Supposed to Be Race-
Neutral. That's Impossible," *Washington Post,* October 16, 2020, https://
www.washingtonpost.com/business/2020/10/16/how-race-affects-your
-credit-score/.

12. Laura Swanson, "Credit Health During the COVID-19 Pandemic,"
Urban Institute, March 8, 2022, https://apps.urban.org/features/credit
-health-during-pandemic/.

13. Elise Gould and Valerie Wilson, "Black Workers Face Two of the
Most Lethal Preexisting Conditions for Coronavirus—Racism and Economic Inequality," Economic Policy Institute, June 1, 2020, https://www.epi
.org/publication/black-workers-covid/#:~:text=Historically%2C%20black
%20workers%20have%20faced,of%206.1%25%20over%20the%20year.

14. Liz Lewis, "Beating Unemployment Bias: How to Build Awareness and Empathy," Indeed, May 26, 2021, https://www.indeed.com/lead/how-to-fight-unemployment-bias.

15. Christian E. Weller, "African Americans Face Systematic Obstacles to Getting Good Jobs," Center for American Progress, December 5, 2019, https://www.americanprogress.org/article/african-americans-face-systematic-obstacles-getting-good-jobs/.

16. Helen Dodson, "Racial Differences Exist in Reports of Workplace Drug Testing," YaleNews, September 25, 2013, https://news.yale.edu/2013/09/25/racial-differences-exist-reports-workplace-drug-testing.

17. "Drugs at Work," American Addiction Centers Detox.net, December 15, 2021, https://detox.net/uncover/drugs-at-work/.

18. Dave Clark, "Update on Our Vision to Be Earth's Best Employer and Earth's Safest Place to Work," Amazon, June 1, 2021, https://www.aboutamazon.com/news/operations/update-on-our-vision-to-be-earths-best-employer-and-earths-safest-place-to-work.

19. ManpowerGroup Employment Outlook Survey, ManpowerGroup, https://go.manpowergroup.com/hubfs/MPG_MEOS_Q4_2021_Global_Report.pdf (accessed July 7, 2022).

20. Ashley Nellis, PhD, "The Color of Justice: Racial and Ethnic Disparity in State Prisons," The Sentencing Project, October 13, 2021, https://www.sentencingproject.org/publications/color-of-justice-racial-and-ethnic-disparity-in-state-prisons/.

21. "Exonerations by Race/Ethnicity and Crime," National Registry of Exonerations, https://www.law.umich.edu/special/exoneration/Pages/ExonerationsRaceByCrime.aspx (accessed July 7, 2022).

22. "Back to Business: How Hiring Formerly Incarcerated Job Seekers Benefits Your Company," Trone Private Sector and Education Advisory Council to the American Civil Liberties Union, https://www.aclu.org/report/back-business-how-hiring-formerly-incarcerated-job-seekers-benefits-your-company (accessed July 7, 2022).

23. Maithreyi Gopalan and Shannon T. Brady, "College Students' Sense of Belonging: A National Perspective," Educational Researcher, December 24, 2019, https://journals.sagepub.com/doi/abs/10.3102/0013189X19897622?journalCode=edra&.

24. "Is the Cost of a Top College Worth It? It Depends," Indeed, https://offers.indeed.com/rs/699-SXJ-715/images/InteractiveResearch_ExecutiveSummary.pdf (accessed July 7, 2022).

25. "Race in the Workplace: The Black Experience in the US Private Sector," McKinsey & Company, February 21, 2021, https://www.mckinsey .com/featured-insights/diversity-and-inclusion/race-in-the-workplace-the -black-experience-in-the-us-private-sector.

26. Tori Fica, "What People Really Want from Onboarding," BambooHR, October 3, 2018, https://www.bamboohr.com/blog/onboarding-infographic.

27. "About Us," Project Implicit, https://implicit.harvard.edu/implicit /aboutus.html (accessed July 7, 2022).

28. Ruchika Tulshyan and Jodi-Ann Burey, "Stop Telling Women They Have Imposter Syndrome," *Harvard Business Review*, February 11, 2021, https://hbr.org/2021/02/stop-telling-women-they-have-imposter-syndrome.

29. Morela Hernandez, Derek R. Avery, Sabrina D. Volpone, and Cheryl R. Kaiser, "Bargaining While Black: The Role of Race in Salary Negotiations," *Journal of Applied Psychology*, https://www.apa.org/pubs/journals /releases/apl-apl0000363.pdf (accessed July 7, 2022).

30. Eileen Patten, "Racial, Gender Wage Gaps Persist in US Despite Some Progress," Pew Research Center, July 1, 2016, https://www .pewresearch.org/fact-tank/2016/07/01/racial-gender-wage-gaps-persist-in -u-s-despite-some-progress/.

31. Hannah Riley Bowles and Linda Babcock, "How Can Women Escape the Compensation Negotiation Dilemma? Relational Accounts Are One Answer," *Psychology of Women Quarterly*, August 24, 2012, https://projects .iq.harvard.edu/files/bbowles/files/psychology_of_women_quarterly-2013 -bowles-80-96_0.pdf.

32. Jasmine Medina-Perez, "Reimagining the Internship to Promote Racial Equity," *Stanford Social Innovation Review*, July 9, 2019, https:// ssir.org/articles/entry/reimagining_the_internship_to_promote_racial _equity.

33. Michael T. Nietzel, "Starbucks Celebrates Largest Graduating Class of Employees in Its College Achievement Program," *Forbes*, May 9, 2022, https://www.forbes.com/sites/michaeltnietzel/2022/05/09 /starbucks-celebrates-largest-class-of-employees-graduating-in-its-college -achievement-program/?sh=218a89386c3c.

34. Gillian B. White, "Black Workers Really Do Need to Be Twice as Good," *The Atlantic*, October 7, 2015, https://www.theatlantic.com/business /archive/2015/10/why-black-workers-really-do-need-to-be-twice-as-good /409276/.

35. Darreonna Davis, "Black Women Are Less Likely to Get Quality Feedback at Work. That Impacts Their Earnings and Leadership Opportunities Over Time," *Forbes*, June 15, 2022, https://www.forbes.com /sites/darreonnadavis/2022/06/15/black-women-are-less-likely-to-get -quality-feedback-at-work-that-impacts-their-earnings-and-leadership -opportunities-over-time/?sh=7ccodof97b7a.

36. Joan C. Williams, Denise Lewin Loyd, Mikayla Boginsky, and Frances Armas-Edwards, "How One Company Worked to Root Out Bias from Performance Reviews," *Harvard Business Review*, April 21, 2021, https://hbr.org /2021/04/how-one-company-worked-to-root-out-bias-from-performance -reviews.

37. "Resolving Conflict across Cultural Boundaries: Using the Intercultural Conflict Style Inventory," ICS Inventory LLC, https://icsinventory .com/ (accessed September 9, 2022).

38. Wenliang Hou and Geoffrey T. Sanzenbacher, "Social Security Is a Great Equalizer," Center for Retirement Research at Boston College, January 2020, https://crr.bc.edu/wp-content/uploads/2020/01/IB_20-2.pdf.

39. Ariel-Schwab Black Investor Survey (2022), Charles Schwab, https:// www.schwabmoneywise.com/tools-resources/ariel-schwab-survey-2022 (accessed July 7, 2022).

Chapter 18

Epigraph: Ayana Young, "Tricia Hersey on Rest as Resistance, Episode 185," For the Wild (podcast) June 8, 2020, https://forthewild.world/podcast -transcripts/tricia-hersey-on-rest-as-resistance-185 (accessed June 2022).

1. "State of the Global Workplace," Gallup 2022, https://www.gallup.com /workplace/349484/state-of-the-global-workplace-2022-report.aspx (accessed June 22, 2022).

2. "Unsafe, Unheard, Unvalued: A State of Inequity," *Hue* 2022, https:// www.stateofinequity.wearehue.org/ (accessed June 22, 2022).

3. "Summary Health Statistics: National Health Interview Survey," Center for Disease Control, 2018, Table A-1a, http://www.cdc.gov/nchs /nhis/shs/tables.htm (accessed June 22, 2022).

4. J. He, Z. Zhu, J. D. Bundy, K. S. Dorans, J. Chen, and L. L. Hamm, "Trends in Cardiovascular Risk Factors in US Adults by Race and Ethnicity and Socioeconomic Status, 1999–2018," *JAMA* 326, no. 13 (2021): 1286–98, doi: 10.1001/jama.2021.15187.

5. A. T. Geronimus, M. T. Hicken, J. A. Pearson, S. J. Seashols, K. L. Brown, and T. D. Cruz, "Do US Black Women Experience Stress-Related Accelerated Biological Aging?: A Novel Theory and First Population-Based Test of Black-White Differences in Telomere Length," *Human Nature* 21, no. 1 (March 10, 2010): 19–38, doi: 10.1007/s12110-010-9078-0. PMID: 20436780; PMCID: PMC2861506.

6. "State of the Global Workplace," Gallup 2022.

7. "Wellness Industry Statistics and Facts," Global Wellness Institute, https://globalwellnessinstitute.org/press-room/statistics-and-facts/#:~: text=The%20wellness%20economy%20includes%20eleven%20sectors%3A %201%20Personal,8%20Mental%20Wellness%20%28%24131%20billion%29 %20More%20items…%20 (accessed June 22, 2022).

8. "Unsafe, Unheard, Unvalued: A State of Inequity," *Hue* 2022.

9. Adewale Maye, "No-Vacation Nation, Revised," Center for Economic and Policy Research, May 2019, https://cepr.net/images/stories/reports/ no-vacation-nation-2019-05.pdf (accessed October 2022).

10. "Paid Time Off Trends in the U.S.," US Travel Association, 2019 https://www.ustravel.org/sites/default/files/media_root/document/Paid%20 Time%20Off%20Trends%20Fact%20Sheet.pdf (accessed October 2022).

11. Jack Zenger and Joseph Folkman, "Are We More Productive When We Have More Time Off?," *Harvard Business Review*, June 17, 2015, https:// hbr.org/2015/06/are-we-more-productive-when-we-have-more-time-off.

12. Danielle Braff, "How to Design a 21st Century Time-Off Program," SHRM, March 20, 2018, https://www.shrm.org/hr today/news/hr-magazine /0418/pages/how-to-design-a-21st-century-time-off-program.aspx.

13. Yekaterina Chzhen, Anna Gromada and Gwyther Rees, "Are the World's Richest Countries Family Friendly? Policy in the OECD and EU," UNICEF Office of Research, Florence, https://www.unicef.org/ media/55696/file/Family-friendly%20policies%20research%202019.pdf (accessed October 2022).

14. Gallup, "Wellbeing: Employee Wellbeing Is Key for Workplace Productivity," 2022, https://www.gallup.com/workplace/215924/well-being .aspx.

15. "2021 Absence and Disability Management Survey Highlights: Employers Revisit Time-Off Benefits," Mercer, https://www.mercer.us /content/dam/mercer/attachments/north-america/us/us-2021-absence-and -disability-infographic.pdf (accessed June 22, 2022)

16. Amit Batish, " Equilar 100: The Highest-Paid CEOs at the Largest U.S. Companies," Equilar, April 18th 2022, https://www.equilar.com/reports/90 -highest-paid-ceos-2022-equilar-100.html.

17. Edward R. Berchick, Jessica C. Barnett, and Rachel D. Upton, "Health Insurance Coverage in the United States," 2018, *Current Population Reports*, P60-267(RV) (Washington, DC: US Government Printing Office, 2019).

18. N. Rhee, "Race and Retirement Security in the United States," National Institute on Retirement Security, 2013, https://www.nirsonline.org/ wp-content/uploads/2017/07/race_and_retirement_insecurity_final.pdf.

19. "Brother You're on My Mind: Mental Health Snapshot of African American Men," National Institute on Minority Health and Health Disparities, https://www.nimhd.nih.gov/docs/byomm_factsheet02.pdf (accessed June 22, 2022).

20. "Unsafe, Unheard, Unvalued: A State of Inequity," *Hue* 2022.

21. "Food Insecurity and Poverty in the United States: Findings from the USDA and US Census Bureau," Feeding America, https://hungerandhealth .feedingamerica.org/wp-content/uploads/2018/10/Food-Insecurity-Poverty -Brief_2018.pdf#:~:text=When%20looking%20across%20racial%20groups %20or%20regions%2C%20additional,Who%20is%20food%20insecure%20in %20the%20United%20States%3F (accessed June 25, 2022).

22. Janet McVittie, Ranjan Datta, Jean Kayira, and Vince Anderson, "Relationality and Decolonisation in Children and Youth Garden Spaces," *Australian Journal of Environmental Education* 35, no. 2 (2019): 93–109, doi:10.1017/aee.2019.7.

23. Ocean Robbins, "Community Gardens Are Growing Health, Food, & Opportunity," *Food Revolution Network,* August 4, 2021, https:// foodrevolution.org/blog/community-gardens/.

Chapter 19

1. "Corporate Pledges for Racial Justice Fall Short, Analysis Finds," *Philanthropy News Digest,* August 24, 2021, https://philanthropynews digest.org/news/corporate-pledges-for-racial-justice-fall-short-analysis -finds.

2. Mary-Frances Winters, *Black Fatigue: How Racism Erodes the Mind, Body, and Spirit* (Oakland, CA: Berrett-Koehler, 2020).

3. Amanda Barroso, "Most Black Adults Say Race Is Central to Their Identity and Feel Connected to a Broader Black Community," Pew Research Center, February 5, 2020, https://www.pewresearch.org/fact-tank/2020

/02/05/most-black-adults-say-race-is-central-to-their-identity-and-feel -connected-to-a-broader-black-community/.

4. Andrew R. Todd, Galen V. Bodenhausen, and Adam D. Galinsky, "Perspective Taking Combats the Denial of Intergroup Discrimination," *Journal of Experimental Social Psychology* 48 (December 27, 2011): 738–45, https:// doi.org/:10.1016/j.jesp.2011.12.011. Andrew R. Todd, Galen V. Bodenhausen, and Adam D. Galinsky, "Perspective Taking Combats Automatic Expressions of Racial Bias," *Journal of Personality and Social Psychology* 100, no. 6 (March 7, 2011): 1027–42, https://doi.org/10.1037/a0022308.

5. "Caucus and Affinity Groups," Racial Equity Tools, https://www .racialequitytools.org/resources/act/strategies/caucus-and-affinity-groups (accessed July 2022).

6. Simone E. Morris, "LinkedIn Joins the Bandwagon by Compensating ERG Leaders for Culture Impacts," *Forbes*, June 17, 2021, https://www.forbes .com/sites/simonemorris/2021/06/17/linkedin-joins-the-bandwagon-by -compensating-erg-leaders-for-culture-impacts/?sh=619c77a42811.

7. Jessica Bantom, "The Lived Experience Quotient: The Most Overlooked and Undervalued Set of Strengths," *The Inclusion Solution*, January 27, 2022, https://doi.org/10.1037/a0022308.

8. Jalen Sherald, "The Buzz: What We Miss When We See 'Firsts,'" *The Inclusion Solution*, June 13, 2019, https://www.theinclusionsolution.me /the-buzz-what-we-miss-when-we-see-firsts-yale-kahlil-greene-president -history-firsts-race-leadership/.

Chapter 20

Epigraph: Marcus Garvey and Amy Jacques Garvey, *The Philosophy and Opinions of Marcus Garvey, Or, African for the Africans* (Dover, MA: Majority Press, 1986), 2.

1. Eric Goldschein, "Racial Funding Gap Shows Black Business Owners Are Shut Out from Accessing Capital," *NerdWallet*, January 8, 2021, https:// www.nerdwallet.com/article/small-business/racial-funding-gap.

2. "History of Supplier Diversity for Minority Business Development," National Minority Supplier Development Council, July 12, 2018, https:// nmsdc.org/history-supplier-diversity-minority-business-development/.

3. "Small Businesses Generate 44 Percent of U.S. Economic Activity," US Small Business Administration Office of Advocacy, January 30, 2019, https://advocacy.sba.gov/2019/01/30/small-businesses-generate-44-percent -of-u-s-economic-activity/.

4. Robert Fairlie, Alicia Robb, and David T. Robinson, "Black and White: Access to Capital among Minority-Owned Startups," Stanford Institute for Economic Policy Research, December 15, 2016, https://drive.google.com /file/d/1QSXobvF3ZgYd_XyIPNeIMI6_GYyMVQx5/view.

5. Rashawn Ray, Andre M. Perry, David Harshbarger, Samantha Elizondo, and Alexandra Gibbons, "Homeownership, Racial Segregation, and Policy Solutions to Racial Wealth Equity," Brookings, September 1, 2021, https://www.brookings.edu/essay/homeownership-racial-segregation-and -policies-for-racial-wealth-equity/.

6. Salvador Rodriguez, "Facebook to Buy $100 Million Worth of Unpaid Invoices from 30,000 Small Businesses Owned by Women and Minorities," CNBC, September 11, 2021, https://www.cnbc.com/2021/09/11/facebook-to -buy-100-million-of-invoices-from-diverse-owned-businesses.html.

Chapter 21

Epigraph: Quoted in Barbican Centre, "Joy Buolamwini: Examining Racial and Gender Bias in Facial Analysis Software," Google Arts & Culture, 2019, https://artsandculture.google.com/story/joy-buolamwini-examining -racial-and-gender-bias-in-facial-analysis-software-barbican-centre/BQW BaNKAVWQPJg?hl=en.

1. Ruha Benjamin, *Race after Technology: Abolitionist Tools for the New Jim Code* (Oxford, England: Polity, 2019), 65.

2. Safiya Umoja Noble, *Algorithms of Oppression: How Search Engines Reinforce Racism* (New York: New York University Press, 2018).

3. Benjamin, *Race after Technology*.

4. Felix Richter, "Women's Representation in Big Tech," Statista, July 1, 2021, https://www.statista.com/chart/4467/female-employees-at-tech -companies/.

5. "2021 Top Companies for Women Technologists Key Findings and Insights Report," AnitaB.org, September 28, 2021, https://anitab.org/research -and-impact/top-companies/2021-results/.

6. Benjamin, *Race after Technology*, 19.

7. "2021 Top Companies for Women Technologists," 3.

8. Slyvia Ann Hewlett, Carolyn Buck Luce, Lisa J. Servon, Laura Sherbin, Peggy Shiller, Eytan Sosnovich, and Karen Sumberg, "The Athena Factor: Reversing the Brain Drain in Science, Engineering, and Technology," *Harvard Business Review Research Report*, no. 10094 (June 2008): https:// www.researchgate.net/publication/268325574_By_RESEARCH_REPORT

_The_Athena_Factor_Reversing_the_Brain_Drain_in_Science_Engineering _and_Technology.

9. "Resetting Tech Culture," Accenture, 2020, https://www.accenture .com/_acnmedia/PDF-134/Accenture-A4-GWC-Report-Final1.pdf.

10. Kerry (Rosvold) Peters, "Gender Inequality Issues in the Technology Industry," *New View Strategies*, November 4, 2021, https://getyournewview .com/tech-industry-gender-inequality/.

11. Sam Dean and Johana Bhuiyan, "Why Are Black and Latino People Still Kept Out of the Tech Industry?" *Los Angeles Times*, June 24, 2020, https://www.latimes.com/business/technology/story/2020-06-24/tech -started-publicly-taking-lack-of-diversity-seriously-in-2014-why-has-so -little-changed-for-black-workers.

12. Todd Feathers, "Major Universities Are Using Race as a 'High Impact Predictor' of Student Success," *The Markup*, March 2, 2021, https:// themarkup.org/machine-learning/2021/03/02/major-universities-are-using -race-as-a-high-impact-predictor-of-student-success.

13. Dean and Bhuiyan, "Why Are Black and Latino People Still Kept Out of the Tech Industry?"

14. Noble, *Algorithms of Oppression*, 70.

15. Dianne Grayce Hendricks and Celina Gunnarsson, "Design and Implementation of an Engineering for Social Justice Curriculum," *American Society for Engineering Education*, Paper ID #24893, 2019.

16. Cathy O'Neil, *Weapons of Math Destruction: How Big Data Increases Inequality and Threatens Democracy* (New York: Crown Publishers, 2016), 223.

17. Benjamin, *Race after Technology*, 13.

18. O'Neil, *Weapons of Math Destruction*, 183.

19. Noble, *Algorithms of Oppression*, 94.

20. O'Neil, *Weapons of Math Destruction*, 225.

21. O'Neil, *Weapons of Math Destruction*, 209.

22. Timnit Gebru, Jamie Morgenstern, Briana Vecchione, Jennifer Wortman Vaughan, Hannah Wallach, Hal Daume III, and Kate Crawford, "Datasheets for Datasets," Microsoft, December 1, 2021.

23. Hahrie Han, "Promoting Electoral Reform and Democratic Participation (PERDP) Initiative," Ford Foundation, April 2016.

24. Han, "Promoting Electoral Reform," 19.

25. Julia Angwin, Jeff Larson, Surya Mattu, and Lauren Kirchner, "Machine Bias," *ProPublica*, May 23, 2016, https://www.propublica.org/article/machine-bias-risk-assessments-in-criminal-sentencing.

26. Noble, *Algorithms of Oppression*, 167.

27. Leon Yin and Aaron Sankin, "How We Discovered Google's Social Justice Blocklist for YouTube Ad Placements," *The Markup*, April 9, 2021, https://themarkup.org/google-the-giant/2021/04/09/how-we-discovered-googles-social-justice-blocklist-for-youtube-ad-placements.

28. Maarten Sap, Dallas Card, Saadia Gabriel, Yejin Choi, and Noah A. Smith, "The Risk of Racial Bias in Hate Speech Detection," University of Washington, 2019, https://homes.cs.washington.edu/~msap/pdfs/sap2019risk.pdf.

29. Quoted in Salma El-Wardany, "Like Our Society, Instagram Is Biased against Women of Color," *Refinery29*, December 10, 2020, https://www.refinery29.com/en-gb/2020/12/10150275/shadow-ban-instagram-censorship-women-of-colour.

30. Noble, *Algorithms of Oppression*, 141.

31. Todd Feathers, "Why It's So Hard to Regulate Algorithms," *The Markup*, January 4, 2022, https://themarkup.org/news/2022/01/04/why-its-so-hard-to-regulate-algorithms.

32. Feathers, "Why It's So Hard."

33. Feathers, "Why It's So Hard."

34. Benjamin, *Race after Technology*, 179.

Chapter 22

1. "Top Lifetime Grosses," Box Office Mojo by IMDbPro, Data as of May 27, 1:40 PDT, https://www.boxofficemojo.com/chart/top_lifetime_gross/?area=XWW (accessed March 15, 2022).

2. Margaret Maurer, "Why It Took So Long to Get a Black Panther Movie," *Screenrant*, February 15, 2018, https://screenrant.com/black-panther-movie-delay/.

3. "Brands Fail to Represent Black Women in Ads," *WARC*, July 16, 2020, https://www.warc.com/newsandopinion/news/brands-fail-to-represent-black-women-in-ads/en-gb/43860.

4. Tracy Jan, "News Media Offers Consistently Warped Portrayals of Black Families, Study Finds," *Washington Post*, December 13, 2017, https://www.washingtonpost.com/news/wonk/wp/2017/12/13/news-media-offers-consistently-warped-portrayals-of-black-families-study-finds/.

5. Felix Kumah-Abiwu, "Media Gatekeeping and Portrayal of Black Men in America," *Journal of Men's Studies*, May 14, 2019, https://doi.org/10.1177 /1060826519846429.

6. "Global Skin Lightening Agents Market Report 2021: Market to Reach $385.8 Million by 2027," ResearchAndMarkets.com, June 3, 2021, https://www.businesswire.com/news/home/20210603005406/en /Global-Skin-Lightening-Agents-Market-Report-2021-Market-to-Reach -385.8-Million-by-2027---U.S.-Market-is-Estimated-at-78.6-Million ---ResearchAndMarkets.com.

7. "Shapewear Market Size, Share & Trends Analysis Report by End User (Male, Female), by Distribution Channel (Hypermarkets & Supermarkets, Specialty Stores, Online), by Region, and Segment Forecasts, 2021–2028," *GVR Report Cover Shapewear Market Size, Share & Trends Report*, https:// www.grandviewresearch.com/industry-analysis/shapewear-market (accessed March 15, 2022).

8. Mike Vuolo, "The Birth of Cool: Coul, coole, koole: How We Got From Cool Temperatures to Cool," *Slate*, October 1, 2013, https://slate.com /human-interest/2013/10/cool-the-etymology-and-history-of-the-concept -of-coolness.html.

9. Patrick Marché, "The Misappropriation of African-American English in Advertising Appreciation of Black Culture or 'Digital Blackface,'" *Medium*, June 22, 2020, https://medium.com/@patmarche2/the-misappropria tion-of-african-american-english-in-advertising-3e256cef5d13.

10. Robert L. Heilbroner, "Capitalism," *Britannica*, https://www .britannica.com/topic/capitalism (accessed March 15, 2022).

11. Ibram X. Kendi, *Stamped from the Beginning* (New York: Bold Type Books, 2016).

12. "Groupm Introduces the Media Inclusion Initiative, an Integrated Investment Strategy to Grow Black-Owned Media Companies and Support Creatorship," press release, May 10, 2021, https://www.groupm.com /newsroom/groupm-introduces-the-media-inclusion-initiative/.

13. "Representations of Black Women in Hollywood," Geena Davis Institute on Gender in Media, https://seejane.org/research-informs-empowers /representations-of-black-women-in-hollywood (accessed March 12, 2022).

14. "Star Trek Discovery Is Paramount+'s Most-Watched Show," *Screenrant*, December 18, 2021, https://screenrant.com/star-trek-discovery -paramount-plus-viewership-details/.

15. Daniel Kurt, "Government Leadership by Race: Minority Group Members are Underrepresented in Elected Office and Federal Courts," *Investopedia*, March 15, 2021, https://www.investopedia.com/government -leadership-by-race-5113457.

16. "Demography of Article III Judges, 1789–2020," Federal Judicial Center, https://www.fjc.gov/history/exhibits/graphs-and-maps/race-and -ethnicity (accessed March 16, 2022).

17. Laura Noonan and Taylor Nicole Rogers, "Share of Black Employees in Senior US Finance Roles Falls Despite Diversity Efforts," *Financial Times*, March 30, 2021, https://www.ft.com/content/887d064a-bd5e-4ce6-9671 -9057e12bd5c7.

18. Peter Eavis, "Diversity Push Barely Budges Corporate Boards to 12.5%, Survey Finds," *New York Times*, September 7, 2020, https://www.nytimes .com/2020/09/15/business/economy/corporate-boards-black-hispanic -directors.html.

19. Paige McGlauflin, "The Number of Black Fortune 500 CEOs Returns to Record High—Meet the 6 Chief Executives," Fortune, May 23, 2022, https://fortune.com/2022/05/23/meet-6-black-ceos-fortune-500-first -black-founder-to-ever-make-list/.

20. Marty Swant, "New Ad Industry Diversity Data Provides a New Benchmark—and Room for Improvement," *Forbes*, September 22, 2020, https://www.forbes.com/sites/martyswant/2020/09/22/new-ad-industry -diversity-data-provides-a-new-benchmark-and-room-for-improvement/ ?sh=79efec7835e4.

21. Christopher Boulton, "Rebranding Diversity: Colorblind Racism Inside the U.S. Advertising Industry" (PhD dissertation, University of Massachusetts Amherst, 2012), 621.

22. Matthew Rutherford et al., "Business Ethics as a Required Course: Investigating the Factors Impacting the Decision to Require Ethics in the Undergraduate Business Core Curriculum," *Academy of Management Learning and Education* 11, no. 2 (June 2012): 174–86, https://doi.org/10 .5465/amle.2011.0039.

Chapter 23

Epigraph: Edgar Villanueva, *Decolonizing Wealth: Indigenous Wisdom to Heal Divides and Restore Balance*, Second Edition.

1. Kenneth P. Pucker and Andrew King, "ESG Investing Isn't Designed to Save the Planet," *Harvard Business Review*, August 1, 2022, https://hbr.org/2022/08/esg-investing-isnt-designed-to-save-the-planet.

2. Tracy Jan, Jena McGregor, and Meghan Hoyer, "Corporate America's $50 Billion Promise," *The Washington Post*, August 24, 2021, https://www.washingtonpost.com/business/interactive/2021/george-floyd-corporate-america-racial-justice/.

3. Kara Baskin, "What Corporate Philanthropy Got Wrong After George Floyd's Murder," MIT Sloan School of Management, March 16, 2022, https://mitsloan.mit.edu/ideas-made-to-matter/what-corporate-philanthropy-got-wrong-after-george-floyds-murder.

4. Dana Doan and Barry Knight, "Measuring What Matters," Global Fund for Community Foundations, https://globalfundcommunityfoundations.org/wp-content/uploads/2020/10/MeasuringWhatMatters.pdf (accessed July 7, 2022).

5. "Outcome Mapping," BetterEvaluation, https://www.betterevaluation.org/en/plan/approach/outcome_mapping (accessed July 7, 2022).

6. "Vital Signs Takes the Pulse of Our Communities," Australian Community Philanthropy, https://www.australiancommunityphilanthropy.org.au/wp-content/uploads/2021/05/Vital-Signs-Backgrounder-2020-update.pdf (accessed July 7, 2022).

ACKNOWLEDGMENTS

MARY-FRANCES WINTERS

Founder and CEO

The Winters Group, Inc.

(she/her/hers)

I am deeply grateful to the entire Winters Group team, who embraced my vision for this collaborative project with the same level of passion and thought leadership that they provide in every endeavor that we engage in to do our part in making this a more equitable and just world. While not every member of the team contributed chapters to the book, it was truly a team effort. I appreciate the hard work that everyone put into writing their chapter(s) as well as the rest of the team who cheered the writers on, provided feedforward, and completely supported the project. I acknowledge authors Kevin A. Carter, Megan Ellinghausen, Scott Ferry, Gabrielle Gayagoy Gonzalez, Terrence Harewood, PhD, Tami Jackson, Megan Larson, EdD, Leigh Morrison, Katelyn Peterson, Mareisha N. Reese, Thamara Subramanian, and Rochelle Younan-Montgomery. I say thank you to all of the other members of The Winters Group team: Karen Anaya Quiroga, Beth Cole, Paul Gonzales, Krystle Nicholas, and Keley Smith. I also want to acknowledge Alice Chin from Your Other Half, our HR partner who has contributed to our quest to be justice-centered in all of our people decisions. Additionally, Tricia M. Taitt from FinCore is fantastic in partnering with us to ensure sound financial stewardship.

I want to give a huge thank you to Gabrielle (Gabby) Gayagoy Gonzalez, who served as special projects editor. She enthusiastically embraced all aspects of the project, bringing her expertise from previous jobs in publishing and journalism. Gabby spent countless hours coordinating the logistics and administrative tasks associated with completing the book. She also spent countless hours writing and editing the manuscript. I so appreciate her subject matter expertise, creativity, and keen eye for detail.

Krystle Nicholas is a senior financial analyst at The Winters Group and also an accomplished artist (kryscreates.com). She designed the artwork for the cover of this book and also the art inside *Black Fatigue: How Racism Erodes the Mind, Body, and Spirit*. I thank her for her creative vision and natural ability to bring the book's messages to life with poignant imagery.

Marketing and branding specialist Megan Ellinghausen is our in-house social media maven and a wellspring of creativity. She redesigned the graphics found throughout the book to ensure accessibility and also coded the book's website, www.racialjusticeatwork.com. I am grateful for her contributions.

I also want to give a special thank you to Beth Cole, executive assistant and project coordinator at The Winters Group, for her unwavering championing of the team and our work. She is a positive force for good not only at The Winters Group but for the world. Beth spreads cheer wherever she goes. I am indebted to her for so expertly performing her duties and making my life not only easier but better.

Mareisha N. Reese is president and chief operating officer of The Winters Group. Even more important than her role as my business partner and her indelible impact on our growth, she is my daughter, and I love her dearly. It is not always easy to navigate the business and the personal aspects of our relationship. Mareisha makes it easier and more joyful.

It is always a pleasure to work with the supportive Berrett-Koehler team.

INDEX

Page numbers followed by an f indicate figures, those followed by an n indicate notes, and those followed by a t indicate tables.

intellectual property/work for hire,
236–237
payment terms, 235–236
third-party risk assessments, 237
Professional, defining, 145–146
Professionalism, 31, 141–146
Black hair and hairstyles and, 146
Promotions, 158–160, 159f
Protected classes, 2, 246
Psycho readiness, 90t

Questioning, 137

Racial equity. *See also specific topics*
measures of, 168
Racial equity analysis (framework), 168,
181
insights from, 183, 184t
Racism, 22. *See also* Systemic racism;
specific topics
prevalence, 142
Racist comments by famous persons,
23–24
Radical Candor, 130, 130f
Reflection, 49, 63, 119, 132, 133f, 137, 138.
See also Self-reflection
Reimagining, 9–10, 181. *See also specific topics*
Relationships, fears related to, 74
Reliability, 131
Reparations (for slavery), 186–188
defined, 187
guilt, scarcity, and individualism as
barriers to, 190–191
HR 40 bill, 186, 187, 189
informed possibility models, 193
making reparations real in your
organization, 196–199
making reparations real in your
personal life, 194–195

practicality, 192–194
who should qualify for receiving, 187
Requests for proposal (RFPs), 233–234
Resiliency, individual, 220–221
Resistance, 73f, 74, 75t, 90t
addressing, 50–51
checklist to address, 89
exercises to address, 89–90
mitigating, 74
Respecting the dignity of people one
disagrees with, 137
Restorative dialogue, 125, 128
in practice, 125–126
purpose, 128
Restorative justice, 17
Retirement benefits, 210–211
Retributive justice, 16–17
RFPs (requests for proposal), 233–234
RFP process, 233–234
Ross, Jovida, 124, 128, 136

Saad, Layla, 149
Safety, bringing employees, 106–107
Salaries. *See* Compensation
Sameness and equality, 62
Scarcity
as barrier to reparations, 190–191
unlearning, 191–192
Scott, Kim, 130
Security, fears related to, 73
Self-reflection, 63–65, 86, 119. *See also*
Reflection
Self-understanding, 168–169, 226
focus on other-understanding and,
132–134, 226
Sensitivity reviews, 264
Silence, 113–116, 119, 122
understanding the history of, 114–115
Simplification, 74
mitigating, 74

ABOUT THE AUTHORS

JONI DELUCCIO

Mary-Frances Winters (she/her/hers) is the best-selling author of *Black Fatigue: How Racism Erodes the Mind, Body, and Spirit* and *We Can't Talk about That at Work! How to Talk about Race, Religion, Politics, and Other Polarizing Topics.* She is the founder and CEO of The Winters Group, Inc., a global diversity, equity, inclusion, and justice consulting firm in business for almost four decades. She came of age during the civil rights movement of the 1960s and is a passionate advocate for justice and equity. Named a top ten diversity and inclusion trailblazer by *Forbes*, Mary-Frances believes in opening doors and amplifying marginalized voices and their allies. She has received many awards and honors, including the ATHENA Award, Diversity Pioneer from *Profiles in Diversity Journal*, and The Winds of Change recognition from The Forum on Workplace Inclusion. As CEO of The Winters Group for the past thirty-nine years, Mary-Frances harnesses her extensive experience in strategic planning, change management, diversity, organization development, training and facilitation, systems thinking, and qualitative and quantitative research methods to work with senior leadership teams to drive meaningful organizational change. This is her seventh book.

TIMELESS ARTS PHOTOGRAPHY

Kevin A. Carter (he/him/his) resides on the ancestral lands and waters of the Coast Salish people who have called Orcas Island home since time immemorial. He is a vegan, video gamer, heart attack survivor, and husband. Kevin has over twenty-five years of diversity, equity, and inclusion (DEI) experience and has served as the DEI leader for BP, Campbell Soup, Ahold, and Safeco Insurance. At The Winters Group, Inc., he is the vice president of strategy and assessments and strives to be a a non-anxious, affirming, and committed presence in meeting people where they are on their journey to center equity and justice. Kevin holds a bachelor of arts, cum laude, in philosophy and public affairs from Vanderbilt University and a master of business administration in finance from the Case Western Reserve University Weatherhead School of Management. He is a certified administrator for the Intercultural Development Inventory (IDI) and LIFO—Life Orientations.

Megan Ellinghausen (she/her/hers) is the marketing and branding specialist for The Winters Group, Inc. She is a white, cisgender, heterosexual, able-bodied Gen-Zer, hoping to amplify the power of possibility in Generation Z. Megan's passions lie at the intersection of communication and social justice, where she

DENISE ELLINGHAUSEN

is committed to creating space for transformative dialogue through truthful and compelling storytelling. She believes in the opportunity to create this type of positive social change through technology and the digital world. She is a graduate of the University of Florida with a bachelor of arts in political science, a bachelor of science in public relations, and a master of mass communication in public interest communications.

Scott Ferry (he/him/his) is the lead instructional designer at The Winters Group, Inc. He's a lifelong learner and long-term educator with a commitment to making his little corner of the world a more just and inclusive place. Having spent fifteen years in education as a teacher, instructional coach, assessment expert, and instructional designer, he has extensive experience designing, implementing, and facilitating curricula. Beyond being a Baltimorean, Cincinnatian, and Michigander, he's perhaps most importantly a Georgia Bulldog. When he's not creating learning experiences focused on driving learners toward equitable action, he's probably out enjoying the scents and subtle sounds of nature.

Gabrielle Gayagoy Gonzalez (she/her/hers) is a Filipina American and marketing and PR strategist for The Winters Group, Inc. Her writing has appeared in *Shape, Self, Women's Health*, and *Seventeen*. As an editor at *Shape*, she increased coverage of women of color and hired the magazine's first Black columnist. A neurodiverse multihyphenate, she is also

a former New York City Teaching Fellow at Harvey Milk High School and a founding teacher at the Academy for Software Engineering, a public high school that expanded access to coding education to Black, Latine, and female students across New York City. Gabrielle earned an advanced diploma in managing workplace diversity and inclusion from New York University, a master of science in education from Hunter College, and a bachelor of arts in journalism from The Ohio State University. She lives in Manhattan with her husband, son, and two TV-loving cats. She remembers the Lenape.

Terrence Harewood, PhD (he/him/his) is vice president of learning and innovation for The Winters Group, Inc., and an experienced diversity, equity, inclusion, and justice (DEIJ) executive coach, master facilitator, and cofounder and principal visionary obstetrician at Synergistic Transformations, LLC. He has earned several coveted awards for his skillful DEIJ facilitation. These include the 2018 IDI Intercultural Competence Award and the 2011 Teacher of the Year Award from the University of Indianapolis, where he served as a professor of multicultural education, teaching courses related to culture, educational leadership, and civil rights for almost two decades. In addition to his teaching, coaching, and training experiences, Harewood is an Intercultural Development Inventory Qualified Administrator and one of fifteen select international IDI Qualifying Seminar Facilitators. A native of Barbados, West Indies, he has engaged his extensive DEIJ expertise globally, including in corporate, education, government, and nonprofit sectors. Harewood is also coauthor of a forthcoming book titled *Intercultural Learning from the Inside Out*, designed to help higher education faculty and staff effectively facilitate intercultural experiential learning through a four-phased developmental approach.

Tami Jackson (she/her/hers) is a Black American descendent of chattel slavery of generous height and size. A writer and instructional designer for The Winters Group, Inc., she has nearly fifteen years of experience in industries including sports/entertainment, advertising, real estate, and tech, with a penchant for justice, equity, diversity, and inclusion. She is a first-generation graduate with a bachelor of arts in Asian languages and culture and American studies from the University of Michigan and a master of arts in Black studies from the University of Texas at Austin. A frequent speaker, panelist, and mentor, Tami profoundly believes in the power and necessity of being one's authentic self and retired from code-switching years ago. Tami is an enthusiastic blerd, gamer, dyslexic, cosplayer, boundary enforcer, and plus-sized fashionista. She don't play about her nerd-centric media, Black American culture, sleep, '70s Soul Music, '90s R&B, and family—bio and chosen. Tami proudly hails from Detroit, Michigan, and rests her head begrudgingly in Austin, Texas.

COURTESY DR. MEGAN LARSON

Megan Larson, EdD (she/her/hers) is obsessed with what makes great leaders and how they connect and communicate with people using empathy and a justice lens. This obsession took her through a bachelor of arts in communications, a master of science in integrated marketing communications, and a doctorate of education in organizational leadership. It also took her through nearly twenty-five years in corporate America in tech, manufacturing, water/wastewater, electrical construction, and other Fortune 500 adventures. As the vice president of marketing and business development at The Winters Group, Inc., Megan has the privilege of partnering with clients on their DEIJ transformations. A lifelong Midwesterner, xennial, unapologetically intersectional feminist, and insatiable learner, Megan has intentionally built the family of her dreams with her husband and teen.

Leigh Morrison (she/her/hers) is a storyteller, educator, and creator. As a queer white woman, she is committed to lifelong (un)learning and self-reflection and supporting others in these practices in the broader pursuit of empathy, equity, and justice. Leigh is currently a manager of learning and innovation at The Winters Group, where she is responsible for designing transformative, human-centered learning experiences for learners in many industries. She is passionate about imagining and amplifying possibility models to correct persistent injustices. Leigh holds a bachelor of arts in gender studies and intersectionality from Wellesley College and a master of arts in educational studies from the University of Michigan.

Katelyn Peterson (she/her/hers) is a communicator that brings energy, empathy, and emotion into each connection, especially in her current role as the lead client success account manager at The Winters Group, Inc. She is a millennial, cisgendered, able-bodied Black woman with a degree in mass communications and public relations and a professional background in small business and entrepreneurial consulting. Katelyn has provided speaking engagements and workshops that provide insight into effective and intentional communication, including grant and loan exposure, public speaking practice, and audience influence. Katelyn's passion also lies in working with individuals with developmental disabilities. This work has involved assistance with personal, social, and career coaching and goal setting, but her true reward has been building long-lasting friendships.

Mareisha N. Reese (she/her/hers) is a xennial Black woman who serves as president and chief operating officer at The Winters Group, Inc. In this role, Mareisha manages and handles the day-to-day operations of the organization, ensuring it runs like a well-oiled machine. In a previous life, Mareisha worked as a software engineer, where she was often one of the only (Black) women in her workspaces. The biases and microaggressions that came along with that caused her to develop a passion for diversity, equity, inclusion, and justice work. Mareisha is a graduate of Spelman College with a bachelor of science in computer science, Georgia Tech with a bachelor of science in electrical engineering, and the University of Maryland Robert H. Smith School of Business with dual master's degrees in business administration and information systems.

Thamara Subramanian (she/her/hers) is a first-gen, South Asian American woman from greater Kansas City. Working within the intersection between health and social justice, she is driven by her passion for tackling the root causes of inequities and creating opportunities for all people to thrive. Thamara is currently an equity audit and strategy

manager for The Winters Group, Inc. She conducts DEIJ audits to help organizations reimagine how their policies and practices can better support equity and justice. When she is not walking her dog or volunteering, she's an avid bookworm, hiker, true-crime fanatic, and vegetarian foodie. Thamara holds a bachelor of science in psychology from the University of Michigan and a master's in public health in social and behavioral sciences from the Harvard T.H. Chan School of Public Health.

Rochelle Younan-Montgomery (she/her/hers) is an instructional designer for The Winters Group, Inc., and has a background in nonprofit leadership, community organizing, and higher education. She is a cisgender, queer, biracial SWANA woman and a lover of the natural world. She strives to cultivate mindfulness and healing in her work, recognizing the collective movement toward racial justice requires deep, personal inner awareness. She holds an undergraduate degree in sociology from Azusa Pacific University and is a YWCA Racial Justice Facilitator. She lives in South Minneapolis (on Dakhóta Land) with her partner and two daughters.

About the Cover Artist

Krystle Nicholas (she/her/hers) is a millennial Black woman who serves as the senior financial analyst at The Winters Group, Inc. She is a first-generation college graduate with a bachelor of science, summa cum laude, in business management from Johnson & Wales University. She is passionate about financial literacy in underserved communities. She's a for-

mer volunteer with Heart Math Tutoring, a program for students in high-poverty elementary schools. She has also volunteered her time with VITA, an IRS initiative that helps low-to-moderate income individuals prepare and e-file their taxes at no cost to them. In addition to her analytical side, she is also a creative. Krystle is a self-taught multimedia artist who uses art as a therapeutic practice to relieve stress and add beauty to the world. She currently lives in Charlotte, North Carolina, with her husband and two daughters.

Berrett–Koehler
Publishers

Berrett-Koehler is an independent publisher dedicated to an ambitious mission: *Connecting people and ideas to create a world that works for all.*

Our publications span many formats, including print, digital, audio, and video. We also offer online resources, training, and gatherings. And we will continue expanding our products and services to advance our mission.

We believe that the solutions to the world's problems will come from all of us, working at all levels: in our society, in our organizations, and in our own lives. Our publications and resources offer pathways to creating a more just, equitable, and sustainable society. They help people make their organizations more humane, democratic, diverse, and effective (and we don't think there's any contradiction there). And they guide people in creating positive change in their own lives and aligning their personal practices with their aspirations for a better world.

And we strive to practice what we preach through what we call "The BK Way." At the core of this approach is *stewardship,* a deep sense of responsibility to administer the company for the benefit of all of our stakeholder groups, including authors, customers, employees, investors, service providers, sales partners, and the communities and environment around us. Everything we do is built around stewardship and our other core values of *quality, partnership, inclusion,* and *sustainability.*

This is why Berrett-Koehler is the first book publishing company to be both a B Corporation (a rigorous certification) and a benefit corporation (a for-profit legal status), which together require us to adhere to the highest standards for corporate, social, and environmental performance. And it is why we have instituted many pioneering practices (which you can learn about at www.bkconnection.com), including the Berrett-Koehler Constitution, the Bill of Rights and Responsibilities for BK Authors, and our unique Author Days.

We are grateful to our readers, authors, and other friends who are supporting our mission. We ask you to share with us examples of how BK publications and resources are making a difference in your lives, organizations, and communities at www.bkconnection.com/impact.

Dear reader,

Thank you for picking up this book and welcome to the worldwide BK community! You're joining a special group of people who have come together to create positive change in their lives, organizations, and communities.

What's BK all about?

Our mission is to connect people and ideas to create a world that works for all.

Why? Our communities, organizations, and lives get bogged down by old paradigms of self-interest, exclusion, hierarchy, and privilege. But we believe that can change. That's why we seek the leading experts on these challenges—and share their actionable ideas with you.

A welcome gift

To help you get started, we'd like to offer you a **free copy** of one of our bestselling ebooks:

www.bkconnection.com/welcome

When you claim your **free ebook**, you'll also be subscribed to our blog.

Our freshest insights

Access the best new tools and ideas for leaders at all levels on our blog at ideas.bkconnection.com.

Sincerely,

Your friends at Berrett-Koehler